WOMAN'S ROLE IN ECONOMIC DEVELOPMENT

by Ester Boserup

CONDITIONS OF AGRICULTURAL GROWTH
reprinted

Woman's Role
in Economic Development

by
ESTER BOSERUP

ST. MARTIN'S PRESS
NEW YORK

Published in the United States of America in 1970
by St. Martin's Press, Inc.
© *George Allen & Unwin Ltd 1970*
Library of Congress Catalog Card Number: 70 118569

Preface

In the vast and ever-growing literature on economic development, reflections on the particular problems of women are few and far between. This book will show, I hope, that this is a serious omission.

Economic and social development unavoidably entails the disintegration of the division of labour among the two sexes traditionally established in the village. With modernization of agriculture and with migration to the towns, a new sex pattern of productive work must emerge, for better or worse. The obvious danger is, however, that in the course of this transition women will be deprived of their productive functions, and the whole process of growth will thereby be retarded. Whether this danger is more or less grave, depends upon the widely varying customs and other preconditions in different parts of the underdeveloped world. My object was to identify these patterns and to explain their significance from the point of view of development policies.

Many of the conclusions drawn in the book are necessarily tentative and provisional, and some aspects of the problem had to be omitted for lack of basic information. I hope that this book will help to stimulate further study, including the provision of fresh statistical evidence.

Of course, no first-hand field enquiries could be made for this study. But the tables here presented are entirely new in the sense that the data culled from censuses, from other official statistics, and from a great number of special surveys were never before collected and collated for the purpose of giving an overview of the pattern of female employment. Nearly all the statistical documentation for the study was prepared by Mr Erling Faurbye of the Danish Statistical Office, and I wish to express my thanks for his valuable assistance.

I owe a debt of gratitude to the Danish Board of Technical Co-operation with Developing Countries, which provided a generous grant to cover the cost of the study, including extensive travel in Asia and Africa. This travel enabled me to make fruitful contacts with numerous scholars and officials in universities, government offices, United Nations agencies and Danish embassies. These persons in Asia and Africa, and many others in Europe and America, gave precious advice for my work and provided much valuable material. I should specially mention that the Department of Agriculture at Makerere University, Kampala, permitted me to quote from unpublished research papers.

Contents

Figures

Tables

PART I

In the Village

Chapter 1

Male and Female Farming Systems

A main characteristic of economic development is the progress towards an increasingly intricate pattern of labour specialization. In communities at the earliest stages of development, practically all goods and services are produced and consumed within the family group, but with economic development more and more people become specialized in particular tasks and the economic autarky of the family group is superseded by the exchange of goods and services.

But even at the most primitive stages of family autarky there is some division of labour within the family, the main criteria for the division being that of age and sex. Some particularly light tasks, such as guarding domestic animals or scaring away wild animals from the crops, are usually left to children or old persons; certain other tasks are performed only by women, while some tasks are the exclusive responsibility of adult men.

Both in primitive and in more developed communities, the traditional division of labour within the farm family is usually considered 'natural' in the sense of being obviously and originally imposed by the sex difference itself. But while the members of any given community may think that their particular division of labour between the sexes is the 'natural' one, because it has undergone little or no change for generations, other communities may have completely different ways of dividing the burden of work among the sexes, and they too may find their ways just as 'natural'.

Many social anthropologists and other scientific observers of human communities have emphasized the similarities in the sex roles in various communities. One very distinguished anthropologist, Margaret Mead, in her book *Male and Female*, gives this summary description of the sex roles: 'The home shared by a man or men and female partners, into which men bring the food and women prepare it, is the basic common picture the world over. But this picture can be modified, and the modifications provide proof that the pattern itself is not something deeply biological'.[1]

It is surprising that Margaret Mead, with her extensive and intensive personal experience of primitive communities throughout the world, should venture upon such a dubious generalization. She is right in describing the preparation of food as a monopoly for women in nearly all communities, but the surmise that the provision of food is a man's prerogative is unwarranted. In fact, an important distinction can be made between two kinds or patterns of subsistence agriculture: one in which food production is taken care of by women, with little help from men, and one where food is produced by the men with relatively little help from women. As a convenient terminology I propose to denote these two systems as the male and the female systems of farming.

The position of women differs in many basic features in these two community groups. Therefore a study of the role of women in economic development may conveniently begin with an examination of women's tasks in agricultural production in various parts of the underdeveloped regions of the world.

THE DIVISION OF LABOUR WITHIN AFRICAN AGRICULTURE

Africa is the region of female farming *par excellence*. In many African tribes, nearly all the tasks connected with food production continue to be left to women. In most of these tribal communities, the agricultural system is that of shifting cultivation: small pieces of land are cultivated for a few years only, until the natural fertility of the soil diminishes. When that happens, i.e. when crop yields decline, the field is abandoned and another plot is taken under cultivation. In this type of agriculture it is necessary to prepare some new plots every year for cultivation by felling trees or removing bush or grass cover. Tree felling is nearly always done by men, most often by young boys of 15 to 18 years, but to women fall all the subsequent operations: the removal and burning of the felled trees; the sowing or planting in the ashes; the weeding of the crop; the harvesting and carrying in the crop for storing or immediate consumption.

Of course, there are exceptions to this general rule. In some African communities with shifting cultivation, the women have some help from the men beyond the felling of trees. For instance, men may hoe the land or take part in the preparatory hoeing before the crops are planted, but even with such help the bulk of the work with the food crops is done by women. In some other tribes, most of the field work is done by the men. Thus, we may identify three main systems of subsistence farming in Africa according to whether the field work is done almost exclusively by women, predominantly by women, and predominantly by men.

The relative importance in the African setting of these three patterns can be gauged from Figure 1. This map was prepared forty years ago by H. Baumann, a German expert on African subsistence farming. It appears that forty years ago female farming with no male help except for the felling of trees predominated in the whole of the Congo region, in large parts of South East and East Africa and in parts of West Africa. Female farming was far more widespread than systems of male farming and it also seems to have been more widespread than systems of predominantly female farming with some help from males in cultivation; this latter type of farming was characteristic of the region immediately south of the Sahara.

Farming systems which are not based on scientific methods and with no modern industrial input are usually described as 'traditional'. It is widely but mistakenly assumed that such 'traditional' systems are necessarily passed on from one generation to the next without ever undergoing changes either in techniques or in the division of labour between the sexes. In historic times, tribes with female farming systems have been known to change over to male systems, and—less frequently— tribes with male farming systems have been known to adopt a female system of farming.[2]

Changes in the division of labour between men and women seem usually to have been related to changes in population density and in farming techniques. For one reason or other, the tribe may have migrated to another region, or local conditions for agriculture may have changed in the region where the tribe used to live. It might be, for instance, that the forest

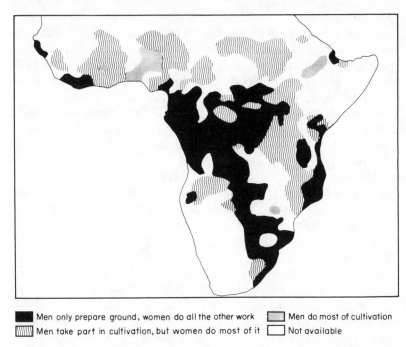

▄ Men only prepare ground, women do all the other work   ▨ Men do most of cultivation
▥ Men take part in cultivation, but women do most of it   ☐ Not available

Figure 1   Areas of Female and Male Farming in Africa, Around 1930

cover was disappearing as the density of population increased, so that the land had to be cultivated more intensively, with shorter periods of rest.

With the gradual disappearance of the tree cover, the men's tasks of felling must decline, as must the opportunities for hunting—another decidedly male form of work. On the other hand, with increasing population density new forest areas become scarce. As the fertility of the old ones diminishes, so will the soil need more careful preparation before it is planted, to offset less frequent periods of lying fallow. In such cases it may be necessary for men to help with the hoeing, or even to take over this operation completely from the women; a predominantly female farming system can thus change to one where the two sexes share more equally the burden of field work. Sometimes the increasing population pressure may induce the men to emigrate from the region in search of wage labour elsewhere. In this case of male depletion the women may have to take over some operations previously performed by men. Many such changes have taken place in various parts of Africa during the rapid growth of population in recent times.

Before the European conquest of Africa, felling, hunting and warfare were the chief occupations of men in the regions of female farming. Gradually, as felling and hunting became less important and inter-tribal warfare was prevented by European domination, little remained for the men to do. The Europeans, accustomed to the male farming systems of their home countries, looked with little sympathy on this unfamiliar distribution of the work load between the sexes and understandably, the concept of the 'lazy African men' was firmly fixed in the minds of settlers and administrators. European extension agents in many parts of Africa tried to induce the under-employed male villagers to cultivate commercial crops for export to Europe, and the system of colonial taxation by poll tax on the house-holds was used as a means to force the Africans to produce cash crops. These were at least partly cultivated by the men, and the sex distribution of agricultural work was thus to some extent modified on the lines encouraged by the Europeans. In many other cases, however, European penetration in Africa resulted in women enlarging their part in agricultural work in the villages, because both colonial officers and white settlers recruited unmarried males for work, voluntary or forced, in road building or other heavy constructional work, in mines and on plantations.

As a result of all these changes, the present pattern of sex roles in African agriculture is more diversified than the one which gave rise to the European concept of the 'lazy African men'. Therefore, the picture presented by Baumann's map of the sex distribution of work for food production must be broadened and brought up to date to take into account the introduction of cash crops and the changes in the sex proportions in African villages brought about by male migrations.

The available data, although insufficient for drawing up a picture for the whole of Africa, gives very useful information about male and female work input in African farming in a number of local case studies. Sometimes these cover some hundred families selected by accepted sampling methods and representative for the district where they live. In other cases, intensive studies have been made of a small number of families, but these studies, while richer in detail, cannot claim to be representative even for the village in question.*

The main results of these various studies of work input by men and women from cultivator families, and of the use of hired labour, are brought together in Table 1. The first thing to note is that in virtually all the studies the number of women in cultivator families taking part in agricultural work was found to be higher than that of the men. A variety of circumstances can help to explain why a relatively small number of men take part in agricultural work. Older men can often stop working by leaving it to their usually younger wives or to their children, while many old women are widows who must fend for themselves. More boys than girls go to school and more young men than young women are away from the villages, working for wages in towns or plantations or attending schools. Since in African villages virtually all the women and many girls even very young ones, take part in the work, the agricultural labour force tends to become predominantly female.

Secondly, the table gives information on the amount of agricultural work performed by those men and women who take any part at all in the work. While women in some cases work shorter hours than men, much more frequently they

* It must be remembered that even a study of a few families is an extremely time-consuming operation if it is based upon observations of the work of each family member in the fields, day by day for a whole year or more. In larger samples, the technique is often to visit the family at regular intervals and question them about their work input of the previous day or week, but, obviously, this procedure is much less reliable than the regular observation of the workers over a long period.

work longer hours or more days per year in agriculture than do the men. Typically, the annual average of work hours per week seems to be between 15 and 20 for women, and around 15 for men, but in some cases women work much less and in

Table 1

WORK INPUT BY WOMEN AND MEN IN AFRICAN AGRICULTURE

Country in which sample villages are located	Percentage of women in family labour force in agriculture	Average hours worked per week on own farm:			Percentage of work in farm performed by:		
		by active female family members	by active male family members	female hours as per cent of male hours	active female family members	active male family members	hired labour of both sexes
Senegal	53	8	15	53	29	66	5
Gambiaª {A	51	19	11	168	64	36	
{B	52	20	9	213	70	30	
Dahomey		2	24	8			
Nigeria	57	3	21	15	9	49	42
Cameroon	62	13	16	81	56	44	
Central African {A	55	15	15	99	55	45	
Republicᵇ {B	58	20	13	150	68	32	
{C	61	10	12	85	57	43	
Congo (Brazzaville)	57	24	15	160	68	32	
{A	67	28	15	193	79	21	
{B	61	20	15	136	68	32	5
{C	53	18	4	450	45	9	15
Ugandaᶜ {D	54	13	13	100	45	37	7
{E	53	13	8	163	56	29	1
{F	61	16	14	114	53	29	4
{G	50	13	15	87	39	52	
Kenya		23					

ª The two samples refer to the same village in the years 1949 and 1962 respectively.

ᵇ The A sample refers to a village where traditional methods were applied, the B sample to a village where improved techniques were used.

ᶜ In the C–G samples respectively 31, 11, 14, 14, 9 per cent of the work waɩ done by children who were not classified by sex.

Note: Some of the sources from which the information was collected failed to specify the length of the work day, or the type of activities classified as agricultural (for instance, it was sometimes not clear whether threshing and transport to and from the field were included). In cases where workdays per year were given without specification of their length, the total number of hours worked per year was calculated on the assumption of a six-hour day, and this figure was then divided by 52 to give average number of hours worked per week. The assumption of a six-hours day may well be on the high side, since shorter hours were recorded in many of the samples, and days of more than six hours were recorded only in a few cases and then in the busiest seasons only. For these reasons, the figures in the table can convey only a broad picture of the input of work in African farming, and it must not be assumed that the table gives a satisfactory picture of differences in work input among the localities mentioned.

other cases men's work in agriculture is very limited. In some Gambia and Uganda samples, men were found to work less than 10 hours per week in agriculture. By contrast, in some samples from the Congo (Brazzaville), Uganda and Kenya women were found to do agricultural work for around 25 hours per week.

The joint result of women's high rate of participation in agricultural work and their generally long working hours was that women, in nearly all the cases recorded, were found to do more than half of the agricultural work; in some cases they were found to do around 70 per cent and in one case nearly 80 per cent of the total. Thus, the available quantitative information about work input by sex seems to indicate that even today village production in Africa south of the Sahara continues to be predominantly female farming. This is all the more remarkable since none of the districts shown in the table is characterized by an agriculture devoted exclusively to subsistence production. All the producers have some cash crops in addition to the food crops cultivated for family consumption, and, as already mentioned, men play a more active part in the production of cash crops than in the production of food crops.

Now it may be asked whether the work done by women tends perhaps to be much lighter than that done by men. The available information does not warrant a hard and fast answer to this question, and only a few suggestions can be offered. Light tasks, such as the guarding of crops against animals and birds, appear to be done mainly by the very young or the very old of both sexes, and able-bodied women are not spared from hard work. One of the sample studies from the Central African Republic mentions that the women generally do the most exhausting and boring tasks, while the performance of the men is sometimes limited simply to being present in the fields to supervise the work of the women.[3]

The samples from Gambia are from a survey and a re-survey of the same village after an interval of ten years during which the number of inhabitants increased and the cultivation of the labour intensive paddy crop expanded. As a result, the women who had been found in the first survey to be already working much longer hours in the fields than the men, were found at the re-survey to be working still longer hours, while the average work input of men had even diminished. In this case, the farming system was thus becoming even more 'female' than it had previously been.

A similar process seems to be under way in the Central African Republic. No re-surveys were done in that country, but two simultaneous surveys were carried out in two different villages, selected for the explicit purpose of identifying the effect of improved and more intensive farming methods. The village of Poyumba (the first line in Table 1 for the Central African Republic) was selected as a specimen of the old-fashioned village, while the village Madomale (the second line), upon advice from the extension service, had introduced intensive methods for the cultivation of cotton, their main cash crop. The figures show that women were doing more work in the 'modernized' village than in the old-fashioned one, while the men were doing less. The reason for this was that women had to do most of the new types of work, while the men had reacted to the higher yields from the new methods by reducing the area of land prepared for cultivation per family below the amount usual in the old-fashioned village with lower crop yields.[4]

The table includes a few cases of 'male farming'. In the sample for Dahomey, and in the sample from Nigeria (which refers to a cocoa producing region inhabited by members of the Yoruba tribe), men's average working hours in agriculture were ten times longer than those of women. Nevertheless, average hours of work for men, at least in the case of Nigeria, were not much longer than is typical for African villages generally. This was possible because the absence of any considerable female contribution to agricultural work was compensated by the use of hired workers for more than 40 per cent of agricultural work. These were immigrant seasonal workers from the Northern regions of Nigeria coming in to help with the cocoa crops, and whom the farmers could afford to use because cocoa production was highly profitable at the time (during the Korean boom) when the sample study was made.[*]

The preceding analysis dealt mainly with Black Africa. This is where female farming systems are most widespread today, but they are by no means unknown in other parts of the world. For instance, in Latin America we find both Indian and Negro

---

[*] The amount of hired labour used in agriculture is specified in a few cases only, but for most of the studies where the amount of hired labour was not recorded, it is known that little or no hired labour was used.

communities where agricultural work is entirely in female hands.[5] In Asia, too, many examples of female farming systems are known. They are widespread among tribal peoples in India, where districts are found with women working more hours in farming than men.[6] These Indian tribal farming systems are similar to the types of shifting agriculture in use among African tribes with female farming.*

In all the countries of South East Asia many tribal peoples subsist by shifting cultivation with female farming, and here, as in India, complaints about 'lazy men' are heard from Europeans as well as from local peoples belonging to communities with male farming systems. Thus, the Vietnamese find that the Laotians, with shifting cultivation and female farming, are lazy farmers,[8] and the Indians have a similar opinion of the tribes of Manipur (in North-East India) which likewise practise shifting cultivation and female farming. They are said to 'take it for granted that women should work and it is quite usual to hear that men while away their time doing nothing very much'.[9]

THE PLOUGH, THE VEIL AND THE LABOURER

The pattern of female farming described above is found mainly in regions of shifting agriculture where the plough is not used. In the regions of plough cultivation, agricultural work is distributed between the two sexes in a very different way. The main farming instrument in those regions, the plough, is used by men helped by draught animals, and only the hand operations—or some of them—are left for women to perform. Table 2 shows the distribution of work between men and women in some regions of Asia where plough cultivation is predominant.

The table is arranged in a similar way to Table 1 which covers African villages with shifting cultivation. A comparison of the two tables gives an impression of women's different roles in these two agricultural systems. The first thing to note is the striking difference in the numbers of women taking part in

---

* In some places, however, the forest protection policy of the Indian Forest Department, through the prohibition of shifting cultivation, has succeeded in modifying the farming system.[7]

field work in African villages and in the Asian regions shown in Table 2. As we have seen, virtually all rural women in Africa take part in farm work, and the agricultural labour force is predominantly female. By contrast, the samples from regions of plough cultivation in Asia show a predominantly

Table 2

WORK INPUT BY WOMEN AND MEN IN AGRICULTURE IN SOME ASIAN COUNTRIES

Country in which sample villages are located	Percentage of women in family labour force in agriculture	Average hours worked per week on own farm:			Percentage of work in farm performed by:		
		by active female family members	by active male family members	female hours as per cent of male hours	active female family members	active male family members	hired labour of both sexes
Western India { A					17	50	33
Western India { B	32	16	33	48	14	57	29
Western India { C	39	19	35	54	20	56	24
Central India { A	21	18	27	64	6	21	73
Central India { B	27	15	29	52	7	20	74
Southern India	40	20	30	67	25	37	38
Delhi territory		31		⊃₁			
Malaya[a] { A		7	17	45			
Malaya[a] { B		9	14	68			
Philippines	21	30	43	70	13	69	18
China[b], average	30			50	13	72	15
Northern China	27			41	9	75	16
Southern China	31			58	16	69	15
of which: sub-region with multi-cropping of paddy	42			76	30	62	9

[a] The A sample refers to a village with one annual crop of paddy; the B sample refers to three villages with multi-cropping of paddy. The farm families were smallholders and both men and women had much wage-labour in addition to their work in own farm.

[b] The figures refer to the period 1929–33.

male family labour force, because a large proportion of women in the cultivator families are completely exempted from work in the fields. The land is prepared for sowing by men using draught animals, and this thorough land preparation leaves little need for weeding the crop, which is usually the women's task. Therefore women contribute mainly to harvest work and to the care of domestic animals. Because village women work less in agriculture, a considerable proportion of them are completely freed from farm work. Sometimes such women perform only purely domestic duties, living in seclusion within their own homes, and appearing in the village street only under the protection of the veil, a phenomenon associated with

25

plough culture, and seemingly unknown in regions of shifting cultivation where women do most of the agricultural toil.

In regions of plough culture, even those women who do take part in agricultural work are less active than the men. In all the Asian sample areas shown in Table 2 women work fewer hours than men in agriculture, while the opposite is usually true in African villages, as seen in Table 1. It is important to note, however, that in the Asian villages covered by Table 2, those women who did play any part in agricultural work were not generally working shorter hours than those which seem usual for African women. The difference arises from the fact that in Asian agriculture men work 25 to 30 hours per week or even more, while in Africa they usually work around 15 hours per week, or less. Hence, the real difference between the use of the African and Asian agricultural labour force, as revealed by a comparison of the two tables, is that Asian men—the operators of the plough—must work longer hours than African men, while many of the wives of Asian men are free from field work.

But there is an additional and very important difference between the distribution of work in African shifting cultivation and in Asian plough cultivation. The plough is used in regions with private ownership of land and with a comparatively numerous class of landless families in the rural population. Therefore, in many regions of plough cultivation, the farm family gets more help from hired labourers than is usual in regions of shifting cultivation. The percentage of agricultural work done by hired labour varies from 15 per cent to over 70 per cent in the samples from Asia, while very few of the culti-vator families in the African samples used significant amounts of hired labour.

Owing to the differences in the use of hired labour and in the technical nature of farming operations under plough cultivation and shifting cultivation, female family labour accounts for a much smaller part of the total agricultural work in the Asian than in the African village. In nearly all cases recorded in Table 1, the female African family members did more than half of the work in agriculture; the comparable figure for Asian cultivator families was less than one-fifth, as seen in Table 2.

To sum up, there seems to be two basic factors which explain the striking contrast between female farmers in regions of shifting cultivation and secluded, domestic women in most other parts of the developing world: one factor is the difference in agricultural systems; the other is the difference in the pattern of social hierarchy between regions of tribal organization and regions of settled farmers with individual ownership of land. Among the latter, a large proportion of the women are able to devote themselves largely or wholly to work within the confines of the home, leaving work in the fields to male family members and to hired workers.

The great advantage of the type of sample studies we have been examining above is that they give information about the actual input of work, measured in hours or days. By the same token, however, most of these surveys are strictly local, covering only a few villages or districts. Far more comprehensive information can of course be had from population censuses if we decide to be content with information on the numbers of hired labourers and of men and women from farm families who take part, more or less extensively, in agricultural work.

Such information is brought together in Table 3. There appears to be two clearly identifiable patterns of labour participation in agriculture. Most African and some South East Asian countries (Thailand, Cambodia) have a high percentage of

Table 3

LABOUR FORCE IN AGRICULTURE BY SEX AND STATUS

Country	Female family labour	Male family labour	Agricultural workers of both sexes
	as percentage of total agricultural labour force as recorded in the most recent population census		
Africa South of the Sahara:			
Sierra Leone	42	57	1
Liberia	42	49	9
Ghana	36	55	9
Union of South Africa	5	29	66
Mauritius	2	13	85

Table 3—contd. Country	Female family labour	Male family labour	Agricultural workers of both sexes
	as percentage of total agricultural labour force as recorded in the most recent population census		
Region of Arab influence:			
Sudan	9	78	13
Morocco	9	72	19
Algeria	37	40	23
Tunisia	38	42	20
Libya	2	79	19
United Arab Republic	2	61	37
Turkey	49	47	4
Jordan	3	70	27
Syria	5	56	39
Iraq	1	74	25
Iran	4	68	28
Pakistan	13	73	14
South and East Asia:			
India	24	48	28
Ceylon	3	43	54
Thailand	50	47	3
Cambodia	75	53	2
Malaya	16	41	43
Singapore	24	49	28
Philippines	13	76	11
Taiwan	19	71	10
Hong Kong	34	46	20
Korea (South)	45	52	3
Latin America:			
Mexico	2	44	54
Honduras	1	73	27
El Salvadore		36	64
Nicaragua	3	50	47
Costa Rica		46	54
Panama	3	83	14
Columbia	3	54	43
Ecuador	3	57	40
Chile	2	29	69
Brazil	8	67	25
Venezuela	2	65	33
Cuba		37	63
Jamaica	9	50	41
Dominican Republic	1	74	25
Puerto Rico	1	18	81

Table 3—contd.

Note: For many of the countries listed in the table, the number of women from farm families participating in agricultural work is understated, either (*a*) because the census records only those women who receive a remuneration for their work, while women who help in the family farm without remuneration are classified as housewives or (*b*) because women who work only in the peak season are classified as housewives. It appears from the figures below for countries which have changed their classification system for rural women that the margin of error for the figures in Table 3 is very wide indeed.

Country	Year	Agricultural labour force (millions)		Percentage of women in agricultural labour force	Agricultural labour force as percentage of total labour force in all occupations
		Women	Men		
Union of South Africa	1936	1·7	1·7	49	64
	1946	0·7	1·7	28	47
	1960	0·2	1·5	12	30
United Arab Republic	1927	0·5	3·0	15	60
	1947	3·9	3·7	51	54
	1960	0·1	3·5	4	53
Philippines	1903	0·2	1·4	13	47
	1948	2·0	2·8	42	66
	1960	0·8	4·4	15	61
	1965	1·3	4·7	21	57
Columbia	1938	1·6	1·8	47	72
	1951	0·1	1·9	4	53
	1964	0·1	2·4	4	41

Because of the wide differences in the system of classification for rural women, a comparison of the female role in economic activities cannot be based upon over-all rates of work participation. For the same reason, the percentage of population engaged in agriculture is not a reliable measure of the stage of development reached by a given country. It appears from the last column in the table above that the statistical elimination of most of the women from the agricultural labour force contributed to reduce the apparent share of population engaged in agriculture in South Africa from 64 to 30 per cent of the active population in a period of twenty-four years while, conversely, the inclusion of more women in the agricultural labour force in the Philippines made the proportion of the agricultural sector appear to have risen from 47 in 1903 to 66 in 1948.

Owing to these differences in the classification of rural women, international comparisons of the proportion of population engaged in agriculture are often based upon figures for male labour only. This, however, is not a valid solution to the problem since women perform a much larger part of agricultural work in some countries than in others. To avoid these difficulties, the criterion for stage of economic development used in this study is *not* the proportion of active population engaged in agriculture, but the proportion of all adults

29

Table 3—contd.

occupied in 'modern occupations', i.e. employees in industry and trade and all personnel in professional, clerical and administrative occupations (see Table 28 and Figures 6, 10, 13). This is thought to minimize the margin of error arising from differences in the classification of women (and men) who work part-time or without remuneration since the numbers of such women (and men) are negligible in the 'modern' occupations.

female participation in agriculture and very few agricultural wage labourers;[10] in contrast many Arab and Latin American countries have a small female participation and agricultural wage labourers form a large part of the agricultural labour force. Where there is a low female participation in farm work, extensive plough cultivation is the rule, and there is little need for female labour except in the harvest season.[11]

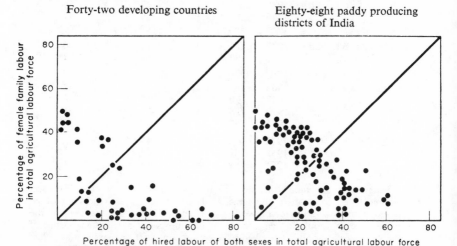

Figure 2 Use of Female Family Labour and Hired Labour in Agriculture

Note: All percentages are based upon number of persons, without regard to hours of work. See Note to Table 3.

Table 3 (and Figure 2, left-hand side) are based upon average figures for whole countries although many of them contain regions with strikingly different types of farming and social organization. Therefore, a more correct picture may emerge if we compare the composition of the agricultural labour force in various districts within the countries. In Figure 2 (right-hand side) such a comparison is made for India. It shows that in rice-producing districts female work participation is high in the farm families where hired labour is little used, but much lower where hired labour accounts for a large part of the labour force.

Thus, it seems to be a general rule, valid for all parts of the developing world, that it is the female members of the farm families who benefit most from the availability of landless families working for wages. As hired labourers are called in, so are the women of cultivator families released from agricultural work. On the other hand, women always seem to bear a large part of the work burden in the more egalitarian communities.

POPULATION PRESSURE AND SEX ROLES IN FARMING

We have seen that male members of farm families work much longer hours in Asian than in African agriculture. To a large extent, differences in animal husbandry and draught power can explain why farmers in Asia are more busy than farmers in Africa.

The shifting cultivator in Africa has no draught animals; he drinks little milk and his consumption of meat is met in some places by hunting and in other places by animals which are kept mostly unguarded and untended in natural grazings far away from the crops and the village. By contrast, the Asian farmer must look after his draught and other domestic animals, which is no small part of his total agricultural effort. The figures below suggest that nearly half the labour input by either male or female family members in Indian farming is accounted for by the labour requirements of draught animals and animal husbandry:

Average hours worked per week by family members:[12]

	With crops		With animals		Total in family farm	
	Women	Men	Women	Men	Women	Men
Western India						
sample B	13	18	3	15	16	33
sample C	16	23	3	12	19	35
Central India	14	14	2	14	16	28
Southern India	9	16	11	14	20	30
Delhi territory	9		22		31	

African cultivators can avoid the heavy burden of keeping and feeding animals because with such a thinly populated continent shifting cultivation can be pursued. It may seem surprising, in view of the primitive tools used in shifting cultivation, that families can produce their food and some cash crops with so small an input of labour as that of the African cultivator families in the villages covered by Table 1. The explanation is that in regions with a favourable land/man ratio, the system of shifting cultivation requires less input of labour per unit of output than primitive systems of permanent cultivation.[13] As long as population densities remain relatively low, labour-intensive systems of land improvement and fertilization need not be applied and it is possible to avoid cultivating land with a low yield due to soil exhaustion after frequent or permanent cultivation without the use of fertilizers.

In other words, the input of labour per family in African subsistence farming can be kept at lower levels than, for instance, in the more densely populated regions of Asia, because the generally much lower population densities in Africa make it possible to stick to an agricultural system with less labour input per unit of agricultural output. It is precisely because such labour-extensive farming systems can be used in most of Africa that it is possible for African villagers to leave most of the farming work to women, while the men work very short hours in agriculture, in comparison to male farmers in densely populated regions of subsistence agriculture.

Female farming systems seem most often to disappear when farming systems with ploughing of permanent fields are introduced in lieu of shifting cultivation. In a typical case, this change is the result of increasing population density which makes it impossible to continue with a system necessitating long fallow periods when the land must be left uncultivated. When a population increase induces the transition to a system where the same fields are used with no or only short fallow periods, this change often goes hand in hand with the transition from hoeing to ploughing; when the land has to be used continuously, it becomes worthwhile, and indeed necessary, to undertake a large initial investment—the removal of tree stumps and bushes and land levelling—which must precede plough cultivation.*

In recent decades, the rapid population increase in developing countries has prompted a change to plough cultivation in many regions of shifting cultivation with a predominantly female pattern of work. And the advent of the plough usually entails a radical shift in sex roles in agriculture; men take over the ploughing even in regions where the hoeing had formerly been women's work. At the same time, the amount of weeding to be done by the women may decline on land ploughed before sowing and planting, and either men or women may get a new job of collecting feed for the animals and feeding them.

It is not an invariable rule that men operate the plough right from the moment it is introduced. Among some Bantu peoples in South Africa, women steer the plough although it was introduced some time ago. Similarly, in India 2 per cent of the ploughing done for farmers by agricultural labourers is done by women.[15] These women probably belong to tribes with female farming traditions, and such examples are no more than sporadic exceptions to the general rule that ploughs are operated by men.

Obviously, the adoption of a farming system where the main farming equipment is operated only by men entails a tremendous change in the economic and social relationship between the sexes. It is understandable that social anthropologists regard the distinction between shifting cultivation and plough cultivation as a fundamental criterion for the identification of different social and cultural patterns, and in later chapters we shall hear much about the more general consequences of this shift. But the male members of tribes who are faced with the problem of changing from shifting cultivation to plough cultivation are not concerned with these long-term effects of their choice. They naturally think mainly in terms of the additional work burden which the ploughing and the care of the draught animals may give them.

* In a district of Nigeria where the change to plough cultivation was contemplated, it was found that, while 20 man-days of work were needed for the preparation of an acre of virgin savannah land and bush for cultivation by the usual method, an investment of 100 man-days was needed to clear similar land before tractor ploughs could operate on it.[14]

Understandably, villagers usually show little enthusiasm for plough cultivation as long as they have land enough to apply shifting cultivation and can cover their protein supply from hunting and fishing or from cattle kept in grazings far from the villages and the crops. And the more the work of hoeing is done by women, the less likely will men be willing to change from hoeing to ploughing. Extension agents may eagerly explain to the farmers how much they can increase their production by ploughing all the land at their disposal and cultivating it permanently with animal manuring instead of having only a part of it hoed and cultivated by their wives. But the husband, measuring his own present work input in agriculture against the prospect of much greater demands for manual work, will be disinclined to change. Many well-meant attempts to foster intensification in African agriculture have been frustrated by this simple mechanism.

In short, the difference in sex distribution of agricultural work in villages of shifting cultivations and in those where the plough is used, is one of the main reasons why shifting cultivators lack enthusiasm for taking to the plough. They seem to agree with the old Arab saying, ascribed to the Prophet himself, that a plough never enters into a farm without servitude entering too.[16]

We saw that when growing population density induces cultivator families to change from shifting cultivation to plough cultivation, men's burden of work usually increases while that of the women diminishes. As long as population density remains low enough to allow extensive plough cultivation without irrigation, there may be little need for weeding, and the animals may need to be hand-fed for only a short period every year, if at all. In such cases, women may have little agricultural work to do.

However, this advantage for the women does not last if the pressure of population increases to the point where it is necessary to use very labour-intensive techniques and to plant very labour-intensive crops in order to maintain the customary income from a smaller area of land. With irrigation, weeding may become a heavy burden for the women, and so may the transplanting of paddy. But men also get more work to do under irrigated farming than under plough cultivation of dry crops, for the digging of irrigation ditches in the fields, the lifting of water from wells and canals, and the repair of terraces and bunds are usually men's work.

Examples of a high degree of work participation by women in densely populated areas are found in Egypt[17] and in China. In the latter, where mostly male farming predominates, women do a large part of the work in the very densely populated regions where agriculture is based upon the double cropping of rice (Table 2).

To sum up, the sex roles in farming can be briefly described as follows: in very sparsely populated regions where shifting cultivation is used, men do little farm work, the women doing most. In somewhat more densely populated regions, where the agricultural system is that of extensive plough cultivation, women do little farm work and men do much more. Finally, in regions of intensive cultivation of irrigated land, both men and women must put hard work into agriculture in order to earn enough to support a family on a small piece of land.

In the last few decades population in developing countries has been increasing at unprecedented rates. The increased population density in rural areas calls for a change of agricultural system towards higher intensity. Unavoidably, this change must affect the balance of work between the sexes and it must often be necessary for one of the sexes to take over some tasks which were normally done by the other sex within that particular community. The authors of some of the studies quoted above complain that agricultural change is being held back because men—or women—refuse to do more work than is customary, or to do work which according to prevailing custom should be done by persons of the other sex.[18]

NOTES TO CHAPTER 1

1. Mead, 1950, 190. 2. Baumann, 296. 3. Guet, Vol. II, 70. 4. Georges, 7–8, 25. 5. Mar, 133; Bastide, 60, 70. 6. Nath, May 1965, 816. 7. Dixit, 22–3. 8. Lévy, 255. 9. Sengupta, 200. 10. Janlekha, 80–2. 11. UN. ECA., *Wom. N. Afr.*, 11; de Moulety, 153; Sweet, 154–6; Fuller

73; Lewis, O., 98; Honigman, 11; Loomis, 27, 102, 134; Corredor, 110.
12. See notes to Table 2.   13. Boserup, 28–34.   14. Galetti, 168.
15. Patnaik, 62; Horrel, 224.   16. Weulersse, 69–70.   17. Seklani, 471,
485; UAR, *Role of W.*, 21.   18. Haswell 1963, 36, 46, 73–4; George, 7–8;
Hailey, 872; Loomis, 102; Lewis, W. A., 43; Winter, 44.

Chapter 2

The Economics of Polygamy

Some years ago, UNESCO held a seminar on the status of women in South Asia. The seminar made this concluding statement after a discussion of the problem of polygamy: 'Polygamy might be due to economic reasons, that is to say, the nature of the principal source of livelihood of the social group concerned, e.g. agriculture, but data available to the Seminar would not permit any conclusions to be drawn on this point.'[1]

It is understandable that such a cautious conclusion should be drawn in Asia where the incidence of polygamy is low and diminishing. In Africa, however, polygamy is widespread, and nobody seems to doubt that its occurrence is closely related to economic conditions. A report by the secretariat of the UN Economic Commission for Africa (ECA) affirms this point: 'One of the strongest appeals of polygyny to men in Africa is precisely its economic aspect, for a man with several wives commands more land, can produce more food for his household and can achieve a high status due to the wealth which he can command.'[2]

It is self explanatory, after our discussion in the preceding chapter of female work input in African farming, that a man can get more food if he has more land and more wives to cultivate it. But why is it that the more wives he has got, the more land he can command, as the ECA statement says? The explanation lies in the fact that individual property in land is far from being the only system of land tenure in Africa. Over much of the continent, tribal rules of land tenure are still in force. This implies that members of a tribe which commands a certain territory have a native right to take land under cultivation for food production and in many cases also for the cultivation of cash crops. Under this tenure system, an additional wife is an additional economic asset which helps the family to expand its production.

In regions of shifting cultivation, where women do all or most of the work of growing food crops, the task of felling the trees in preparation of new plots is usually done by older boys and very young men, as already mentioned. An elderly cultivator with several wives is likely to have a number of such boys who can be used for this purpose. By the combined efforts of young sons and young wives he may gradually expand his cultivation and become more and more prosperous, while a man with a single wife has less help in cultivation and is likely to have little or no help for felling. Hence, there is a direct relationship between the size of the area cultivated by a family and the number of wives in the family. For instance, in the Bwamba region of Uganda, in East Africa, it appeared from a sample study that men with one wife cultivated an average of 1·67 acres of land, while men with two wives cultivated 2·94 acres, or nearly twice as much. The author of the study describes women in this region as 'the cornerstone and the limiting factor in the sphere of agricultural production' and notes that almost all the men desire to have additional wives. A polygamic family is 'the ideal family organization from the man's point of view'.[3]

In female farming communities, a man with more than one wife can cultivate more land than a man with only one wife. Hence, the institution of polygamy is a significant element in the process of economic development in regions where additional land is available for cultivation under the long fallow system. In Chapter 1 we found an inverse correlation between the use of female family labour and the use of hired labour. It seems that farmers usually either have a great deal of help from their wives, or else they hire labour. Thus farmers in polygamic communities have a wider choice in this than have farmers in monogamic communities. In the former community, the use of additional female family labour is not limited to the amount of work that one wife and her children can perform; the total input of labour can be expanded by the acquisition of one or more additional wives.

This economic significance of polygamy is not restricted to the long fallow system of cultivation. In many regions, farmers have a choice between an expansion of cultivation by the use of more labour in long fallow cultivation, with a hoe, or an expansion by the transition to shorter fallow with ploughs drawn by animals.[4] In such cases, three possible ways of development present themselves to the farmer: expansion by technical change (the plough); expansion by hierarchization of the community (hired labour); or expansion by the traditional method of acquiring additional wives. In a study of economic development in Uganda, Audrey Richards pointed to this crucial role of polygamy as one of the possible ways to agricultural expansion: 'It is rare to find Africans passing out of the subsistence farm level without either the use of additional labour (read: hired labour E.B.), the introduction of the plough, which is not a practical proposition in Buganda; or by the maintenance of a large family unit, which is not a feature of Ganda social structure at the moment.'[5]

In the same vein, Little's classical study of the Mende in the West African state of Sierra Leone concluded that 'a plurality of wives is an agricultural asset, since a large number of women makes it unnecessary to employ much wage labour'.[6] At the time of Little's study (i.e. in the 1930s), it was accepted in the more rural areas that nobody could run a proper farm unless he had at least four wives. Little found sixty-seven wives to the twenty-three cultivators included in his sample and an average of 2·3 wives per married man in a sample of 842 households. He describes how the work of one wife enables him to acquire an additional one: 'He says to his first wife, "I like such and such a girl. Let us make a bigger farm this year." As soon as the harvest is over for that year, he sells the rice and so acquires the fourth wife'.[7]

Little's study is thirty years old, and the incidence of polygamy has declined since then. But, although households with large numbers of wives seem to have more or less disappeared in most of Africa, polygamy is still extremely widespread and is considered an economic advantage in many rural areas. The present situation can be gleaned from Table 4, which brings together the results of a number of sample studies about the incidence of polygamy. It is seen that none of the more recent studies shows such a high incidence of polygamic marriages as in the period of Little's old study. Most of the studies show an average number of around 1·3 wives per married man.*

Table 4

INCIDENCE OF POLYGAMY IN AFRICA

Country in which sample areas are located		Average number of wives per married man	Polygamic marriages as percentage of all existing marriages
Senegal	A	1·1	24
	B	1·3	23
	C	1·3	21
Sierra Leone		2·3	51
Ivory Coast		1·3	27
Nigeria	A	2·1[a]	63
	B	1·5	
Cameroon		1·0–1·3[b]	
Congo	A	1·3	11
	B	1·2	17
South Africa			14
Uganda	A	1·7	45
	B	1·2	

[a] The figures refer to male head of families, while married sons living with these seem to be excluded.

[b] The lowest ratio refers to unskilled workers, the highest ratio to own-account workers.

In most cases over one-fifth of all married men were found to have more than one wife at the time of enquiry.†

The acquisition of an additional wife is not always used as a means of becoming richer through the expansion of cultivation. In some cases, the economic role of the additional wife enables

* Some of the samples were taken in urban areas, where the incidence of polygamy is often, though not always, lower than in rural areas.

† To evaluate correctly this figure for the incidence of polygamy it must be taken that some of the married men, at the time of the enquiry, had one wife only because they were at an early stage of their married life, while others were older men living in monogamous marriage because they had lost other wives by death or divorce. Therefore, the figure for the incidence of polygamy would have been considerably higher if it were to show the proportion of men who have more than one wife at some stage of their married life.

the husband to enjoy more leisure. The village study from Gambia mentioned in Chapter 1 showed that in this village, where rice is produced by women, men who had several wives to produce rice for them produced less millet (which is a crop produced by men) than did men with only one wife.[8] Likewise, in the villages in the Central African Republic men with two wives worked less than men with one wife, and they found more time for hunting, the most cherished spare time occupation for the male members of the village population.[9]

Undoubtedly, future changes in marriage patterns in rural Africa will be closely linked to future changes in farming systems which may lessen (or enhance) the economic incentive for polygamic marriages. Of course, motives other than purely economic considerations are behind a man's decision to acquire an additional wife. The desire for numerous progeny is no doubt often the main incentive. Where both the desire for children and the economic considerations are at work, the incentives for polygamy are likely to be so powerful that religious or legal prohibition avails little.

The study of the Yoruba farmers of Nigeria mentioned in Chapter 1 has this to say: 'There are no doubt other reasons why polygamy prevails in the Yoruba country as in other regions of the world; but the two which seem to be most prominent in the minds of Yoruba farmers are that wives contribute much more to the family income than the value of their keep and that the dignity and standing of the family is enhanced by an increase of progeny. While these beliefs persist the institution of polygamy will be enduring, even in families which have otherwise accepted Christian doctrine. The Yoruba farmer argues that the increased output from his farms obtainable without cash expense when he has wives to help him outweighs the economic burden of providing more food, more clothing and larger houses.'[10]

THE STATUS OF YOUNGER WIVES

It is easy to understand the point of view of the Yoruba farmers quoted above when one considers the contribution to family support which women make in this region. Economic relations between husband and wife among the Yoruba differ widely from the common practise of countries where wives are normally supported by their husbands. Only 5 per cent of the Yoruba women in the sample reproduced in Table 5 received from their

Table 5

RIGHTS AND DUTIES OF YORUBA WOMEN

Percentage of women with the following rights and duties:

Wife receives from husband	Wife contributes to household:				
	as self-employed, family aid and housewife	as self-employed, and housewife	as family aid and housewife	as housewife	Total
Nothing	8	11			19
Part of food	32	16			48
All food	15	11	1	1	28
Food, clothing and cash	1		3	1	5
Total	56	38	4	2	100

husbands everything they needed—food, clothing and some cash—and only 2 per cent of them did no work other than domestic activities. A large majority were self-employed (in agriculture, trade or crafts) and many helped a husband on his farm in addition to their self-employment and their domestic duties. Most of these self-employed women had to provide at least part of the food for the family as well as clothing and cash out of their own earnings. Nearly one-fifth of the women received nothing from their husband and had to provide everything out of their own earnings; nevertheless they performed domestic duties for the husband and half of them also helped him on his farm.

There may not be many tribes in Africa where women contribute as much as the Yorubas to the upkeep of the family, but it is normal in traditional African marriages for women to support themselves and their children and to cook for the husband, often using food they produce themselves. A small sample from Bamenda in the West African Cameroons showed that the women contributed 44 per cent of the gross income of the family.[11] Many women of pastoral tribes, for instance the Fulani tribe of Northern Nigeria and Niger, are expected to provide a large part of the cash expenses of the family out of their own earnings from the sale of the milk and butter they produce. They cover the expenditure on clothing for their children and themselves as well as buying food for the family.[12] In many regions of East Africa, women are traditionally expected to support themselves and many women are said to prefer to marry Moslems because a Moslem has a religious duty to support his wife.

In a family system where wives are supposed both to provide food for the family—or a large part of it—and to perform the usual domestic duties for the husband, a wife will naturally welcome one or more co-wives to share with them the burden of daily work. Therefore, educated girls in Africa who support the cause of monogamous marriage as part of a modern outlook are unable to rally the majority of women behind them.[13] In the Ivory Coast, an opinion study indicated that 85 per cent of the women preferred to live in polygamous rather than monogamous marriage. Most of them mentioned domestic and economic reasons for their choice.[14]

In many cases, the first wife takes the initiative in suggesting that a second wife, who can take over the most tiresome jobs in the household, should be procured. A woman marrying a man who already has a number of wives often joins the household more or less in the capacity of a servant for the first wife, unless it happens to be a love match.[15] It was said above that in most parts of the world there seems to be an inverse correlation between the use of female labour and the use of hired labour in agriculture, i.e. that most farmers have some help either from their wives or from hired labour. However, in some regions with widespread polygamy, hired labour is *a supplement* to the labour provided by several wives, in the sense that the tasks for which male strength is needed are done by hired labour, while the other tasks are done by wives. In such cases the husband or his adult sons act only as supervisors.

Reports from different parts of Africa, ranging from the Sudan to Nigeria and the Ivory Coast, have drawn attention to this frequent combination of male labourers and wives of polygamous cultivators working together in the fields under the supervision of one or more male family members.[16] In such cases, the availability of male labour for hire is not a factor which lessens the incentive to polygamous marriages. On the contrary, it provides an additional incentive to polygamous marriages as a means of expanding the family business without changing the customary division of labour between the two sexes. Little reported that in Sierra Leone men with several wives sometimes used them to ensnare male agricultural labourers and get them to work for them without pay.[17]

Table 6

AGE DISTRIBUTION OF MARRIED MOSLEM POPULATION OF DAKAR IN SENEGAL

Percentages

Age group:	First wives	Later wives	Husbands
Below 25 years	12	35	
25–34 years	49	44	10
35–49 years	35	19	59
50 years and over	4	2	31
All ages	100	100	100

In regions where polygamy is the rule, it is likely, for obvious demographic reasons, that many males will have to postpone marriage, or even forego it. Widespread prostitution or adultery is therefore likely to accompany widespread polygamy, marriage payments are likely to be insignificant or non-existant for the bride's family and high for the bridegroom's family, sometimes amounting to several years' earnings of a seasonal labourer.[18] This will induce parents to marry off their daughters rather young, but in a period like the present, where each generation of girls is numerically larger than the previous one, the difference in age between the spouses will be narrower than it was previously.

Figures from Dakar, the capital of Senegal, shown in Table 6, illustrate the importance of the age difference between the spouses. Here, the average marriage age for women is 18 years, and the average age of first marriage for men is between 27 and 28 years. The average age difference between men and their second wives is over 15 years, and nearly all wives belong to age groups which are larger than those to which their husbands belong.[19] No less than 90 per cent of married men belong to the relatively small generations over 35, as can be seen from the table, while only 39 per cent of their first wives and 21 per cent of their second wives belong to these generations.

Economic policy during the period of colonial rule in Africa contributed to the introduction or reinforcement of the customary wide difference in marriage age of young men and girls. In order to obtain labour for head transport, construction works, mines and plantations, the Europeans recruited young villagers at an age where they might have married had they stayed on in the village. Instead they married after their return several years later. The result was an age structure in the villages with very few young men in the age group between 20 and 35 and the need to marry young girls to much older men who had returned from wage labour.

The difference between the numbers of boys and girls in villages where the custom of taking away wage labourers before marriage persists, can be seen from Figure 3 which gives the age distribution in Rhodesian villages as reported in a study by J. Clyde Mitchell.[20] In the age groups 20–35 nearly all the men are away and the number of women in these age groups is several times higher than that of the men. In many other parts of Africa, recruitment for mines, plantations and urban industries results in similarly abnormal age distributions in the villages where the labourers are recruited.

Normally, the status of the younger wife is inferior as befits the assistant or even servant to the first wife. This can be explained partly as a result of the wide age difference between husband and wife and between first and younger wife, but the historical background of the institution of polygamy must also be kept in mind. Domestic slavery survived until fairly recently in many parts of Africa, and the legal ban on slavery introduced by European colonial powers provided an incentive for men to marry girls whom otherwise they might have kept as slaves.

In a paper published as recently as 1959, it is mentioned that in the Ivory Coast women were still being pawned by husbands or fathers to work in their creditor's fields, together with his own wives and daughters and without pay until the debt was paid off, when they were free to return to their own families.[21] Today, such arrangements may be rare in Africa, but it is probable that the bride price for an additional wife is sometimes settled by the cancellation of a debt from the girl's family to the future husband, which would come to much the same thing in terms of real economic relationships.

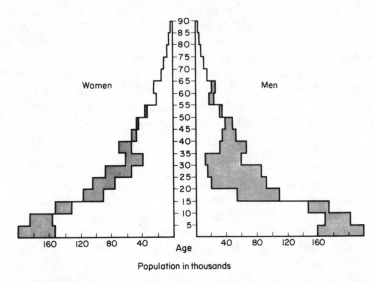

Shaded portion represents persons absent from the African areas

Figure 3 Sex and Age Structure of Population in African Areas of South Rhodesia in 1956

Embodied in Moslem law is the well-known rule that all wives must be treated equally, which implies that the younger wives must not be used as servants for the senior wives. Moreover, a limit is set to the use of wives for expansion of the family business, partly by limiting the allowable number of wives to four, and partly by making the husband responsible for the support of his wives. We have already mentioned that this serves to make Moslem men desirable marriage partners for many African girls in regions where girls married to non-Moslems are expected to support themselves and their children by hard work in the fields. Because of this principle of equal treatment, first wives in orthodox Moslem marriages may desist from making the younger wives perform the most unpleasant tasks. Often in African families—Moslem and non-Moslem—each wife has her own hut or house and cooks independently, while the husband in regular succession will live and eat with each of his wives. Even so, the wife gains by not having to feed her husband all the time, and we sometimes find that women prefer polygamy even where the wives are treated equally.

In most of Africa the rule is that a wife may leave her husband provided that she pays back the bride price. In regions where wives must do hard agricultural work, many young girls wish to find money to enable them to leave a much older husband, and many husbands fear that their young wives will be able to do so.[22] This makes older men take an interest on one hand in keeping bride prices at a level which makes it difficult for women to earn enough to pay them back and on the other hand in preventing their young wives from obtaining money incomes. Later, we shall see what role these conflicting interests between men and women are playing in development policy.

WORK INPUT AND WOMEN'S STATUS

Polygamy offers fewer incentives in those parts of the world where, because they are more densely populated than Africa, the system of shifting cultivation has been replaced by the permanent cultivation of fields ploughed before sowing. However, in some regions where the latter system prevails, polygamy may have advantages. This is true particularly where the main crop is cotton, since women and children are of great help in the plucking season.[23] But in farming systems where men do most of the agricultural work, a second wife can be an economic burden rather than an asset. In order to feed an additional wife the husband must either work harder himself or he must hire labourers to do part of the work. In such regions, polygamy is either non-existent or is a luxury in which only a small minority of rich farmers can indulge. The proportion of polygamic marriages is reported to be below 4 per cent in Egypt, 2 per cent in Algeria, 3 per cent in Pakistan and Indonesia.[24] There is a striking contrast between this low incidence of polygamy and the fact that in many parts of Africa South of the Sahara one-third to one-fourth of all married men have more than one wife.

In regions where women do most of the agricultural work it is the bridegroom who must pay bridewealth, as already mentioned, but where women are less actively engaged in agriculture, marriage payments come usually from the girl's family. In South and East Asia the connection between the work of women and the direction of marriage payments is close and unmistakable. For instance, in Burma, Malaya and Laos women seem to do most of the agricultural work and bride prices are customary.[25] The same is true of Indian tribal people, and of low-caste peoples whose women work. By contrast, in the Hindu communities, women are less active in agriculture, and instead of a bride price being paid by the bridegroom, a dowry has to be paid by the bride's family.[26] A dowry paid by the girl's family is a means of securing for her a good position in her husband's family. In the middle of the nineteenth century it was legal for a husband in Thailand to sell a wife for whom he had paid a bride price, but not a wife whose parents had paid a dowry to the husband.[27]

Not only the payment of a dowry but also the use of the veil is a means of distinguishing the status of the upper class wife from that of the 'servant wife'. In ancient Arab society, the use of the veil and the retirement into seclusion were means of distinguishing the honoured wife from the slave girl who was exposed to the public gaze in the slave market.[28] In the Sudan even today it appears to be a mark of distinction and sophistica-tion for an educated girl to retire into seclusion when she has finished her education.[29]

In communities where girls live in seclusion, and a large dowry must be paid when they marry, parents naturally come to dread the burden of having daughters. In some of the farming communities in Northern India, where women do little work in agriculture and the parents know that a daughter will in due course cost them the payment of a dowry, it was customary in earlier times to limit the number of surviving daughters by infanticide. This practise has disappeared, in its outward forms, but nevertheless the ratio of female to male population in these districts continues to be abnormal compared to other regions of India and to tribes with working women living in the same region. A recent study of regional variations in the sex ratio of population in India[30] reached the conclusion that the small number of women in the Northern districts could not be explained either by undernumeration of females, or by migration, or by a low female birthrate. The only plausible hypothesis would be that mortality among girls was higher than among boys. The conclusion drawn was that 'the persistence of socio-cultural factors are believed to be largely responsible for the excess of female mortality over the male'.[31] One of these socio-cultural factors seem to be a widespread supposition that milk is not good for girls, but is good for boys. There is also a tendency to care more for sick boys than for sick girls.[32]

In a study from a district in Central India with a deficit of women, the author is very outspoken about the neglect of girls: 'The Rajputs always preferred male children.... Female infanticide, therefore, was a tolerated practise.... Although in the past 80 years the proportion of the females to males has steadily risen yet there was always a shortage of women in the region.... When interrogated about the possibility of existence of female infanticide, the villagers emphatically deny its existence.... It was admitted on all hands that if a female child fell ill, then the care taken was very cursory and if she died there was little sorrow. In fact, in a nearby village a cultivator had twelve children—six sons and six daughters. All the daughters fell ill from time to time and died. The sons also fell ill but they survived. The villagers know that it was by omissions that these children had died. Perhaps there has been a transition from violence to non-violence in keeping with the spirit of the times.'[33] The report adds that 'no records of birth or deaths are kept.... it was enjoined upon the Panchayat (village council) to keep these statistics, but they were never able to fulfil the task.'[34] It is explicitly said in the study that the district is one where wives and daughters of cultivators take no part in field work.*

To summarize the analysis of the position of women in rural communities, two broad groups may be identified: the first type is found in regions where shifting cultivation predominates and the major part of agricultural work is done by women. In such communities, we can expect to find a high incidence of polygamy, and bride wealth being paid by the future husband or his family. The women are hard working and have only a limited right of support from their husbands, but they often enjoy considerable freedom of movement and some economic independence from the sale of their own crops.

The second group is found where plough cultivation predominates and where women do less agricultural work than men. In such communities we may expect to find that only a tiny minority of marriages, if any, are polygamous; that a dowry is usually paid by the girl's family; that a wife is entirely dependent upon her husband for economic support; and that the husband has an obligation to support his wife and children, at least as long as the marriage is in force.

We find the first type of rural community in Africa South of the Sahara, in many parts of South East Asia and in tribal regions in many parts of the world. We also find this type among descendents of negro slaves in certain parts of America.[37] The second type predominates in regions influenced by Arab, Hindu and Chinese culture.

Of course, this distinction between two major types of community is a simplification, like any other generalization about social and economic matters. This must be so because many rural communities are already in transition from one type of technical and cultural system to another, and in this process of change some elements in a culture lag behind others to a

* In some cases, the shortage of women in rural communities in North India induce the cultivators to acquire low caste women from other districts, or from other Indian States, against the payment of a bride price.[35] This need not be an infringement on caste rules. Although it is usually forbidden for a man to marry a woman of a higher caste, men of higher caste may have the right to marry women of lower castes.[36] This may then entail the payment of a bride price instead of the receipt of a dowry as would be customary in the husband's own subcaste.

varying degree. For example, some communities may continue to have a fairly high incidence of polygamy or continue to follow the custom of paying bride price long after the economic incentive for such customs has disappeared as agricultural techniques changed.

It was mentioned in Chapter 1 that in many rural communities hired labour is replacing the work of women belonging to the cultivator family. Where this happens, the economic incentive for polygamy may disappear, since additional wives are liable to become an economic burden. This, of course, is true only if it is assumed that the women who give up farm work retire into the purely domestic sphere. It is another matter if the women substitute farming by another economic activity such as trade. We shall revert to the problems of trading women in a later chapter.

In the type of rural community where women work hard, it is a characteristic that they are valued both as workers and as mothers of the next generation and, therefore, that the men keenly desire to have more than one wife. On the other hand, in a rural community where women take little part in field work, they are valued as mothers only and the status of the barren woman is very low in comparison with that of the mother of numerous male children. There is a danger in such a community that the propaganda for birth control, if successful, may further lower the status of women both in the eyes of men and in their own eyes. This risk is less in communities where women are valued because they contribute to the well-being of the family in other ways, as well as breeding sons.

NOTES TO CHAPTER 2

1. Appadorai, 19.   2. UN. ECA., *Wom. Trad. Soc.*, 5.   3. Winter, 24.
4. Simons, 79–80.   5. Richards 1952, 204.   6. Little 1951, 141–2.
7. Little 1951, 141–2, 145.   8. Haswell, 10.   9. Georges, 18, 25, 31.
10. Galetti, 77.   11. Kaberry, 141.   12. Forde, 203; Dupire 1960, 79.
13. UN. ECA., *Polygamy*, 32.   14. Boutillier 1960, 120.   15. Little 1951, 133.   16. Baumann, 307; Forde, 45; Boutillier 1960, 97; Gosselin, 521.
17. Little 1951, 141; 1948, 11.   18. Forde, 75n.   19. UN. ECA., *Polygamy*, 24.   20. Mitchell, *Soc. Backgr.*, 80.   21. d'Aby, 49.   22. Winter, 23.
23. Arnaldez, 50.   24. UN. ECA., *Wom. N. Afr.*, 41; Appadorai, 18.

25. MiMi Khaing, 109; Swift, 271; Lévy, 264.   26. Mitham, 283–4.
27. Purcell, 295.   28. Izzedin, 299.   29. Tothill, 245.   30. Visaria, 334–71.
31. Visaria, 370.   32. Karve, 103–4.   33. Bhatnagar, 61–2.   34. Bhatnagar,
65.   35. Nath, May 1965, 816.   36. Majumdar, 61.   37. Bastide, 37ff.

Chapter 3

Loss of Status under European Rule

In primitive agricultural systems, the difference in productivity between male and female agricultural labour is roughly proportional to the difference in physical strength. As agriculture becomes less dependent upon human muscular power, the difference in labour productivity between the two sexes might be expected to narrow. In actual fact, however, this is far from being so. It is usually the men who learn to operate the new types of equipment while women continue to work with the old hand tools. With the introduction of improved agricultural equipment, there is less need for male muscular strength; nevertheless, the productivity gap tends to widen because men monopolize the use of the new equipment and the modern agricultural methods. In all developing countries—and in most industrialized countries—women perform the simple manual tasks in agriculture while the more efficient types of equipment, operated by animal or mechanical power, are used primarily by the men. Often, men apply modern scientific methods in the cultivation of cash crops, while their wives continue to cultivate food crops by traditional methods. Thus, in the course of agricultural development, men's labour productivity tends to increase while women's remains more or less static. The corollary of the relative decline in women's labour productivity is a decline in their relative status within agriculture, and, as a further result, women will want either to abandon cultivation and retire to domestic life, or to leave for the town.

THE RESPONSIBILITY OF THE EUROPEANS

European settlers, colonial administrators and technical advisers are largely responsible for the deterioration in the status of women in the agricultural sectors of developing countries. It was they who neglected the female agricultural labour force when they helped to introduce modern commercial agriculture to the overseas world and promoted the productivity of male labour.

It has already been mentioned that the Europeans showed little sympathy for the female farming systems which they found in many of their colonies and in those independent countries where they settled. Their European acceptance that cultivation is naturally a job for men persuaded them to believe that men could become far better farmers than women, if only they would abandon their customary 'laziness'. They wanted proof of their belief, and they found it. Baumann noted that cultivation with the hoe was very superficial when undertaken by women, and that the intensity of hoe culture increased in proportion to the men's share in it.[1] Also Daryll Forde noted that a higher standard of yam cultivation was achieved where men worked with women and supervised them.[2]

How to explain the higher intensity of cultivation and better yields where men help the women is an open question. One possible explanation could be found in the superior physical strength of the men; but it may just as well be contended that the higher productivity simply reflects the fact, mentioned in chapter 1, that men take part in cultivation where population is dense and where, therefore, relatively intensive methods are *needed*, while women work alone where fertile land is abundant and there is no need to apply labour-intensive methods. In any case, virtually all Europeans shared the opinion that men are superior to women in the art of farming; and it then seemed to follow that for the development of agriculture male farming ought to be promoted to replace female farming. Many Europeans did all they could to achieve this.

In Uganda women began the cultivation of cotton, yet in 1923 the European director of agriculture in the territory had stated that 'cotton growing could not be left to the women and old people', and one decade later most of the men were growing cotton and coffee, and importing hired labour from other tribes to do most of the work.[3]

In those parts of Uganda where cultivation continued to be

done mainly by women, the Europeans neglected to instruct the female cultivators when they introduced new agricultural methods, teaching only the men in an agricultural setting of traditional female farming, with particularly unfortunate results in regions with large male emigration, as observed by A. W. Southall: 'Now that new agricultural rules are being introduced for contouring, strip cropping, weed bunding, etc., the wife with husband away will be at a worse disadvantage or rather it is in her fields that such rules will not be observed, for all these new tasks fall mainly within the men's province, and only men are subjected to the propaganda in their favour.'[4]

This warning against teaching modern farming techniques to men but not to women dates back to 1952. Many more recent warnings against the neglect of women cultivators by the extension services could be quoted.[5] One of the studies from the Central African Republic, mentioned in Chapter 1, has this to say: 'Although women play such an important role in agricultural production, the extension services never approach her, but always her husband or brother. The education of the women, even as regards labour productivity, must be done immediately.'[6]

In spite of these warnings, nearly all technical advisers further the policy of promoting male work as initiated by the colonial administrators. And this is true not only of European and American experts. In Senegal, West Africa, Chinese instructors (from Taiwan) failed in their efforts to introduce better techniques in paddy production because they taught only the men, who took no notice since their wives were the culti-vators and the wives being untaught, continued, of course, in the old way, subdividing the carefully improved fields into small traditional plots.[7]

As a result of the attitudes of the extension services, the gap between labour productivity of men and women continues to widen. Men are taught to apply modern methods in the cultiva-tion of a given crop, while women continue to use the traditional methods in the cultivation of the same crop, thus getting much less out of their efforts than the men. The inevitable result is that women are discouraged from participating in agriculture,

55

and are glad to abandon cultivation whenever the increase in their husband's income makes it possible.

And this is not all. The tendency towards a widening gap in labour productivity and income of the two sexes is exacerbated by the fact that it is the cash crops that the men are taught to cultivate by modern methods. These crops are gradually being improved by means of systematic research and other government investment, while the cultivation of the women's food crops is favoured by no government support or research activities, at least not until recently. Moreover, men can use part of their earnings from cash crops to invest in the improvement of their production, while women who produce food crops for family use have no cash income for improving their farming techniques. Farming improvements are thus concentrated in the male sector, while the female sector continued with traditional low-productivity methods.[8]

Such a development has the unavoidable effect of enhancing the prestige of men and of lowering the status of women.[9] It is the men who do the modern things. They handle industrial inputs while women perform the degrading manual jobs; men often have the task of spreading fertilizer in the fields, while women spread manure; men ride the bicycle and drive the lorry, while women carry headloads, as did their grandmothers. In short, men represent modern farming in the village, women represent the old drudgery.

Of course, not only the methods of agricultural training and instruction are responsible for this peculiar polarization of sex roles, with men at the progressive end and women at the traditional end. In many regions, the spread of primary education has helped to create a technical and cultural gap between men and women. Everywhere, boys were sent to school before the girls, or many more boys than girls went to school. Therefore, while illiteracy, traditional behaviour, and superstition had once been common among all the villagers, these signs of backwardness gradually became more characteristic of the women than of the men in rural communities. And there is a cumulative process at work: in a rural community where young men have been to school and have gained at least an acquaintance with the scientific approach, while girls are taught only traditional beliefs by illiterate mothers, it is unquestionably true that it is more effective to teach modern agricultural methods to male than to female farmers.[10] In short, by their discriminatory policy in education and training the Europeans created a productivity gap between male and female farmers, and subsequently this gap seemed to justify their prejudice against female farmers.

FROM CULTIVATOR TO FAMILY AID

As was seen, the change from traditional to modern farming tends to enhance men's prestige at the expense of women's by widening the gap in their levels of knowledge and training. In some cases this tendency is further strengthened by the change in production pattern which gives men the role of independent cultivators who take the decisions, while women's role is reduced to that of family aids or of hired workers on land belonging to male farmers, with a correspondingly enhanced male status over women.

This change in women's status is connected with the change from shifting cultivation in regions of tribal tenure to permanent cultivation of privately owned land. It was mentioned in Chapter 2 that under shifting cultivation each member of the tribe which dominates a given territory has the right to take land under cultivation. In cases where women are the farmers, it is they who make use of this right, although it is said in some tribes that the women own only the crops, while the men own the land.[11] The same distinction is often made in descriptions of the rights of tribal chiefs—who are said to own the land—and the ordinary members of the tribe—who are said to own the crop. But the word 'ownership' is ambigious in relation to tribal tenure and is often used by chiefs in order to justify a claim for ownership rights in land belonging to the tribe as such, when land is becoming scarce and therefore a valuable asset.[12] Similarly, in the relationship between man and women, the use of the European concept of ownership can give the impression of an absolute right for men which may not exist in the community in question.[13]

In a tribal area, the clearing of a strip of land for cultivation does not establish ownership of that land. The person who clears the land, or who cultivates it, owns the crops and he (she) may continue to cultivate the land as long as he (she) needs it. If the population is sparse, the cultivation of a plot of land is usually given up after a few years and replaced by a new plot, no one caring about what happens to the abandoned one. By contrast, when population increases so that it becomes difficult to find suitable land for new fields, cultivators will naturally begin to keep an eye on their old fields and prevent others from taking them under cultivation. In this way, a sort of *de facto* private property in land may emerge in regions where land is gradually becoming scarce, through population increase or the expansion of the cultivation of cash crops. This scarcity of land may result in the loss of women's rights to land.[14]

In a study of a region of the Cameroons in West Africa, Phyllis Kaberry showed a possible danger for the economic welfare of women in the idea that men own the land, women the crops. As long as land is not scarce, such ideas are harmless to women's welfare. But it is a different matter when pressure on land increases to the point of shortage, or when the practice of renting or selling land is started, since only the men would reap the gains. Phyllis Kaberry suggested that in such cases women should be given the right to acquire land on equal terms with men.[15]

We must distinguish between the type of *de facto* permanent user right which may appear spontaneously when land is becoming scarce, and, on the other hand, the outright private ownership of land. The latter means that individuals can freely sell land to other members of the tribe or to outsiders, while the former may mean only that the right of occupancy for a given piece of land can be passed on from parents to their children. In many tribal regions, land tenure seems to be at an intermediate stage between traditional tribal rights to clear plots and the full private ownership of land. We often find that land can be passed on from fathers to sons in patrilinear tribes, and from mothers to daughters in matrilinear tribes, but that the sale of land is not allowed, or is exceptional. When sales of land increase women are at a disadvantage, because they usually cultivate subsistence crops for the family, while men cultivate cash crops or work for a wage. Therefore, it is the men who have money and can purchase land. Thus the possession of land is likely to pass gradually from women to men, even in tribes where women have the right to inherit land.

Little information seems to be available about the amount of land in tribal communities owned by men and women respectively. However, we do have a survey of the ownership of 960 plots of land in three villages in a district of Tanzania in East Africa (Table 7). Land tenure in the district is in a transitional

Table 7

OWNERSHIP OF LAND IN TANZANIA VILLAGES

Percentages of all plots of land in sample villages

Method by which owner had obtained possession of the plot:	Female owner	Male owner	Together
Clearing of land	17	32	49
Inheritance	18	21	39
Purchase		6	6
Other means (including marriage)	4	2	6
Total	39	61	100

stage, and rights to clear plots exist side by side with rights to inherit land and to sell it. Women were in possession of nearly 40 per cent of the plots in the villages surveyed and they had inherited nearly as many plots as the men, whereas only men had purchased land. The three villages had been selected with the object of throwing light on different stages of economic development. In one of the villages, situated far from any modern activities, women were in possession of 46 per cent of the plots. In the second village, situated in a district with large plantations, women had 38 per cent of the plots, and in the third village, which was adjacent to a plantation, women had only 26 per cent of the plots.[16] This survey thus tends to confirm the generalizations made above, but, admittedly, it is no more than one suggestive example.

If the possession of land is passing from women to men, it

does not necessarily follow that women lose their traditional right to grow crops of their own. They may preserve a customary right to use land belonging to their husbands for the growing of food for the family, together with the right to sell the surplus of such crops and use the proceeds freely.[17] But even in such cases, the position of women has changed from that of an independent cultivator with her own farming rights, to a person who is farming land belonging to another person. Moreover, this position may be no more than a transitional step to the stage where women are unpaid helpers in the production of crops belonging to their husbands.

The loss of women's right to land is sometimes the result of land reforms introduced by European administrations. The Europeans everywhere seem to have objected to the peculiar position of African women, which was so different from anything the Europeans were accustomed to. In the Congo, female predominance in farming is very evident: in one region it was found that there were 38,000 female cultivators, but only 18,000 male cultivators.[18] But Suzanne Comhaire-Sylvain says that in the Congo there was 'always very strong propaganda coming from the Missions and the Government against matrilinear custom. Emphasis was laid upon the teachings of the Bible where all authority comes from God through the father.'[19]

In the Congo, the Belgians did recognize women as cultivators in the modernized farming system,[20] but in other parts of Africa, where female farming predominated, women were eliminated by European-styled land reforms, and the land was given to their husbands, although before the reforms the women had been independent cultivators.* For instance, in the Bikita Reserve in Rhodesia, a female farming area, the land reform completed in 1957 allocated the land to men and widows only, but not to married women.† This meant that

* In many communities in developing countries, married women have, besides their land, livestock of their own. Among both the Haussa and the Fulani tribes of Northern Nigeria, women own domestic animals and men cannot dispose of them without the consent of their wives. But when the British administration made a census, by asking only the men they excluded the stock belonging to the women.[21]

† Also in Mexico, women lose their right to have parcels in the 'ejido', the communally owned areas, when they marry.[22]

23 per cent of those who received land were absent men, who worked as wage labourers outside the region, while their wives lived as cultivators in the Reserve.[23] The position of the women became precarious, because the men could—and often did—divorce and marry other women, in which case their former wives were deprived of the land they had considered their own, and with good reason, since they had cultivation rights in it.

European administration made a similar transfer of land from women to men in the Union of South Africa. In 1898 a proclamation in the Transkei denied the right of each wife of a polygamist to have her own plot and introduced the rule of 'one man one plot' with the result that the wives not only had to cultivate in common the land belonging to their husbands but lost it to his male heirs after his death.[24] A similar transfer of rights in land took place in the Taung reserve when the land was irrigated. Although women are the main cultivators, the irrigated fields were allocated to the men who alone were taught the techniques of irrigated farming.[25]

In South East Asia, European administrations have similarly transferred rights in land from women to men. For instance, in the Negri Sembilan area of Malaya, land was held by women cultivators. Both paddy land and the land on which the women had their homesteads was traditionally passed on from mother to daughter, or from sister to sister. The British administration took the first step in the change favourable to the men when it was decided that only the land which was under actual cultivation by the women would continue to pass in the female line, whereas the areas serving as fallow land in shifting cultivation had to be registered to ensure the continuance of female inheritance. In this way the women lost their right to forest land, and later this proved to have been a significant loss, when the men began to plant rubber trees in the forest areas.[26]

Since the concepts of male and female rights in land are highly ambiguous, we cannot expect statistics to give a faithful picture of the extent to which women are cultivators of their own land or family helpers in their husbands' farms. Nevertheless, Table 8 brings out the difference between the male farming of Arab and Latin American countries, where women are a tiny minority among the own-account farmers, and, on the other hand some

Table 8

SEX DISTRIBUTION OF PERSONS WHO ARE FARMING ON OWN-ACCOUNT

	Percentage of women among:		
Country:	persons employing hired labour	persons not employing hired labour	all own-account farmers
Africa South of the Sahara:			
Sierra Leone			10
Liberia			18
Ghana			37
Mauritius	4	12	11
Region of Arab influence:			
Morocco	5	2	3
Algeria			2
United Arab Republic	2	1	1
Jordan	2	1	1
Syria	1	1	1
Iran	5	2	2
Pakistan			4
South and East Asia:			
Ceylon			3
Thailand	18	14	14
Cambodia			10
Malaya			19
Philippines	9	4	4
Taiwan			8
Korea (South)			13
Latin America:			
Mexico			5
Honduras	5	1	1
El Salvadore	2	1	1
Nicaragua			5
Costa Rica	1	1	1
Panama	3	1	1
Columbia			5
Ecuador			5

Table 8—contd.

Chile	12	6	6
Brazil			5
Venezuela	5	4	4
Cuba			1
Jamaica			13
Dominican Republic			1
Puerto Rico			2

countries in West Africa and South East Asia, where women form a significant proportion of own-account farmers. It is worth noting that Jamaica shows a pattern similar to that of West Africa rather than Latin America. The Jamaican population consists mainly of descendants of African slaves, and some African farming traditions appear to have been preserved there.

THE REVOLT OF THE WOMEN

African women have not always accepted without protest the deterioration in their position. The transfer of rights from women to men was often felt to be an injustice committed by the Europeans. It is said about the transfer of rights in the Transkei that 'the people want to restore to women the rights they had to land in the old society. But all attempts to bring about the change have failed to persuade an inflexible bureaucracy which is not responsible to the people.'[27]

A more vigorous protest against colonial action hostile to women was launched by the famous 1929 women's revolt in the Abo region of Nigeria organized in response to a tax imposed by the British administration.[28] In 1959 women revolted in the Kon region of Eastern Nigeria, while that region was still part of the British Cameroons. The Kon revolt was studied by an American anthropologist, Robert E. Ritzenthaler.[29] Women's resistance to the deterioration of their position as farmers coupled to their fear of losing their land to male farmers led to major upheavals. The Kon is a region of female farming with some Fulani sheep farming. The unrest among the women sparked off when the Fulani flocks trespassed into the women's farming area and damaged the crops. This was fanned into a major revolt by rumours spread among the women that the Government was

63

selling their land to the Ibo tribe. These rumours were unfounded, having apparently been spread by some men who wanted to gain the women's support in the 1959 elections. Ritzenthaler stresses in his report of the uprising that, although there were no Ibos in that region, the almost neurotic hatred of them was shared by most people in the region. The illiterate women regard their land as almost sacred, and the fear that their land might be sold was by far the most important reason for the uprising.

During the uprising, some two thousand women, led by the traditional women's organization in the region, marched in procession to a neighbouring town, occupied the market and set fire to it. They agreed on a number of resolutions; among these the elimination of all foreign institutions, such as courts and schools, and the expulsion from the region of all foreigners, including Ibos, members of other tribes and Europeans.

The unrest among the Kon women spread to neighbouring tribes. In one of them, the introduction of new farming techniques was the immediate cause of the uprising. Ritzenthaler shows that the women resisted by desperate means, and he finds that many of their complaints were legitimate.[30]

These dramatic events in Nigeria are not the only evidence of female resistance against the loss of opportunities for cultivation on their own account. Phyllis Kaberry reports from the Cameroons that the men, although they held themselves to be owners of the land, as mentioned above, would always consult their wives before they pledged or sold land. They did this because they feared that their wives might leave them if they parted with land without consulting them.[31] There are many reports from Africa about husbands whose wives refuse to help them in the production of cash crops, or to perform household chores, unless they are paid a wage for their work.[32] Other reports concern women who refuse to help their husbands in the cultivation of cash crops because they want to grow only their own food crops. This is considered an obstacle to the progress from subsistence agriculture to commercial production for the market. In the Bwamba region of Uganda, for instance, women's preference for growing subsistence crops is held to be an important factor restrianing the cultivation of cash crops.[33]

NOTES TO CHAPTER 3

1. Baumann, 295ff. 2. Forde, 67n. 3. Powesland, 20–2. 4. Southall, 1952, 158–9. 5. Pauw, 72. 6. Georges, 7. 7. Delalande, 61. 8. Leurquin, 251–2; *Wills Time Allocation*, 8. 9. UN., *Role Wom. Ec. Dev.*, 1968, 35. 10. Boismenu, 10. 11. Kaberry, 42; Richards 1939, 190. 12. Boserup, 83n, 92–3. 13. Simons, 196ff. 14. Simons, 261–9 *passim*. 15. Kaberry, 148. 16. Tanner, 16–19. 17. Finnegan, 66, 92–3. 18. Soyer-Poskin, 144. 19. Comhaire-Sylvain, 123. 20. Soyer-Poskin, 145. 21. Forde, 123, 128n, 203. 22. Redfield, 57. 23. Floyd, 30. 24. Simons, 262. 25. Pauw, 72. 26. Swift, 276–7. 27. Simons, 266. 28. Leith-Ross, 23–9. 29. Ritzenthaler, 151–6. 30. Ritzenthaler, 156. 31. Kaberry, 147. 32. Clignet, 211; Galetti, 76; Little 1948, 11; Kaberry, 147. 33. Winter, 15.

Chapter 4

The Casual Worker

In developing countries, as already mentioned, two main types of rural community can be identified; one in which wage labourers are few, and women are very active in agricultural work, and the other type where women take little part in agricultural work while the male cultivators employ much hired help. In some countries where these hired workers are men, we have a genuine type of male farming with little female participation, but other countries show a more intricate social and sex pattern where women work as casual labourers for male cultivators belonging to another caste or ethnic group than the workers.

This pattern seems to exist primarily where peoples with male and peoples with female farming traditions have come to live together within the same region. In such cases, those with male farming traditions most often dominate the people with female farming traditions who are a subjugated group subsisting by casual labour, possibly supplemented by shifting cultivation on poor or hilly land. The social gap between cultivators and agricultural labourers is always wide, and particularly so where female agricultural workers of a low caste or tribal group work for male farmers belonging to communities with non-working women living in seclusion. Here the three status differences—social class, ethnic group and sex—culminate in the creation of an abyss between employer and employee.

Another inevitable effect of this social gap is to encourage the cultivator's wife to retire into seclusion and to avoid all manual work outside the household, in order to distinguish herself from the despised and hard-working female labourers, even if this means that she must live in utter poverty.

66

This social pattern, where women from subjugated communities serve as agricultural workers for members of landowning communities, is found the world over. From Africa comes a notorious example of a clash between the Tutsi and the Hutu in Burundi, caused by the conflict of these social patterns which created such acute tension that the Hutu massacred many Tutsi. The Hutu is a tribe with a female farming tradition and both Hutu men and Hutu women worked as labourers for the Tutsi upper class. Until the recent massacre in Burundi, the Tutsi and the Hutu were living in a symbiotic social structure which may be characterized as an elaborate caste system, where women in each caste, although subservient to men of their own caste, were vastly superior to all men of lower castes.[1] The wives of the Tutsi chiefs had absolute power over most male members of the local communities, while the Hutu women were at the bottom of the social hierarchy, doing the hard labour and subordinate to all other groups in the communities, including their own husbands. In the Hutu tribe, the firm traditions of female work have given rise to folklore tales about women who are much better agricultural workers than men and are capable of carrying twice as heavy loads than men, etc.[2]

A tribal population, subjugated and deprived of land by another ethnic group, may end by inter-marrying with the dominating group and thus becoming integrated with it in a less rigid social pattern. However, in the hierarchical rural communities in many parts of Asia, deeply ingrained customs and attitudes have prevented the integration of land-owning and landless groups. This is particularly true of India, where the caste system precluded both inter-marriage and the acquisition of land by low-caste people. Therefore, landless and landowning groups with different farming traditions continue to co-exist; side by side with high-caste Hindu women, who take no part in farming activities, some 15 million women belonging to tribal and low-caste groups earn their living as casual labourers on farms belonging to the higher-caste Hindus. India, together with Ceylon and Malaya, seem to be the only countries where more than 10 per cent of all adult women earn their living as agricultural labourers (Table 9). But while most female

Table 9

SEX DISTRIBUTION OF AGRICULTURAL WAGE LABOURERS AND OF PERSONNEL IN MINING, CONSTRUCTION AND TRANSPORT

Country	Female agricultural wage labourers as percentage of all adult women	Percentage of women among agricultural wage labourers	Percentage of women in total labour force[a] in:		
			mining	construction	transport
Africa South of the Sahara:					
Sierra Leone		5	1	1	2
Liberia		4	3	1	2
Ghana		6	5	3	1
South Africa	2	10	1	1	8
Mauritius	7	20	21		2
Uganda		2	4	1	10
Kenya	2	27	b	b	b
Region of Arab influence:					
Sudan		4		2	
Morocco	1	5	2	1	3
Tunisia		2	2	1	3
United Arab Republic	1	4	1		1
Turkey	1	23	2	1	2
Syria	1	8	5	1	1
Iraq		2	3	1	
Iran	1	4	1		1
Pakistan	1	6	1	1	1
South and East Asia:					
India	12	44	19	12	2
Ceylon	12	40	13	6	5
Burma	b	b	8[c]	3[c]	2[c]
Thailand	2	35	25	9	5

a The percentages refer to total personnel, including clerical staff and persons working on own-account.

b No information is available.   c In urban areas only.

68

Table 9—contd.

Cambodia	1	24	b	b	b
Malaya	12	39	16	8	2
Singapore		13	10	7	2
Indonesia	b	b	12	4	4
Philippines	1	12	4	1	2
Hong Kong		25	17	8	1
Korea (South)		10	4	1	3
Latin America:					
Mexico	5	16	7	3	5
Honduras		6	1	1	7
El Salvadore	2	4	1		2
Nicaragua	1	3	3	1	2
Costa Rica	1	2	1	1	1
Panama		2	4	1	12
Columbia	1	3	26	1	5
Ecuador	1	4	6	2	3
Chile	1	2	2	1	5
Brazil	1	5	9	1	4
Venezuela		3	5	1	4
Cuba	1	2	3	1	4
Jamaica	3	17	14	2	12
Dominican Republic		2	1		1
Puerto Rico		1	1	2	7

agricultural labourers in Ceylon and Malaya work in the plantations, most of the Indian women work on family farms belonging to men with non-working wives. More than 40 per cent of the agricultural workers in India are women and according to major sample enquiries they did 37 per cent of all the agricultural work done by casual labourers in 1956–7.[3]

THE INFLUENCE OF CASTE ON WOMEN'S WORK AND WAGES

A large number of village studies from all parts of India describe the intricate hierarchical pattern of work in Indian villages. The description of the social pattern of a village in Andhra Pradesh in South East India may be mentioned as an example. The author of that study, S. C. Dube, found four main social groups. In the top group of high-caste people women took no part in any outdoor activities and many observed *purdah*, i.e. they never left the house unveiled. Their husbands' agricultural work was restricted to the supervision of those who performed the actual manual work. Below this top group was the local cultivator caste. Their women were occupied mainly with domestic duties and never earned money for the support of the family, while the men would plough their own fields. In the third group of ordinary low-caste people, women assisted their husbands in the fields and they also went to the market. They worked mainly within the family framework and in their own fields, although they might work for a wage in the busy season. The fourth and lowest social group was composed of women belonging to the poorest of the low castes who were expected regularly to seek paid work for the support of their families.[4]

Thus, within the social microcosm of a single Indian village we can clearly identify the different types of female work pattern which we have described as being characteristic of various parts of the world at large. First, there is the veiled, non-working woman of the Middle East. Secondly, we have the domestic wife who contributes very little to farming; this we recognize as the characteristic type of many Latin American countries. The third type is that of the active family worker who must carry a large share of the burden of work in the family farm and who may occasionally work for others. She is characteristic of the South East Asian scene. And, fourthly, we find the 'African type' of woman who cannot expect to be supported by her husband, but must fend independently for her own support and for that of the family by accepting whatever work she can find.

It is well known that the social variables of caste status and of ethnic group in India are highly correlated, and women with the different work characteristics just described can often be identified as belonging to different ethnic groups. Indeed, India is a meeting place for peoples with different cultural traditions and this is reflected in the work pattern of its women —and of its men. Sometimes, a given village is exclusively or predominantly inhabited by members of one particular ethnic group: there are tribal villages with no Hindus, and Hindu villages with no tribal and few low-caste people. In other instances, among them the particular village mentioned above, the different groups live in the same place, subjected to a rigid sex-caste-ethnic pattern of division of labour and leisure.

Tribal and low-caste families of agricultural labourers are far more numerous in some parts of India than in others. Some of the North Indian States have little tribal population and relatively few low-caste families. By contrast, in Central India, tribal and low-caste people are a large minority, in some cases approaching one-half of the population. And in South India, many communities have female farming traditions. Hence, female participation rates in farming are much higher in Central and South India than in North India and Pakistan. As appears from Table 10, female wage workers account for 18 per cent

Table 10

AGRICULTURAL LABOUR FORCE IN INDIA AND PAKISTAN BY SEX AND STATUS

Status and Sex:	South India	Central India	North India	Pakistan
		Percentages		
Labourers, women	18	13	6	1
Labourers, men	17	13	11	13
Family members, women[a]	23	30	24	13
Family members, men	42	44	59	73
Total	100	100	100	100

[a] Include all female family members who take part in agricultural work for at least one hour per day during most of the working season.

of the total agricultural labour force in South India, for 13 per cent in Central India, but for only 6 per cent in Northern India and one per cent in Pakistan.

Thus, the India-Pakistan sub-continent can be divided into two rather sharply demarcated regions with strikingly different patterns of female employment. In North India and Pakistan the pattern of female work participation resembles that of the West Asian and North African Arab countries, while Central and South India have a pattern more like that of South East

Asia, where female work participation rates are very high. Obviously, the influence from West Asian culture was strong in the Northern part of the India-Pakistan Sub-continent and only slight in the Southern part.

In some of the regions with a numerous population of agricultural labour families, women workers do a very large part of the total agricultural work. This is the case, for instance, in two districts of Central India, where one-third of all agricultural work is done by women from landless families working as casual labourers (Table 11), while women from cultivator families do no more than 6–7 per cent of the field work in the family farms.*

Table 11

WORK INPUT IN AGRICULTURE IN TWO DISTRICTS OF CENTRAL INDIA BY SEX AND STATUS

Percentages of total hours worked in agriculture in the sample farms

	Akola district			Amraoti district		
			Both			Both
Status of worker:	Women	Men	sexes	Women	Men	sexes
Casual labourer	35	8	43	30	5	35
Farm servant		13	13		13	13
Member of farm family:						
Hours worked as hired on other farms	6	11	17	7	18	25
Hours worked on own farm	6	21	27	7	20	27
Total	47	53	100	44	56	100

Such examples of women of cultivator families doing very little farm work in their own farms can also be found in other parts of the world. As mentioned in Chapter 1, the Yoruba women in Nigeria were found to do only 7 per cent of the agricultural work, while male family members and male labourers did 93 per cent of the work. But there is an important difference

* The two districts do not seem to be exceptional as regards under-utilization of female family labour. Gadgil says that the population in these districts has 'almost no sentiment against field work by women', in contrast to the restrictive attitudes to female family labour in other parts of India.[5]

between this and the Indian case; the Yoruba women contribute little to farming but make up for this by taking an extremely active part in trading and crafts, while women of the Hindu cultivator families usually do no work other than their domestic activities except for their small participation in farming. Moreover, it must be taken into account that the survey of the Yoruba was made in an exceptionally prosperous year in one of the most prosperous farming districts of Africa, while the Indian survey covers a normal year in a poor region of India. When women from the cultivator families hardly take any part in farming, even in such a poor region, and leave nearly all the female tasks to tribal and low-caste women working as casual labourers, it is difficult to avoid concluding that the prejudice against women's work in the field is an important cause of the region's poverty.*

The contrasting patterns of female work participation in Northern and Southern India has a corollary in the different ratios between female and male wages in agriculture. The difference between the wages paid to women and to men for the same agricultural tasks is less in many parts of Northern India than is usual in Southern India and it seems reasonable to explain this as a result of the disinclination of North Indian women to leave the domestic sphere and temporarily accept the low status of an agricultural wage labourer. Table 12 gives information on the ratio between women's and men's wages in Indian agriculture, based upon data concerning the three tasks of weeding, transplanting and harvesting in thirteen States in two different years. It appears that in about two-thirds of the cases the average ratio of female to male wages was between 0·6 and 0·8, but in nine cases out of seventy-seven the ratio was over 0·9. None of these untypical cases of small or non-existing wage differential were found in South India, where the supply of female labour is ample, as just mentioned. In that region, the abundant supply of female

---

* It would be a fallacy to suggest that if the women of the cultivator families were more inclined to work, the results would be necessarily be to deprive the low-caste women of an opportunity of employment and thus to leave poverty unchanged or even exacerbated by a more uneven distribution. For the survey in question was made in a region of India where there are plenty of possibilities for expansion and intensification of agricultural production if more labour were available in the farm families.

73

labour keeps women's wages very low in relation to men's wages.*

Owing to this cheap female labour in South India, half the women in cultivator families can avoid agricultural work (as shown by Table 10). But the low level of wages resulting from

Table 12

RATIO OF FEMALE TO MALE AGRICULTURAL WAGES IN INDIA

Ratio:	13 Indian States	6 North Indian States	3 Central Indian States	4 South Indian States	16 Villages in the State of Uttar Pradesh
	Number of observations (localities)				
Below 0·50	2	2			
0·50–0·59	5	2		3	1
0·60–0·69	23	8	8	7	1
0·70–0·79	27	11	5	11	3
0·80–0·89	11	7	2	2	3
0·90–0·99	4	2	2		6
1·00 and more	5	4	1		2
Total	77[a]	36	18	23[a]	16

Note: The data for Indian States refer to average wages paid in the years 1950–1 and 1956–7 for weeding, transplanting and harvesting, i.e. six wage differentials for each State. The data for the State of Uttar Pradesh are wages paid in 1956–7 for hoeing and weeding, i.e. one wage-differential for each village.

[a] No information is available about male wages for weeding in Kerala in one of the years covered in the investigation.

the large supply of female labour in South India has another and more favourable effect: it provides an incentive for the use of labour-intensive farming methods, with well irrigation and cultivation of transplanted paddy. As a result, the men too,

* Similarly, the plantations in North India apply smaller wage differentials between the sexes than do plantations in the south. In Northern India, average daily earnings of female and male unskilled labour differ by only some 5 to 15 per cent, and the difference in wage rates for similar work is sometimes even smaller. In South Indian plantations, sex differentials in wages are considerably larger.[6]

who do most of the watering, can find fairly continuous employment throughout the year.[7]

The ratios of female to male wages show a much wider spread in North India, where the supply of tribal and low-caste female labour is small. In some cases the ratio is 0·5 or even lower, and in other cases equal wages seem to be paid to the two sexes. Of the ten extreme cases of very narrow or very wide wage differentials in North India (Table 12, column 2) half refer to the Punjab, the most prosperous farming area in India, where tribal and low-caste labour is rare and where attitudes to female farm work are restrictive. The difficulty of drawing women into the agricultural labour market when they are needed seems in some cases to have led to the payment of equal wages for men and women, but in other cases we find extremely high wages— by Indian standards—for male workers, and thus very wide differentials.*

Some more detailed information about wages for hoeing and weeding in sixteen villages of the State of Uttar Pradesh in North India seems to confirm that wage differentials tend to disappear when female labour is in short supply. These data are summarized in column 5 of Table 12. In half the villages, the ratio of female to male wages for hoeing and weeding was above 0·9. These cases of narrow wage differentials are highly interesting, because Uttar Pradesh is one of the Indian States with a most restrictive attitude to women's work. Even agricultural labourers keep their women at home, and employment as a wage labourer is shunned by half the women in agricultural labouring families. Likewise, the participation rate for female family labour in their own fields is among the lowest in India. The high frequency, in this region, of equal wages for the same type of work seems to confirm that restrictive attitudes to women's work tend to create a shortage of female labour and thereby to eliminate the customary wage differential between men and women.†

* In Central India too, where there is much tribal labour, equal wages were in some cases paid to men and women for weeding and transplanting. But this equality was due to unusually low wages for male (tribal) labour. It would seem that in this case the absence of the usual male prejudice against such types of 'female' tasks had the effect of eliminating wage differentials between male and female labour, by lowering the price of male labour.

† These sixteen villages are from the more prosperous part of the State of Uttar Pradesh. Another investigation in the poor Eastern part of the State gave

CHEAP LABOUR FOR THE EXPORT SECTOR

In Asia, and in many parts of Africa, a large proportion of the cash crops are produced in plantations established in colonial times and still owned and run by Europeans. Recru tment policy for these plantations differed widely from region to region. In some cases only men were employed, in other cases the whole family, and these differences have often survived the end of colonial rule.

In most Asian plantations with a family employment policy, women and children continue to work together with the male workers. In Ceylon and Vietnam, women account for over 50 per cent of the labour force in plantations. In Malaya and India the share is over 40 per cent and in Pakistan and the Philippines it is around 35 per cent.[9] Because plantations predominate in Malayan and Ceylonese agriculture, women wage labourers account for no less than 16 and 22 per cent, respectively, of the whole agricultural labour force in these countries.

Recruitment policies similar to those of Asian plantations are found in plantations and large foreign owned farms in some parts of East Africa. In many other parts of Africa, employment in plantations is reserved for men. The most widespread colonial system of recruitment for plantations in Africa was to employ young unmarried men, as already mentioned. The Europeans not only restricted the recruitment to men; they often made sure that his wife and children did not follow the man to his new residence, but stayed behind in the village. In other cases, the low wages paid to the men and the dormitories put at their disposal were sufficient to deter the women.

The Congo was among the African countries where the European recruited only men for the plantations, even for jobs like weeding which in the village was never done by men. Being cut off from his family, and being obliged to perform the despised

---

similar results. In thirty-four localities, wages were collected for female work and for different types of male work. In twenty-three out of these thirty-four cases, women were paid a wage which corresponded to the lowest wage paid for male labour (usually for 'miscellaneous work', but sometimes for transplanting), in two cases women were paid more than the lowest rate for men, and only in nine cases were they paid less.[8]

'female tasks', the worker naturally tended to be dissatisfied and to absent himself frequently to return to his village to see his family.[10] After independence, there has been a tendency for African plantation workers to take their families with them, and the report of the Second African Regional Conference of the International Labour Organization says that 'on plantations and large farms employers welcomed women joining their husbands; the women made a home, helped to stabilize the workers, helped to feed the families by cultivating a small plot of land and were available to help in light seasonal agricultural work such as harvesting and weeding as wage-earning workers'.[11] However, according to statistics presented in the same report, the number of women working for wages in agriculture remains very small. African women cultivate land belonging to themselves or to their husbands, but in most African countries the majority of agricultural wage labourers are men.

Thus, the African woman contributes little to production of cash crops (and thereby to production for export), both because plantation labour consists mainly of men, and because men are more active in producing export crops in family farming. In the production of food crops, on the other hand, the African woman plays a major role, as already explained. In Asia, the situation is quite different: a major share of Asian agricultural exports is produced in the plantations, where women have an important role to play, while their role in food production for the home market is relatively small.

We may now ask how these striking contrasts in the use of female labour in Asia and in Africa are to be explained. Do they reflect only differences in colonial recruitment policy, or more fundamental differences between African and Asian farming systems? Is it a matter of mere historical accident or is there an explanation in terms of economic motive?

It seems that the clue is to be found in considerations of cost in the plantation sector. In each of these continents the division of labour between the sexes depends upon what factor makes labour costs for the export sector the lowest feasible in the given local circumstances. In Africa, the methods of food production are such that women can do nearly all the operations unaided by men. It is therefore possible to economize on labour costs in plantations (as well as in mines and industries) by employing only male workers, leaving the dependents—women, children and old people—to be supported in the home village by the able-bodied women. The Asian pattern is in sharp contrast; there the predominating agricultural system requires the presence of men in the village and therefore men cannot be recruited on the assumption that their women can be left behind to support themselves and their dependents in the village. Hence, the plantation owner must face the fact that the whole family must get its livelihood from the plantation, and this, of course, can be arranged most cheaply by having every able-bodied member of the family working at the plantation. Thus, in the Asian as well as the African case, the plantation (or the European farm) can avoid paying the male wages sufficient to support a whole family.

It is worthy of note that both these ways of holding down labour costs in the export sector are at the expense of the women. The woman at the Asian plantation has a double job, as housewife and as full-time labourer, at least for a large part of the year, while the men are at leisure when work in the plantation is over. In some cases, women workers in Asian plantations work even longer hours than the men. In the North Indian tea gardens, the work system for men is that of 'task work', which means that they can leave when the task set for the day is done, normally after four or five hours of work. Women's work is leaf plucking at piece rates which often means working for seven or eight hours in order to earn an adequate daily wage. A woman's day begins at 4 or 5 a.m. with cooking for the family. Then, after seven or eight hours of plantation work, she must fetch water and firewood and cook another meal. Children are often brought to the fields, the smallest one strapped to the back of the mother.[12]

Likewise, the African women must do double the amount of work when most of the younger men are away working in plantation or mines. There is some disagreement among writers as to the maximum amount of work African women can do in villages deserted by young men.[13] One author suggests that in Zambia the predominant farming system can function normally, as long as not more than half of all adult men are permanently away.[14] Another author reports that around Lake Nyassa the farming system can function normally with 60–75 per cent of adult men absent.[15] Again, others stress the deterioration of farming in the many cases where women must do the work almost unaided by men.[16] This burden African women take on in the manless villages is their contribution to Africa's export production. Only in quite a superficial sense can it be said that this export effort is based solely upon male labour.

THE FEMALE COOLIE

Many of the women who take on casual agricultural labour are also prepared to accept other kinds of manual, unskilled employment that happen to be available in the rural area where they live. Everywhere we find such female general labourers who work alone or in groups recruited and supervised by contractors. They often move from district to district in response to the shifting demand for labour for transplanting, harvesting, road work and other construction, and work in mines and transport.

A high proportion of women labourers in agriculture often goes with a large number of women working in mines, construction and transport, as can be seen from Table 9. In a number of Asian countries, and in some Latin American countries, women are used for surface work at mines, for transport and for the loading and unloading of railway waggons. In some of these countries women account for up to one-fourth of the labour force in the mines. Women are also used in many countries for transporting materials on building sites. Even in Arab countries, we find women in heavy outdoor jobs. In Syria, the task of putting up the nomad's tent in the desert is traditionally a woman's job, and in the towns women work as masons and in house construction generally.[17] Many African contractors employ women on road construction, for drawing water and carrying sand and other road making materials, as well as in mines.[18]

However, the use of women on building sites is most widespread in Asia. Vietnamese women are load carriers and dock labourers,[19] and in Malaya, Chinese women from the Kwantung province in China do the unskilled work in the building trade, such as earth moving, foundation-digging, etc.[20] In India, the job of women on building sites in both rural and urban areas is to pass bricks along a line to the bricklayers or to carry cement, lime and mortar on their heads.*

Women are preferred to men in these jobs because they are willing to accept lower wages and more often accept unauthorized deductions, false accounts and delayed payments. According to an Indian investigation 'some of the labour contractors were very frank indeed when they stated that without female labour much of the charm of the construction industry would be lost and that the labour cost of construction would increase very substantially'.[22]

Both in Indian rural areas and in the towns, the female construction workers are tribal and low-caste women of rural origin, and so are the women working in the mines.[23] But the employment of women in the mines is declining because women are now forbidden to work underground, and many open-cast mines are being mechanized and the women replaced by machines operated by male workers.[24]

THE IMPACT OF AGRICULTURAL MODERNIZATION ON THE EMPLOYMENT OF WOMEN

Since women are used for the hand operations in agriculture it might be suggested that the use of female labour will gradually disappear as agriculture is modernized. But the problem is not so simple as that.

Owing to the rapid rise of population in developing countries, combined with shortage of capital, many countries will probably be unable to solve their agricultural problems exclusively by means of capital-intensive techniques, and therefore the total demand for female labour is likely to increase. Indeed, a half-mechanized agriculture often seems to raise the demand for female labour.[25] If there is to be a decline of female agricultural labour it will more likely be due to a change in labour supply; rural women may increasingly refuse to toil in the fields and insist on doing only non-agricultural or domestic work. In the

* In India, waggon-loading is considered a woman's job, and men are reluctant to accept such work.[21] However, when the railways introduced a penalty for slow loading and unloading, the contractors began to replace the female loaders with men.

latter case, we must expect to see the reduction of wage differentials between the sexes as a means of containing the female exodus from agriculture.

Female wage labour rarely contributes to the agriculture of industrialized countries, but in many of them the wives of small farmers are becoming more burdened by agricultural work because their husbands also take on non-agricultural jobs. In Japan's agricultural labour force there are now more women than men, and a new type of 'housewife farming family' is becoming increasingly frequent.[26] In the United States, the shrinking of the agricultural labour force is accompanied by an increase in the proportion of women in it, and in Canada the number of women occupied in agriculture is increasing.[27] Thus the modernization of agriculture does not necessarily oust women from agricultural employment.

If women must continue to play a major role in the agriculture of some developing countries, then it would seem to be vitally important that steps should be taken to eliminate sex discrimination in admission to courses and schools where modern agricultural methods are taught, and that women farmers should also be helped to improve their farming practices instead of being overlooked by the extension services or even ousted from their farms. Fortunately, some developing countries are beginning to take steps to improve agricultural education for women and to help women farmers. We shall return to these problems in Part III.

NOTES TO CHAPTER 4

1. Albert, 182.   2. Albert, 185–6.   3. India Min. of L. 1960, 91.   4. Dube 1956, 174–5.   5. Gadgil, 10–11.   6. India Labour Statistics 1962, 55; *India Labour Year book* 1965, 51–2.   7. India Min. of F. Madras, 43, 144.   8. Shrivasta, 179–89.   9. Doctor, 565; Tran Van Minh, 317.   10. Doucy, 184–5.   11. ILO, *Afr. Conf. Report*, 6.   12. Deshpande, 84.   13. Mitchell, *Lab. and Pop.*, 236–7.   14. Watson, 34.   15. van Velsen, 266ff.   16. Southall 1952, 158–9; Richards 1939, 298, 404–5.   17. Weulersse, 309; Sweet, 154; Fuller, 73.   18. CCTA, 127; Baker, 78ff.; Razafy, 205.   19. Coughlin, 135.   20. Wee, 162.   21. Deshpande, 80.   22. Deshmukh, 192.   23. Sengupta, 155; ILO *Rev.* 1956, I, 290.   24. India Min. of L., Delhi 1964, 12–13, 29.   25. de la Rivière, 10.   26. Koyama, 81–2.   27. Farrag, 32.

PART II

In the Town

Chapter 5

Women in a Men's World

Many towns in developing countries are of fairly recent origin. They have grown up around major European enterprises or around sea ports, railway or road centres where exports to and imports from Europe were handled. Other towns grew up as centres of colonial administration or as marketing and service centres in areas where Europeans settled. Sex proportions in such towns continue to reflect the principles of selection which the Europeans used in their recruitment of indigenous labour. In regions where only men were recruited, we find towns with a large surplus of men. Some African towns have several men to each woman, and in other continents we also find towns with a large male surplus.

Extreme examples of 'male towns' are found in South Africa and Rhodesia, where mining companies recruited men, supplied quarters to single men only, and paid wages which were insufficient to support a family. Moreover, access to the towns was often legally barred for women without a special permit which was difficult to obtain. Almost exclusively male townships resulted, such as Witwatersrand, where less than one per cent of African employees have their wives living with them. All the miners are either unmarried or have left their wives in their home village, and only office workers and policemen are able to live with their wives.[1]

On the other hand, in the Copper Belt in Zambia, the mining companies always had a different recruitment policy. They provided family quarters and plots of five acres where a miner's wife could grow food for the family. Therefore, even in colonial times, two-thirds of the miners were married and four-fifths of the married men had their wives living with them.[2]

Some administrative centres have nearly as large a surplus of men as the mining centres. Before independence, Nairobi had five men to each woman in the African areas, and other towns in Kenya and Uganda had more than two men to each woman.[3] Likewise, Leopoldville (now Kinshasa) in the Congo had twice as many men as women.[4] Although the surplus of men is gradually becoming smaller in 'male' African towns, it will be a long time before normal sex proportions are established in the adult population.

'Male towns' are also to be found in Asia. The big Indian towns have 25 per cent more men than women.[5] By contrast, Latin American towns usually have a surplus of women, and in the rural areas there is, correspondingly, a surplus of men. This, of course, is a result of a predominantly female flow of rural-urban migration.[6]

But towns with a big surplus of men are not the only kind of 'male towns' to be found in developing countries. Many towns of ancient origin with a balanced sex pattern may nevertheless be described as 'male towns', although in another sense; the economic life of the town and all outdoor activities are taken care of by men, while women live in seclusion within the family dwelling. With women confined to the homes, the streets, market places, shops, factories, offices, restaurants and cinemas become a male world with an enormous surplus of men over women. In the Arab towns, the veil is gradually disappearing, but this does not necessarily mean that women now take more part in urban life than they did before. The main change may be that women now stay within the protecting walls of their own homes, instead of venturing into the streets protected by the veil. In villages in North African and Asian countries, few women stay indoors, even if they do no field work, for they have their daily chores, such as the fetching of water and fuel for the household. But in towns in Arab countries, India and Pakistan, many women leave even the daily shopping to their men (unless they can afford to keep servants) and hardly ever appear outside the house. It is true that the surplus of men in the streets, cinemas, etc., is declining gradually with the advent of new, less timid generations of girls, but even in this type of 'male towns' it will be a long time before more balanced sex proportions are established in outdoor life.

In sharp contrast to 'male towns' of the two types described above, there is a third type of town in which streets and market places are dominated by women, since most of the retail market trade is in female hands, while the whole of the modern sector, modern shops, industries and offices, is almost exclusively taken care of by men. This type of 'semi-male town' is characteristic of Africa, but it also exists in other parts of the world.

Since the participation of women in trade distinguishes the 'semi-male' type of town from the two types of 'male town' in developing countries, we shall begin the analysis of the role of women in urban development with a discussion of the role of women in market trade.

SEX AND RACE IN MARKET TRADE

In no other field do ideas about the proper role of women contrast more vividly than in the case of market trade. To most Hindus and Arabs, the idea of female participation in trade is an abomination. Hindu and Arab women are not only absent from the sellers in the markets, they are in a minority even among the customers, since men do the shopping of both food and of women's clothing.[7] Among African and most people in South East Asia, on the other hand, a very large share of market trading, selling as well as buying, is left entirely to women.

There are striking differences between the roles which men and women play in trade in various parts of the world (Table 13). Women account for a half or more of the labour force in trade in many African countries, and for less than 1 per cent in most Arab countries. The few trading women in Arab countries either belong to European or other minority groups, or they are village women, selling eggs, poultry and other home-craft products, mainly in village markets.[8] By contrast, the trading women of West Africa are famous. In Ghana, women account for 80 per cent of the labour force in trade, and they handle both village and urban trade. Likewise in the Yoruba region of West Nigeria,

Table 13

WOMEN IN TRADE AND COMMERCE

Country:	All women in trade and commerce as percentage of:		Women trading on own-account as percentage of all women in trade and commerce
	all adult women	total labour force in trade and commerce	
Africa South of the Sahara:			
Sierra Leone	3	47	75
Liberia	1	35	78
Ghana	15	80	94
Nigeria[a]	b	46	b
Mauritius	1	8	47
Region of Arab influence:			
Sudan		8	b
Morocco		4	48
Libya			b
United Arab Republic		6	81
Turkey		1	56
Jordan			b
Syria		1	48
Iraq		2	b
Iran		2	59
Pakistan		2	83
South and East Asia:			
India	1	11	b
Ceylon		6	66
Burma	b	47[c]	85[c]
Thailand	5	56	40
Cambodia	4	46	b
Malaya	1	10	74
Singapore	2	10	53
Indonesia	2	31	b
Philippines	3	51	61
Taiwan	1	13	b
Hong Kong	3	18	60
Korea (South)	3	33	64

[a] Eastern region only.
[b] Urban areas only.

Table 13—contd.

Latin America:

Mexico	3	29	b
Honduras	2	36	62
El Salvadore	3	54	69
Nicaragua	4	59	77
Costa Rica	2	19	25
Panama	2	32	27
Columbia	2	26	25
Ecuador	2	23	68
Chile	2	27	63
Venezuela	1	9	50
Cuba	1	10	10
Jamaica	6	65	b
Dominican Republic	1	20	68
Puerto Rico	1	18	17

market trade is dominated by women, and in Eastern Nigeria, women account for about half the labour force in trade.*

South and East Asia have regions with female traders and regions with male traders, as can be seen from Figure 4. Women account for around half the trading labour force in Burma, Thailand, Cambodia, Laos, the Philippines and Vietnam.[11] The contrasting picture is found in areas inhabited by a Chinese population, such as Singapore, Taiwan and Hong Kong, where women account for no more than 10 to 15 per cent of the labour force in trade. The small role women play in trade in the latter countries is consistent with the traditional pattern of trade in China. Before the communist revolution, only 7 per cent of the Chinese labour force in trade were women.[12] In India, too, trade is in male hands, as already mentioned, but there are significant differences between North India and Pakistan, where women account for only 6 and 2 per cent, respectively, of the labour force in trade, Central India with 11 per cent and South India with 17 per cent (Table 14). As is the case with the farming pattern, there is a significant difference between the roles of women in the Northern and the Southern parts of the Indian

* Also in other West African countries, most of the market trade is in female hands. In Dakar, the capital of Senegal, 60 per cent of sellers in the markets are women.[9] Women also dominate the markets in the Congo and in many parts of East Africa. In Rhodesia, Zambia and Malawi, there are more women than men among the sellers, and in the Luo tribe in Kenya it is rare to find a woman who does not trade in some small way.[10]

subcontinent; the West Asian pattern of seclusion of women exerts a stronger influence in North India than in South India.

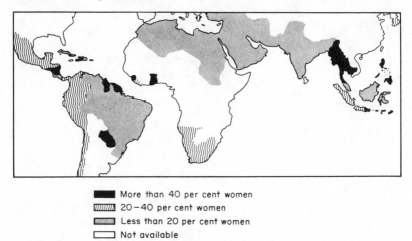

■ More than 40 per cent women
▨ 20–40 per cent women
▨ Less than 20 per cent women
☐ Not available

Figure 4　Sex distribution of Labour Force in Trade

In Indonesia, the regional variations in the degree to which women participate in trade are even larger than in India, but here the dividing line is between West and East rather than between North and South as it is in India. In Sumatra, women account for 15 per cent of the labour force in trade, and in East Java

Table 14

REGIONAL DIFFERENCES IN WOMEN'S ACTIVITIES IN INDIA PAKISTAN AND INDONESIA

Percentage of women in the labour force

| | India | | | Pakistan | Indonesia | |
	South	Central	North		Sumatra	East Java
Agriculture	40	42	29	14	33	27
Home industry	41	38	37 ⎫	11	18	34
Other industry	17	9	6 ⎭			
Construction	17	16	5	1	5	3
Trade	17	11	6	2	15	44
Transport and other services	27	22	13	8	21	39
Total labour force	36	37	26	12	30	30

90

44 per cent. Thus, in South East Asia we seem to have a basically 'female trade pattern' but, owing perhaps to Arab and Chinese influence, there is a belt of male trade running from North India and Pakistan through Malaya to Western Indonesia. Within this belt, only one-tenth of the traders are women, as against one-half outside this belt.

In Latin America, different cultural patterns are reflected in opposing attitudes to female participation in trade. In some countries with a predominantly Negro or Indian population, more women than men are in trade,[13] while women account for less than 10 per cent of the labour force in trade in countries on the Atlantic coast where Arab influence, transmitted through the Spanish upper class, has penetrated more deeply. Latin America differs from other developing countries in having a larger modern trade sector with both male and female shop assistants. Outside Latin America, most of the women occupied in the trade sector are trading on their own account, while only a minority, sometimes a very small minority, work for wages or are helping relatives (Table 13, Column 3).

We must now ask why market trade has come into women's hands in some regions while in others only men go to market to sell and buy. We get a clue from looking at the products sold by women. These are primarily agricultural products; fruits, vegetables, milk, eggs and poultry (while meat is usually sold by men). It is noteworthy, furthermore, that those regions where women dominate the food trade of rural and urban markets are usually the regions which are characterized by female farming traditions. Conversely, in the regions where we find market trade dominated by men, we also find that men do most of the agricultural work, while women give only occasional help. In other words, where agriculture is a male occupation, men usually also take care of the trading, but where women are actively engaged in producing the crops, and particularly when they are farmers on their own account, they also take the crops to the market where they may also sell articles which they have not produced themselves.*

* In some communities, for instance in Indian communities in Latin America, women cultivate and men trade,[14] but this type of division of labour seems to be exceptional.

91

In regions where Moslem women take no part in trade it is often taken for granted that this is because women's trading is supposed to be incompatible with the Moslem religion. But this is an unwarranted inference, for in regions with female predominance in trade, religion does not prevent Moslem women from taking part in it. The market women in Dakar, mentioned above, are Moslem women, and in Khartoum, in the Sudan, where Arab women, at least the younger ones, keep away from the market, the peanut market is handled by Nigerian female pilgrims who have settled in the Sudan on their way to or from Mecca.[15]

Men usually despise occupations manned predominantly by women, be it agriculture or trade, and they will normally hesitate to take part in such work. This helps to explain why we so often find the peculiar pattern of trade being handled partly by local women and partly by male immigrants. This combination is quite frequent in West Africa, where much of the wholesale trade and some of the retail trade is in the hands of Lebanese men, while local women do the rest. We see it in East Africa, where Indian or Arab immigrants and local women combine; and in South East Asia with Burmese women and Indian men; Thai and Vietnamese women and Chinese men; Indonesian and Philippine women and Chinese men, etc. Indeed, at a certain stage of development it seems to be a normal feature for immigrant tradesmen from communities with an old tradition of money transactions to penetrate the markets for at least some articles. Such foreigners can most easily dominate the markets where indigenous men keep away from trade and consider it a feminine occupation. A Vietnamese man regards trade as debasing for men and thinks that women are more economical and thrifty,[16] and the Philippine man regards himself as being too sensitive for the coarse language and aggressive behaviour necessary in a good tradesman.[17] Therefore they willingly let their wives handle small scale market trade and for similar reasons they may be content to leave large-scale trade to the more aggressive—and despised—foreigners.

WORK INPUT AND EARNINGS OF MARKET WOMEN

Market trade is sometimes the main occupation for women who belong to communities where married women, having no right to support from their husbands, must support themselves and their children. This is the case in the Yoruba region of Nigeria, where two-thirds of all adult women are trading, half of them with trade as their main occupation. For the others, trade is a subsidiary to agriculture or crafts, for these women sell their own products in the market.[18]

According to a study of a town in Ghana, 70 per cent of adult women are engaged in trading activities. It goes without saying that when such a large majority of adult urban women are active traders, the average turnover must be very small indeed. But women spend a lot of time on this trade. Out of seventy-eight women who were interviewed in the Ghana study, seventy went to the market at least five times a week, forty women said that they would spend six to eight hours in the market, the rest said more.[19] If these facts are not overstated, the women had little time left for cultivation. Nevertheless, half of them claimed that they were cultivating although they were vague as to the frequency of their agricultural work. These were women who had to support themselves, and partly support their children, from their trading and farming profits, the money their husbands gave them having to be spent on the food they had to cook for their husbands, and on some of the food for the children.

The fact that nearly all women in some communities trade in the market, although most of them derive very little income from it, is more understandable if it is remembered that these women, most of them illiterate, have few alternative opportunities for earning. Moreover, for many women the daily visits to the market, where they spend much of the time chatting with neighbours while waiting for customers, is an agreeable pastime, preferable to the hard work they would have to do if they were farming instead of trading.[20] In other words, like many men, they prefer a small profit from trade to a larger one from farming. Therefore, if agricultural development were to release the farmer's wife from farm work and favour the use of hired labourers, we should expect to see more women take to trading in the market.

Yoruba women have turned more and more to trading in imported goods, and some Ghana women are said to have credits of thousands of pounds sterling with overseas firms and to act as intermediaries to women retailers.[21] Likewise, in South East Asia, for instance in the Philippines, large profits are said to be earned by some women traders.[22]

The extent to which women travel in order to carry out their trade varies widely. West African women often travel long distances to carry on their business.[23] Women wholesale dealers in Dahomey go from village to village, buying cheaply and stocking the goods for resale in times of scarcity.[24] Sometimes women in sparsely populated areas waste a lot of time travelling in order to make trivial sales. There are reports of women from pastoral tribes in North Nigeria and the Republic of Niger who in the dry season would walk fifteen to twenty miles to the market to sell one or two litres of milk.* [25]

West African women traders use a variety of devices to keep prices uniform or to limit the number of competitors in a given market, but it seems that they rarely succeed. In his study of West African trade, Peter Bauer mentions that unions of women traders sometimes persuade the authorities to limit permits for stalls in the market to members of the association, and to decree that non-members are allowed to trade only on the outskirts of the towns while the Central market is reserved for members of the union.[27] But licensing arrangements in markets may also be used as a weapon against female trade. In the Cameroons, an attempt was made to deny the women access to the market, as a means of inducing them to spend more time in the fields; but the authorities had to retract because of the deep resentment among the women.[28] In Kenya, in the last years of colonial rule, market women were less lucky. They got only 20 per cent of the hawkers' licences issued by the city council of Nairobi, and probably because of this, prosecution for illegal hawking accounted for a very high proportion of all criminal acts committed by women in Nairobi.[29]

In independent Africa, women traders are actively trying to oust immigrant traders. A resolution from a meeting held under UN auspices in 1963 demanded that 'access to the market place

---

* In regions with more dense population and better means of transport, small producers sell to intermediaries, and only the ones with larger quantities travel to market, often by bus. Women from a Thai village would walk to Bangkok themselves only if they had 200–300 eggs to sell; otherwise, they would accept the lower prices offered by the intermediary.[26]

should be opened to the women of all African countries and where certain market places are monopolized by men, mostly by foreigners, governments and local authorities should not hesitate to break this *de facto* monopoly by means of legal and fiscal measures in favour of indigenous women'.[30]

FROM THE MARKET PLACE TO THE SUPER-MARKET

Market women may create organizations for a more or less effective defence of their interests against outsiders, but they are unable to prevent keen competition and underbidding within their own ranks, and, therefore, they cannot compensate for a small turnover by a high profit per transaction. Hence, female market trade can compete quite successfully with more modern types of trade, such as department stores and super-markets. Therefore, in many developing countries the modern trade sector remains small compared to the traditional trade sector, at least outside the big cities.

In the modern trade sector, most shop assistants are men, even in countries where market women dominate the traditional trade sector. Given the high rate of illiteracy and the high average age of the market women,* it was not to be expected that they would be recruited as shop-assistants in the modern trade sector. On the other hand, it could perhaps have been expected that in countries with traditions of female trade, many young literate girls would be recruited as shop-assistants. But this is not so. In Ghana where female literacy is high by African standards, and where over 80 per cent of own-account traders are women, the proportion of women among employees in trade is no more than 24 per cent. A similar contrast is found in Thailand, where 60 per cent of own-account traders are women as are 22 per cent of

---

* A study of 200 market women in Dakar[31] revealed the following age composition, which corresponds well with what one would expect from visits to African and Asian markets:

below 19 years	0 per cent
20–29 years	9 per cent
30–39 years	27 per cent
40–49 years	35 per cent
50–59 years	20 per cent
60 and more	9 per cent

employees in trade.* The only developing country outside the Western Hemisphere with a high proportion of women among trade employees is the Philippines with 40 per cent as against 55 per cent women among own-account traders.

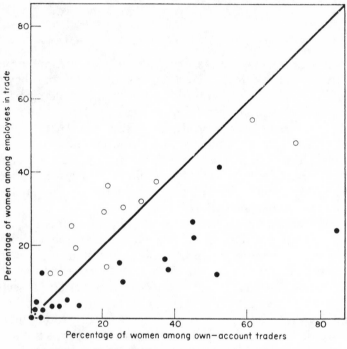

○ Latin American countries
● Other developing countries

Figure 5 Status and Sex of Labour Force in Trade

Thus, in Africa and Asia, the number of women employees in trade is smaller than among own-account traders. In Latin America, the typical sex distribution in the trade sector is exactly the opposite (Figure 5). In nearly all Latin American countries, the proportion of shop girls employed in trade is higher than the proportion of women among own-account

* This has probably something to do with the fact that large shops in Thailand are mostly owned by Chinese merchants who, as already mentioned, tend to employ male assistants.

traders.* In Latin America, therefore, the modernization of the trade sector, which substitutes shops with shop assistants for the traditional small-scale market trade, has the effect of strengthening the female element in the labour force in trade, while a similar development in other parts of the world results in an increasing 'masculinization' of the trade sector.

Two possible explanations suggest themselves to account for the difference in sex proportions in the trade personnel in Latin America and in other developing countries. One explanation could be that the Western Hemisphere has different cultural traditions, and a higher rate of female literacy. Alternatively the higher stage of economic development reached in most countries of Latin America, compared with most developing countries in Africa and Asia, could by itself account for the difference in sex proportions in the trade sector. As can be seen in Figure 6, the proportion of women among trade employees is in fact high in all industrialized countries. In the nine industrialized countries shown in the chart, ranging from Japan to New Zealand to Western Europe and North America, the proportion of women among trade employees is between 35 and 55 per cent.

When countries are arranged according to the stage of economic development, as in Figure 6, there appears to be little correlation between the proportion of women employees in the trade sector and the degree of development. Some countries at low stages of development have a high proportion of women employees in trade, apparently because they have traditions of female market trade. In other countries, where market trade is traditionally in the care of men, the number of women in the modern trade sector is correspondingly small. In other words, cultural traditions, including the role of women in the traditional sector of market trade, seem to be a more important factor in determining the place of women in the modern trade sector than is the stage of general 'modernization' achieved by the country. Thus, even in the modern cities of Singapore and Hong-Kong, the traditional Chinese pattern of male dominance in

---

* The few exceptions to this are Latin American countries with predominantly Negro and Indian populations and with a very high proportion of women both in market trade and in modern shops.

trade is reflected in a remarkably low participation by women—5 and 10 per cent, respectively—of employees in trade.

To sum up, women's role in trade in the modern sector in developing countries can be described as follows: Very few women are found in the modern trade sector in Arab countries,

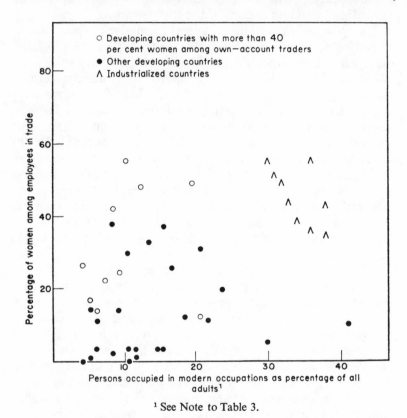

¹ See Note to Table 3.

Figure 6 Sex Distribution of Employees in Trade in Countries at Different Stages of Development

in India, in countries and towns with a Chinese population, and in Atlantic countries of Latin America where the impact of Spanish culture was strong. In all these countries there is a deep-seated cultural resistance to women's participation in trade. In the countries with a tradition of female trading, on the other

98

hand, we sometimes find a high proportion of women among employees in trade, especially in South East Asia, but in many other cases, particularly in Africa, the participation of women in modern trade is held down by their low level of literacy and by a general tendency to give priority to men in the employment recruitment in the modern sector.

FEMALE SERVICES IN MALE TOWNS

It is not unusual, in countries where food trade is a female occupation, for some of the market women to prepare meals ready for consumption on the spot. Most market places in developing countries are also open-air restaurants where owners of stalls and peddlers sell ready-cooked food. In towns with a large surplus of single men, many take their meals in the market or in small restaurants where women cook and sell food. In those parts of Africa where it is a customary duty for village women to brew beer for ceremonial occasions, women living in urban areas often take to commercial brewing, their homes becoming popular meeting places for the men. The sale of such home-brewed beer is a widespread feature in many parts of Africa. In the Union of South Africa, this trade, although illegal, is an important occupation for urban women,[32] whose husbands' friends usually form the nucleus of her beer customers. The beer is sold on credit, and at the beginning of the month the customers may have to hand over most of their wages to settle their account. These women, therefore, may often contribute considerably to the support of their families.

In towns with a large surplus of single men, there is heavy demand not only for restaurant services, but also for the services of prostitutes, and for female company in the shape of bar personnel, dancers, singers, etc. Naturally, beer houses and bars tend to be centres of prostitution, whether it be that professional prostitutes meet their customers there, or that the owners and employees in the establishment indulge in semi-prostitution.

The large demand for prostitutes is not limited to the towns with a big male surplus. A similar situation is found where many men marry late, or even remain unmarried, because many men who can afford to marry have more than one wife. Finally, in the type of town where seclusion keeps ordinary women away from the streets, and indeed from male company, except that of the closest relatives, prostitutes and semi-prostitutes are in demand as feminine companions in dancing establishments and bars.

In some tribes with self-supporting women, no social stigma is attached to prostitution and semi-prostitution. Balandier reports from the Congo (Brazzaville) about an 'elite of young women, for whom the designation "*hétaire*" is more suitable than prostitute'. Some of these women enjoyed great prestige and a very favourable economic position. They set up a number of professional associations with president, vice president, treasurer, etc., for the purpose of providing mutual aid for members in difficulty, and to organize festivals, funerals, etc.[33] In Ghana and Nigeria prostitutes have professional unions of a similar type,[34] and of one large tribe it has been said that to their women 'prostitution . . . is merely a new calling like any other and they became prostitutes as reasonably and as self-righteously as they would have become typists or telephone girls.[35]

The conflicting views on prostitution in Africa must be kept in mind when patterns of female employment in urban areas are considered. African men from patrilinear tribes often fear that their wives may take to prostitution, repay their bride price with the money thus earned, and then leave them.[36] Therefore, the men may choose to leave their wives behind in the village or to keep them away from jobs which may offer opportunities for prostitution. In so doing they continue the endeavours of European missionaries and administrators in the colonial period to keep down the number of urban women, and their employment, as a means of limiting the scope for prostitution. The Europeans prevented single women from going alone to find work in the copper belt[37]; in both Central and West Africa, they expelled from the towns those women who were living alone and were thus not under the authority of a male relative.[38] Even now African women are forbidden to migrate to towns in the Union of South Africa without special permission.[39]

It is doubtful, however, whether these restrictions on the potential supply of prostitutes did in effect reduce the amount of prostitution. It is possible that they even enhanced it by making the urban sex ratio still more biased in favour of men. In any case, despite all these restrictions in the colonial period, women living singly accounted in many African towns for no less than 25–30 per cent of all women.[40] But if the effect of the colonial policy on the amount of prostitution is dubious, another effect of this policy is beyond doubt; it served as a barrier to women's emancipation from tribal and family authority, and to their efforts to obtain genuine urban employment.

Since independence, many of these restrictions on women's movements and employment have been lifted. African tribes which used to take stern measures against sexual self-emancipation by their women, such as the death penalty or the forced transport of prostitutes back to their home villages, now take a more detached view of illegal child-bearing than before.[41] But the fear of female prostitution continues to be an important factor in the attitude to female employment in Africa, as in other parts of the world. In East Africa, there seems to be a tendency to regard as 'sexually loose' all well-dressed urban women who work outside the home, and this prejudice seems to lower the esteem in which the highly educated girls who work in professions and as secretaries are held.[42]

The differences between the position of women in towns where they dominate the trade sector and in towns where they stay indoors is also reflected in the patterns and kinds of prostitution. In countries where women are traders, prostitution is centred on markets and bars, and it is either unorganized, or the prostitutes have their own mutual voluntary organizations, as mentioned above. In those countries, on the other hand, where men dominate the market place, while their wives stay at home, the prostitutes also live in secluded quarters and houses.[43]

With independence, however, change has occurred in many of these countries. Restrictions have been abandoned, houses have been closed, and the prostitutes have appeared in streets and bars, or they have changed from professionals to semi-professionals.[44] This development probably implies a partial emancipation of the prostitutes, and an improvement in their social status. But, on the other hand, the public appearance of prostitutes may strengthen the tendency to regard working women as *eo ipso* semi-prostitutes. In any case, this prejudice continues to be a major deterrent to job seeking by middle class girls in India as well as in Arab countries.[45]

Table 15

WOMEN IN PRIVATE DOMESTIC SERVICE

| | Women in private domestic service[a] as percentage of | | |
Country:	all adult women	all women in non-agricultural occupation	total labour force in private domestic service
Africa South of the Sahara:			
South Africa	12	52	78
Kenya		b	10
Region of Arab influence:			
Sudan		19	28
Morocco	2	30	86
Libya	1	6	41
United Arab Republic	1	32	53
Turkey		9	12
Jordan		31	42
Syria		3	17
Iraq		21	49
South and East Asia:			
India		5	36
Thailand	1	5	78
Malaya	1	17	98
Taiwan	1	6	65
Hong Kong	8	26	57
Latin America:			
El Salvadore	5	26	97
Costa Rica	6	34	100
Columbia	7	37	94
Chile	8	35	92
Venezuela	5	26	94
Dominican Republic	4	22	92
Puerto Rico	3	13	94

a Includes domestic servants occupied in private households, but excludes personnel in domestic service establishments.

b No information is available.

In Latin America, semi-prostitution seems to be widespread among the group of domestic servants, which is particularly numerous in the towns of that part of the world (Table 15). They are mainly rural girls who have immigrated to the towns, alone and young.[46] In some Latin American countries, more than one-third of all women in non-agricultural employment are domestic servants. This is true also of some Arab countries, but there the over-all number of women employed as domestic servants or otherwise, is very low, while women's rate of participation in economic activities is high in Latin American towns.

DOMESTIC SERVANTS

As just mentioned, the number of domestic servants is particularly high in Latin America which is not surprising, as it is a characteristic feature of countries at an intermediate stage of economic development for a large number of women to be engaged in paid housework. By contrast, in countries at very early stages of development, domestic tasks like cooking, serving of meals, washing, etc., are done within the family, usually by the women. At the intermediate stages of development, many such services have become commercialized, being performed for wages by either male or female domestic servants. And at still higher levels, some of these services have become commercialized outside the household by men or women specializing in one or other of these service activities, as owners and employees in bars, cafeterias, restaurants, laundries, house and office cleaning services, etc. In industrialized countries, the number of people employed in such service establishments is large, whereas domestic servants are few; these two domestic service groups taken together seem to account, in the typical industrialized country, for from 4 to 6 per cent of all adults, 60 to 70 per cent of them being women.

In developing countries, wide variations are found in the proportion of women working as domestic servants and in domestic service establishments. In most of Latin America, the whole group of domestic servants and employees in service establishments seems to be as large as or larger than in industrialized countries and here, too, all these activities are predominantly

103

'women's work' (Figure 7). But in most other developing countries the service sector is much smaller, and in many Arab, African and Asian countries these jobs are held mostly by men.[47] In

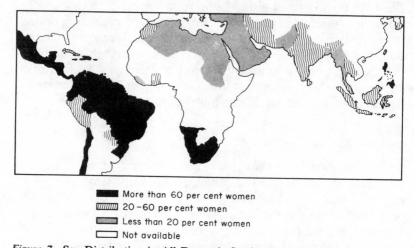

More than 60 per cent women
20–60 per cent women
Less than 20 per cent women
Not available

Figure 7   Sex Distribution in All Domestic Service Occupations[a]

[a] Includes private domestic services, personnel in restaurants, bars, laundries.

general the whole domestic service sector grows with economic development and, at the same time, tends to become more exclusively 'feminine'.

NOTES TO CHAPTER 5

1. Philipps, 174; Simons, 281–2.   2. Mitchell, *Lab. and Pop.*, 238.
3. Southall 1961, 46.   4. UN. ECA., *Urb. Trop. Afr.*, 5.   5. Desai, 383–5.
6. UN. Soc. Aff. Urb. Lat. Am., 100.   7. Cormack, 80–1.   8. Fuller, 77;
Sweet 154; UN. ECA., *Wom. N. Afr.*, 12.   9. Inst. Sc. Ec. Dakar, App. I,
22.   10. Ominde, 55.   11. Coughlin, 137; Lévy, 246.   12. Ta-Chung Liu,
182, 188.   13. Belshaw, 58; Jimenez, 22.   14. Mar, 133.   15. UN. ECA.,
Wom. N. Afr., 12.   16. Coughlin, 137.   17. Fox, 363.   18. Galetti, 200.
19. McCall, 295–6.   20. Galetti, 561.   21. Galetti, 291; McCall, 290.
22. Pecson, 345.   23. Peddler, Vol. 18, 1948, 268–9.   24. Tardit, 275.
25. Dupire, 78.   26. Janlekha, 45.   27. Bauer, 391.   28. Kaberry, 71–2.
29. Carlebach, 5, 10–11.   30. UN. ECA., *Role Wom. Urb. Dev.*, 31.
31. Inst. Sc. Ec. Dakar, App. I, 4.   32. Hellman, 184; Hunter, 192.
33. Balandier 1955, 146–8.   34. Sicot, 132.   35. Leith-Ross, 267–8.

36. Leith-Ross, 268.   37. Watson, 44.   38. Southall 1961, 223.   39. Van der Horst, 35.   40. Southall 1961, 51.   41. Wilson, 111; Ominde, 42. 42. Southall 1961, 51; Oloo, 27–9.   43. Servais, 347–8; Sicot, 127. 44. Sicot, 127.   45. M'Rabat, 37–8 *passim*.   46. Sicot, 126.   47. ILO *Afr. Conf. Report*, 10–11.

Chapter 6

Industry: From the Hut to the Factory

In very primitive communities, women usually devote a fairly large part of their time to the production of a variety of goods for household use, such as containers for food, cooking utensils, mats and carpets, and to making clothing for the family. Moreover, in many regions women help in the construction of houses; they collect building materials, plaster the walls, make the necessary furnishings, etc. At this stage of subsistence economy, although nearly all the women take part in such activities, none of them—and none of the men for that matter—spend all their time at it.

At a later stage, certain of the goods used in daily life begin to be exchanged between people within a village or with people in neighbouring villages. Usually, some men as well as women begin to produce for sale some of the goods hitherto produced for family consumption only. Some women may specialize in preparing for sale ready-made dishes, or in brewing of beer for sale. Others specialize in the production of clothing, mats and carpets for sale, and many women are professional potters or basket weavers at village level.

With further economic development and improvement in the transport system, markets for professionally made artisan products may widen, and some villages, where such things are made for sale, may grow into small towns, with an economy based partly upon such home industries and partly upon market trade for the surrounding region. If such a centre of home industries appears to have specialized in products which are traditionally produced by women we may find a very high female participation in them.

Clifford Geertz has studied the changes which take place when production for domestic use is transformed into a home industry producing goods for sale. In a study of a small Indonesian town, Geertz found that some goods which in the villages were produced for family use in slack periods of farming, were produced in the town on a larger scale for sale in the markets, but with the use of the same techniques. The processes were simple and known by virtually everybody—men, women and children. In one neighbourhood he found five home industries producing bean curd (a soy bean sauce for rice dishes).[1] In that neighbourhood, almost every man, woman and child over the age of nine or ten was giving some time every month to the manufacture of bean-curd, but none drew a full living from it. Because the method of production was so simple that almost anybody could do any job, the organization of work was extremely flexible. People might come and go more or less freely, working when they wished and being replaced by others from the neighbourhood when they gave up working. Women were not only active as workers in these home industries; one enterprise had been started by a woman and was being run by her.

We can see the next stage in this development in a study of another Javanese industry, the Batik industry, which is centred on Jogjakarta in Central Java.[2] When the survey was made, the industry had 43,000 full-time workers, half of them women. In addition, 1 million part-time workers, all of them women, were employed. These were mainly the wives of farmers in the surrounding villages who had to work in the fields as well as in industry. Some women took work home while others practically lived on the job. The industry in Jogjakarta came into the hands of women because the men had to serve the king for such low wages that the women had to supplement them by producing batik for sale as well as for their own use. It has remained a predominantly female industry in this district.

Women are employers as well as workers. They managed a quarter of the total number of enterprises; one quarter were run by men and a half jointly by men and their wives. Men managed the largest and women the smallest. Among the full-time workers, the men were the printers while the women did the waxing and scraping which was no easier than printing but was paid lower

107

wages, because work done by women was called 'trained' and not 'skilled'.[3]

In many developing countries women form a large part of the home industries' labour force, and not only in those countries of Africa, South East Asia and Latin America where women are active in market trading, but also in some countries where women take little or no part in trade, such as Morocco and Iran. In these countries, with their tradition of female seclusion, women comprise one-fourth and one-third respectively of own-account work and family aids in industrial occupations (Table 16). This is because women who live in seclusion have no way of earning money except by working in home industries. Because they have no choice they tend to accept very low rates of pay from these industries which can therefore compete successfully with larger industries based upon relatively expensive male labour.

In the countries of the Middle East we find some women even employing hired labour; in Iran they account for 10 per cent of all industrial employers of hired labour. This is connected with the technical procedure in the carpet industry, where one adult woman weaver supervises three to six small girls.[4]

Female home industries are often located in regions where women keep completely away from other remunerative activities.* The social ban on other activities compel secluded women to take to the only activity by which they can earn money without the loss of social esteem within their community. We found in our investigation of Indian rural scene (in Chapter 4) that social restrictions on women's work sometimes result in relatively high wages for those women who dare to break the taboo. Here we have the other side of the picture; the social restrictions on women's work resulting in a large supply of women for the few types of work they can do without opprobium. As a result, earnings in such activities are small.

In India, seven million men and five million women are engaged in home industries. Indian artisans belong to low castes

* The industrially employed women in Southern Iraq are mainly engaged in the production of mats and baskets in their own homes.[5] Another example of industrial activity by strictly secluded women is found in East Pakistan where women account for 40 per cent of the labour force in the cotton textile home industry.[6]

Table 16

WOMEN IN INDUSTRIAL OCCUPATIONS

Country:	Female own-account workers (incl. employers)	Female family aids	Female employees	Total	Percentage of women in family labour force[a] in industrial occupations	among employees in industrial occupations
	as percentage of all women in industrial occupations:					
Africa South of the Sahara:						
Sierre Leone	70	22	8	100	15	2
Liberia	51	14	35	100	8	2
Ghana	91	3	6	100	39	3
Mauritius	26	3	71	100	9	4
Region of Arab influence:						
Morocco	51	4	35	100	25	15
United Arab Republic	36	8	56	100	7	2
Turkey	37	14	49	100	17	10
Syria	27	13	60	100	14	6
Iran	35	6	59	100	36	18
Pakistan	64	30	6	100	11	2
South and East Asia:						
India	b	b	16	100	35	12
Ceylon	30	4	66	100	47	11
Burma	b	b	b	100	36[b]	29[c]
Thailand	22	20	58	100	47	27
Cambodia	36	29	35	100	36	14
Malaya	20	3	77	100	17	11
Singapore	11	5	84	100	20	14
Philippines	57	10	33	100	68	20
Hong Kong	5	6	89	100	19	41
Korea (South)	24	13	63	100	15	11
Latin America:						
Honduras	61	10	29	100	46	9
Nicaragua	62	5	33	100	48	14
Costa Rica	31	3	66	100	27	13
Panama	45	4	51	100	21	9
Columbia	55	5	40	100	33	13
Ecuador	71	7	22	100	39	10
Chile	37	1	62	100	35	12
Venezuela	56	1	43	100	34	9
Cuba	16	1	83	100	15	14
Jamaica	53	11	36	100	54	16
Dominican Republic	47	1	52	100	23	9
Puerto Rico	8		92	100	26	24

[a] Family labour force includes own-account workers (including employers) and family aids.
[b] No information is available.   [c] Urban areas only.

Note: Industrial occupations include home industries, manufacturing industries and construction activities. Clerical, administrative and sales personnel in industries is excluded.

where it is normal for women to work. As in the Batik industry in Java, many Indian home industries employ women who do part-time work, which they often take home.* Some tribal areas of India have completely female home industries. Manipur was mentioned in a previous chapter as notable for its active women and inactive men. In addition to being farmers and traders, the women of Manipur account for 84 per cent of the labour force in home industries.[8] Likewise, in some Latin American countries on the coast of the Pacific, we find as many women as men among the own-account workers and family aids in industrial jobs.

WOMEN'S DROP-OUT FROM INDUSTRY

The proportion of adults working on their own account or as family aids in industry varies from one country to another. In some as much as 3 to 5 per cent of the adult population are employed in this way, and in others only 1 to 2 per cent. There may be several explanations for this low percentage; one could be that when much of the rural population is still at the stage of producing non-agricultural goods for home use in their daily lives, the market for the sale of such goods is very restricted. A second explanation could be that when cheap imported wares fill the market, there is little demand for home-produced goods. Yet another possibility could be that when the market is supplied with products from a large, modern home-based factory, family industries are unable to compete with these products and the demand for family labour ceases.

When, in a given country, a manufacturing industry is gradually being built up in competition with existing home industries manned by family labour, much of this labour is likely to change over to wage employment in the larger industries, be it successful enterprises in the home industries which expand and move to special premises, or a foreign or domestic large-scale industry which is recruiting labour. The important problem in the context of the present study is how this process of change will affect the large female labour force in the family industries. In other words,

* An investigation of small-scale industries in Bombay showed that out of 239,000 women employed in small industry, 192,000 worked in the industry producing cheap hand-made cigarettes (Bidis). This work they could do in their own homes.[7]

will the expanding employment of wage labour in industry proper absorb not only the male labour force released from home industries, but also the female labour force formerly occupied in such industries?

Figure 8 helps to provide an answer to this question. The pattern emerging from the figure is remarkably uniform. *All*

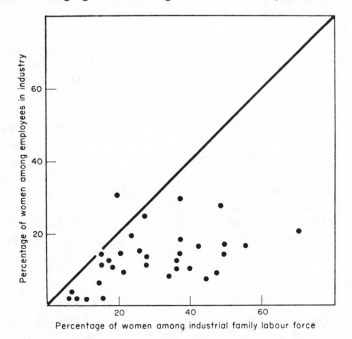

Figure 8 Status and Sex of Labour Force in Industrial Occupations

the countries represented have a lower percentage of women among hired workers than among own-account workers and family aids in industrial occupations* and this strongly suggests that when larger industries gradually drive the home industries out of business, women lose their jobs, because the type of products they were making (home spun cloth, hand made cigars, hand made matches, etc.) are replaced by products factory made by a labour force composed of many more men than women. In fact, it appears from the figure that in nearly all developing

* The only exception is Hong-Kong, with its very large textile industry.

111

countries women in industrial occupations account for less than one-fifth of the employees while they often account for one-third to a half of own-account workers and family aids.

In India, where in 1927 the percentage of women among factory workers was 17, it has since declined and seems now to be static at around 11 per cent.[9] The explanation for this is to be found in a steady and continuous decline in the percentage of women workers in the textile industries which outweighs the increases in some other industries.* In many other countries, the proportion of women workers in textile factories is very high, but in India women number less than 6 per cent of the textile workers. This is less than half of the percentage of women in the construction industry, where women have the special tasks of carrying headloads of building materials and of passing bricks from hand to hand to the bricklayers, as already mentioned.

With the gradual ousting of women from the old textile industries the regional distribution of women's industrial employment in India has changed considerably in favour of the South. Manufacturing industry now employs only 6 per cent of women in North India, but 9 per cent in Central India and no less than 17 per cent in South India. Here, again, we find a correlation between traditional and modern patterns of female employment. It was seen that women are much more active in both agriculture and trade in Southern India than in the North. This pattern is now seen to be repeated in the modern industrial sector. It would be a mistake, however, to assume that this is the general rule. In West Africa, where women's activity rates in agriculture and trade are at record levels, most modern factories keep their doors closed to women applicants.

WHY EMPLOYERS PREFER MALE WORKERS

Why is it that we find so few women among the industrial workers, when there are so many among the independent producers and family aids in home industries? It seems that we must

---

* The decline was particularly steep in the jute industries where the number of women employed declined from 33,000 in 1952 to 9,000 in 1962, while employment of men declined from 260,000 to 234,000.[10] The work the women had been doing was taken over by machines and the women were given no other work instead, while men were usually given other work when their former jobs had been eliminated by mechanization.

look for the explanation both on the supply and the demand sides of the female labour market. For various reasons, most employers prefer male labour and the women themselves (and their relatives) prefer work in home industries rather than work for wages in larger enterprises.

It is often suggested that rules about obligatory benefits for women workers contribute to the preferential recruitment of male labour to large-scale industries, which cannot violate the rules so easily as the smaller ones. Many developing countries have adopted the principle of paying equal wages to men and women doing identical jobs.[11] If, in addition, women get special benefits, such as the right to maternity-leave, crèches for their children, the right of exemption from night work and underground work in mines, etc., the result may indeed be to make it more profitable to employ men than women workers.[12] One of these benefits, the prohibition of women's work on night shifts, seems to be a serious impediment to the employment of women in large-scale industries.*

Understandably, it has been questioned whether it is wise to introduce the usual prohibition of women's work on night shifts in regions where the climate, at least in certain seasons, makes night shift work seem preferable to work in daytime.†[15]

It is less convincing to argue that rules for maternity leave and for the provision of crèches prevent the employment of women, since it would be easy to shift the financial burden of these special benefits from the employer of the women who benefit from them, to all employers, independently of whether they employ women or men. Where such financial equalization is not carried out, in spite of complaints of negative employment effects for the women, it may be suspected that for other and undisclosed reasons it is thought undesirable to increase the recruitment of women for industry. In some European countries where women workers are keen to get employment in industry, their trade unions have been reluctant to ask for special benefits, and

---

* It appeared from an investigation in Northern Nigeria that the textile industry refrained from hiring women workers, despite good experience with them, because they were not allowed to work on the night shifts.[13] The same was the case in Uganda.[14]

† An Indian committee report recommended that 'night shifts should be so arranged as to enable the employment of women in such shifts'.[16]

113

sometimes they have even refrained from pressing the claim of equal pay for male and female workers in order to make female labour competitive in spite of lower productivity, higher turnover or more frequent absence from work. When trade unions and governments in developing countries frequently endorse *both* the principle of equal pay for equal work *and* the practise of giving special benefits for women workers, it could be that these authorities feel that it is a small disadvantage, or even an advantage, if the application of these principles leads to preferential recruitment of male labour in industry, so that only those jobs which no men care to apply for are given to women.

A report by the International Labour Organization concerning the employment of women in Africa, posed the question whether it was the need to pay for maternity leave or the very fact that the women workers were often absent for child birth that made employers hesitate to recruit women workers.[17] It must be remembered that childbirth is a much more frequent event among women workers in Africa than in Europe and North America. This is partly because African women marry so young that married female workers make up a large share of all women workers, and partly because the frequency of pregnancy among married African women is much higher than in the industrialized world.

WHY WOMEN SHUN THE FACTORY

In order to explain the low rates of female employment in industry, we should not look at the demand side alone. Often the women themselves tend to prefer work in home industries or in service trades rather than in wage employment in large-scale industry. The more flexible working hours in home industries are a great advantage for married women, and particularly for women with small children. Whether the work takes place in the woman's own home or in that of a neighbour, it is possible to keep an eye on the children during work. Moreover, it is usually possible, as mentioned above, to come and go fairly freely and to interrupt the work when domestic duties require attention. And it is possible to obtain part-time employment in home industries but impossible or at least difficult in larger industries with a more rigorous rhythm of work. It is true that work in home industries often continues long after modern industries have closed down for the day, but this does not necessarily mean that individual workers in these industries are working longer hours than in modern industries. Some of them may do so, but, because of the relatively free coming and going, others may work much shorter hours or fewer days per month than workers in modern industries in the same country.*

In many developing countries, employment in home industry is preferred because it does not entail contact with persons outside the woman's own family, and particularly because the woman does not have to risk being under the supervision of men who are not members of the family. These advantages are frequently mentioned not only in Arab countries and in India but also in Latin American and African countries.

It seems that factory work by women is frowned upon in all parts of the under-developed world. This is particularly so in Arab countries, where the women workers in factories, few as they are, work mostly in what a Western observer has described as 'harem conditions'. Women work apart from the men and have no contact with them beyond what is absolutely necessary for the work. The women themselves insist on having these conditions observed, and cases have been reported from West Asian factories where the women workers refused the male supervisors access to the premises.†[20]

Both in India and Pakistan public opinion makes a sharp distinction between work in home industries and 'literate work', which are regarded as respectable occupations, and factory work which is not regarded as respectable for women.[22]

* A manpower survey in the Philippines showed that among self-employed women in home industries and women who were helping in family industries, i.e. among those who could decide more or less freely on their own working hours, only 36–38 per cent worked 40 hours or more per week, while 68 per cent of women wage workers in industry worked 40 hours or more per week.[18] In Indonesia, modern industries *attract women workers* by offering part time employment.[19]

† An official report in Calcutta suggested that a similar arrangement in the factories might be a suitable method to attract middle class women to industrial employment.[21]

In Puerto Rico, the percentage of women among the workers is particularly high (24 per cent). But when the United States-owned large-scale industries in Puerto Rico began to recruit women workers, particularly workers from small towns or rural areas, the moral standard of the factory had to be established before the suspicions of the conservative elders and husbands could be overcome and the women could get permission to take employment in the factories.[23] Among the Maya Indians in the Guatamala highlands, factory work was also considered 'a not quite fitting job' for women. But the prejudice is not an absolute one; when Latin America's largest textile mill was set up in the region, the Indian women accepted employment in large numbers, since they could thereby add handsomely to family income, and recruited small girls as domestic servants to take care of their children during factory hours.[24]

Even in Africa, the exceedingly low rate of female employment in factories is partly explained by the fear that women might be exposed to a demoralizing influence in factory surroundings. This was revealed, for instance, in an investigation of factory labour in Jinja, the new industrial centre of Uganda,[25] and it is stated in more general terms in a report by the International Labour Office: 'The idea of being employed by an outsider except in a post requiring education is distasteful both to her (the woman) and to her family and husband, though there is the possibility of some exception if a woman is working along with her husband, e.g. in agricultural employment on farms or plantations.'[26] Nevertheless, women often seem keen to obtain factory work in Africa. In 1952, when the first factory in Stanleyville in the Congo opened its gates to women, there was a rush of applicants.[27] In North Nigeria, there seems to be a large potential female labour supply and industrial vacancies could be filled several times over by women applicants, but men form 99 per cent of the factory workers partly because of the prohibition of night work for women mentioned above.[28]

Because there are few women among industrial workers proper and many women among own-account workers and family aids in home industries, we find that in most developing countries a large proportion of the industrially employed women are in home industries, while only a small proportion of the industrially employed men have remained in this low-productivity branch of the industrial sector. The figures below show that in twenty out of twenty-eight developing countries less than 30 per cent of the industrially employed men worked on their own account or as family aids in home industries, while in only four countries were less than 30 per cent of the women in this category.*

Number of developing countries where the share of industrially occupied men, resp. women, working on own-account or as family helpers was within indicated ranges:

	Men	Women
less than 30 per cent	20	4
30–59 per cent	7	12
60–89 per cent	1	9
90 and over		3
Total number of countries	28	28

We found a similar division of labour in the trade sector in many countries, where men are employees in the modern shops while women handle small-scale market trade in food and other daily necessities. This type of polarized division of labour creates a wide gap in productivity and income between men and women within the same sector, lowering the position of women in relation to that of men. The gap between the productivity and earnings of men and women is further widened because those few women who are employed in modern industry are mostly doing unskilled jobs. This will be discussed more thoroughly in Chapter 8. But first let us consider how the employment pattern for educated women changes in the course of economic development.

NOTES TO CHAPTER 6

1. Geertz, 66–70.   2. Kertanegara, 351ff.   3. Kertanegara, 379. 4. Woodsmall 1960, 71.   5. Langley, 278.   6. Husain 1956, Vol. I, 55. 7. Lakdawala, 88.   8. India 1961, census.   9. Giri, 380. ILO India, 14. 10. India Min. of L. Delhi 1964, 7–11.   11. ILO Rev. 1956, I, 189–92; ILO *Afr. Conf. Report*, 51–2, 139–40.   12. India Min. of L. Simla 1964,

* The contrast would be even more pronounced if owners of industrial establishments employing hired labour were excluded from the category of own-account workers and family aids, since nearly all such owners are men.

24; India Min. of L. Delhi 1964, 29–30; Sison, 128; Fonseca, 173–5.
13. Wells, 103–4, 113.   14. Lefauchaud, 25.   15. Lefauchaud, 25.
16. Shah, 209.   17. ILO 1964, *Afr. Conf. Report*, 24.   18. *Philippines Survey of Households* 1960.   19. Dobby, 373.   20. Woodsmall 1936, 265; Nouacer, 190.   21. India W. Bengal 1959, 37.   22. Husain 1956, Vol. I, 240; Sengupta, 223.   23. Gregory, 151–2.   24. Nash, 317–20.   25. Sofer, 611.   26. ILO, *Afr. Conf. Report*, 7.   27. Xydias, 287–88.   28. Wells, 103, 116.

Chapter 7

The Educated Woman

'Higher' education, however defined, is enjoyed by only a tiny minority of girls in developing countries. Obviously, the number of students receiving advance education and training is closely related to the general level of development. On the one hand, a country must have reached a certain level before it can afford to give most of its young people lengthy education, and, on the other hand, the opportunities for using highly educated people in an efficient way occur more or less *pari passu* with economic development.

Of course, drawing the line of demarcation between 'secondary' and 'higher' education is somewhat arbitrary. Mainly for reasons of statistical convenience, we shall here define 'higher' education as all formal education beyond the age of 14. Table 17 shows that those students who according to this definition are receiving higher education—let us call them 'adult students'—account for no more than two or three per cent of all adults in the relatively poor countries belonging to the Arab group, in the low-income countries in Asia (India, Burma and Indonesia) and in such backward American countries as Honduras and El Salvador. By contrast, in the more advanced countries of Latin America, and in Asian towns like Singapore and Hong Kong more than 5 per cent of all adults are receiving education. But the spread of education is sometimes determined by factors other than economic levels. In some relatively poor countries like the Philippines and South Korea, adult students account for between 6 and 7 per cent of all adults.

The table gives not only the total number of students but shows how many of these adult students are girls. Here the link with economic factors is less evident. Even in the poorest country, some parents are rich enough to provide education not only for their sons but also for their daughters. If they wish to do so and

Table 17

ADULT STUDENTS BY SEX AND AGE

Country:	Percentage of all adults who are:		Women students as per cent of all students:		
	students	women students	15–19 years	20–24 years	15 years and over
Africa South of the Sahara:					
Ghana	4·2	0·9	24	10	22
Mauritius	4·9	1·6	34	20	33
Region of Arab Influence:					
Morocco	2·3	0·5	22	11	21
Iran	1·9	0·4	22	11	19
South and East Asia:					
India	2·6	0·5			19
Burma	a	a	26[b]	29[b]	27[b]
Malaya	4·7	1·4	30	24	29
Singapore	5·8	2·1	36	32	36
Indonesia	2·9	0·9	33	23	31
Philippines	6·8	3·0	46	40	44
Taiwan	2·9	0·7	26	15	24
Hong Kong	4·9	2·2	45	43	44
China					23
Korea (South)	6·4	2·0			32
Latin America:					
Honduras	2·2	1·1	49	34	48
El Salvadore	3·4	1·6	47	40	46
Costa Rica	4·4	2·1	48	44	48
Panama	4·9	2·5	50	46	50
Venezuela	6·1	2·8	47	39	46
Puerto Rico	9·3	4·6	50	47	50

a No information is not available.   b In urban areas only.

if the government fails to establish public schools for girls, private schools for them are likely to be set up. Thus, if a poor country belongs to a culture with a positive attitude to higher education for girls we find a high proportion of girls among the relatively few adult students. By contrast, if the dominant culture is hostile or indifferent to the higher education of girls, we find few girls among the adult students even if the country is economically relatively advanced.

This cultural factor is clearly reflected in Table 17. Consider, for instance, the figures for Latin American countries where the total number of students varies according to the degree of economic development, as already mentioned. Yet there is virtually no difference in the sex proportions among students in the 15–19 years age group, because Latin American parents who can afford to educate their children beyond the age of fourteen do so both for their boys and their girls, so that girls account for very nearly half the student population in those age groups in every Latin American country represented in the table. Only at the University level, i.e. in the age group 20–24, do the boys outnumber the girls, but even at this level the difference is slight in some of the Latin American countries. This, then, is the sex pattern of education in a cultural setting where a positive attitude is taken to the education of girls, although there are reservations about employing married women.*

Among the towns and countries of the Far East shown in Table 17, only in Hong Kong and the Philippines does the girl student population compare with that of Latin American countries. The fact that girls account for such a high proportion of the students in the Philippines is highly significant, for it alone among the former colonies in the Far East was under American and not European dominance. The student population of the Philippines ranks first in size (7 per cent of adults), and, barring Hong Kong, it is the only Asian country to have nearly as many girl students as boys.

In Chinese-speaking areas (other than Hong Kong) there are two to three boy students for each girl, and this is true even of Singapore, a city with a high income level by Asian standards. It would seem that the traditional Chinese hostility towards

* In some regions in Latin America attitudes to the education of girls are less positive. Among the poor Indian population in Southern Peru, as late as 1958, the rural schools had only 28 per cent girls among the pupils, but these poor populations do not contribute to the supply of adult male students either.[1]

female education is dying only slowly and this seems to hold good for the overseas Chinese as well as for the Mainland of China.* This traditional hostility towards education for girls is reflected to a still greater extent in the sex proportion among students in India and in the Arab countries, where there are four boys to each girl in the age group 15 to 19, and up to ten boys to one girl in the age group 20 to 24.

Several factors contribute to the drop-out of girls after the age of nineteen. For one thing, there is a deep-seated fear of marriages where the wife is more educated than the husband.[3] This attitude is ubiquitous; we find it even in the Philippines, the top-ranking Asian country as regards female education,[4] and it encourages many parents and girls to stop education at a stage when it is still possible to find husbands at similar (or higher) educational levels. All informants in an enquiry among Indian girl students at American Universities agreed that, while an Indian girl improves her marriage chances by having high school education, to continue further is to penalize her chances of marriage.[5] This fear of being unable to find a husband is probably a more important factor in the drop-out in education than the young marriage age for girls, since the low wages of domestic servants and the system of extended family would usually make it possible for a girl to further her studies after marriage, if she so desired. Many Asian women do continue after marriage if their husbands are willing for them to finish their studies, either to take up careers or because of the social prestige of education.

In most of Africa, higher education for girls is quite a recent phenomenon. In the colonial period the curricula of missionary schools for African girls stressed domestic activities, dress-making and embroidery, in addition to religious education. It was a 'training for the home' and in some regions literary instruction was kept to a minimum.[6] But it is interesting to note that in places where African parents had the chance to give their daughters higher education, the female student population was not so low. Around 1960, 40 per cent of the Bantu students of

---

* In 1932, girls accounted for 12 per cent of Chinese University students. In 1946 the percentage had risen to 18, and as late as 1958 it was 23 per cent only. In that year, the share of girls in secondary schools was 31 per cent and in primary schools 39 per cent.[2]

South Africa were girls, and the Ghana students, 15 to 19 year age-group had one girl to three boys.

SECLUSION IN THE PROFESSIONS

Most boy students who have received higher education find jobs in administration or in the professions. But how can girls in developing countries make use of their education? Some light is thrown on this question in Figure 9 in which the sex proportion

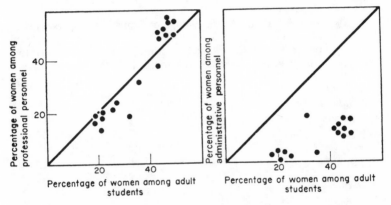

Figure 9 Sex Distribution of Adult Students and of Persons in Professional and Administrative Occupations

among students is compared to that of administrative and professional personnel in a number of developing countries.

It appears that the proportion of women among administrative personnel is always very much lower than the proportion of women among students. In countries with relatively few girl students, women account for less than 3 per cent of the administrative personnel, and in countries where the number of boy and girl students is about equal, little more than 10 per cent of the administrative personnel are women. In effect, administrative work is a male monopoly in developing countries, just as it is in nearly all industrialized countries.* But it is worth noting again

* Even in the Soviet Union where women account for more than half the non-manual labour force, the percentage of women in top administrative jobs is as low as 12 per cent.[7]

that it is in those developing countries where American influence is most pronounced—Latin American countries, the Philippines and South Korea—that women exceed 10 per cent of administrative personnel, Table 18, column 3.

Table 18

WOMEN IN CLERICAL AND ADMINISTRATIVE OCCUPATIONS

Country:	Women in clerical and administrative occupations as per cent of all adult women	Percentage of women of all personnel		
		in clerical occupations	in administrative occupations	in clerical and administrative occupations
Africa South of the Sahara:				
Sierra Leone		16	9	14
Liberia		13	9	12
Ghana		7	3	6
Mauritius	1	24	4	19
Region of Arab influence:				
Sudan		2		2
Morocco		27	1	21
Libya		6	1	5
United Arab Republic		a	a	5
Turkey	1	a	a	12
Jordan		6		5
Syria		6	4	6
Iraq		5	2	2
Iran		4	3	4
Pakistan		1		1
South and East Asia:				
India		3	3	3
Ceylon		6	3	6
Burma		a	a	9[b]
Thailand		14	9	13

[a] No information is available.   [b] Urban areas only.

Table 18—contd.

Cambodia		6	12	7
Malaya		7	2	6
Singapore	2	10	7	9
Philippines	1	23	14	21
Taiwan	1	13	7	11
Hong Kong	2	a	a	13
Korea (South)		6	18	10

Latin America:

Mexico	2	30	12	28
Honduras	1	33	11	28
El Salvadore	1	33	17	28
Nicaragua	1	25	11	24
Costa Rica	2	27	11	24
Panama	4	a	a	41
Columbia	2	36	15	28
Ecuador	1	28	7	26
Chile	2	30	17	27
Venezuela	3	34	11	30
Cuba	2	25	5	17
Jamaica	3	50	18	45
Dominican Republic	1	27	12	25
Puerto Rico	3	a	a	32

Turning from the administrative work to the professions, we find a completely different pattern. In all the developing countries represented in Figure 9 the percentage[3] of women in the professions and among the students are similar. Far from being a male monopoly, the professions would seem to be open, without discrimination, to both sexes and to be equally attractive to educated women and educated men. This seems to be true of African, Arab, Asian and American countries, despite the wide differences in attitudes to women's roles.

Prima facie, this is a striking fact that needs some further explanation. We get the clue when we consider the particular type of work professional women are doing. In most countries, two-thirds or more of all women in the professions are teachers, and a large proportion of the remaining one-third are nurses or perform other medical services (Table 19). Even in countries with a tradition of seclusion for women and with few girls among the students there is a demand for professional women, simply because custom requires that if a girl is to be educated, she should be educated by female teachers, in special schools for girls. Similarly, it is thought that decency requires women to be taken care of by female health personnel, female social workers, etc. In other words, in countries where women live in seclusion,

Table 19

WOMEN IN THE PROFESSIONS

Country:	Percentage of all adult women occupied				Percentage of women of all personnel				Women in the professions as percentage of all women in non-agricultural occupations
	as teachers	as nurses	in other professions	in all professions	in teaching	in nursing	in other professions	in all professions	
Africa South of the Sahara:									
Ghana	0·3	0·2	0·2	0·6	22	61	10	20	2·5
South Africa	0·8	0·8	0·2	1·8	50	93	13	42	7·6
Kenya	0·3	a	a	a	23	a	a	a	a
Region of Arab influence:									
Sudan	0·1	0·1		0·1	14	32	1	8	8·7
Morocco	0·3	a	a	0·4	15	a	a	13	6·7
Libya	0·3	0·2		0·5	16	31	3	14	10·9
United Arab Republic	0·5	0·1		0·6	30	100	3	22	18·3
Turkey	0·4	a	a	0·7	31	a	a	21	19·8
Jordan	0·7	0·3		1·0	35	54	3	30	32·6
Syria	0·4	0·1		0·5	34	50	1	27	19·0
South and East Asia:									
India	0·3	0·1		0·4	20	71	6	16	4·8
Thailand	0·6	0·1	0·1	0·8	33	76	25	34	6·3
Malaya	0·7	0·3	0·1	1·1	30	70	9	28	14·0
Philippines	1·3	0·2	0·2	1·6	67	78	19	51	8·4
Taiwan	0·5	a	a	0·9	31	a	a	26	11·4
Hong Kong	1·3	0·4	0·6	2·3	53	92	19	38	6·7
Latin America:									
El Salvador	1·0	a	a	1·5	68	a	a	52	8·2
Costa Rica	2·3	a	a	3·3	72	a	a	56	18·9
Venezuela	1·7	a	a	3·2	73	a	a	50	16·0

a No information is available.

the demand for professional women does not violate the rules of seclusion, but indeed is a necessary *result* of those rules. Such modern facilities as schools and hospitals can be introduced without danger to the system of seclusion only on condition that a staff of professional women is available so that contacts between men and women belonging to different families may be avoided. The employment of a limited number of women in the professions makes it possible for the great majority of women to avoid exposure to contacts with male professional staff. Moreover, even the professional women staff can avoid male contacts if they are educated in establishments staffed by women, and when their education ends they serve only other women and girls. 'The veil could still be retained' said an American observer of professional women workers in Moslem countries thirty years ago.[8]

Since then, the veil has fallen in many Moslem countries, but young women teachers in Morocco still think of teaching jobs as particularly suitable because there 'women are in contact only with other women or with children'.[9] This explains why the proportion of women among professional staffs is usually as high as between 15 and 30 per cent in countries in the Arab group. And this is why we find a close correlation between the extent to which girls are educated and the proportion of women in the professions. Under this system, the rate of expansion of the education of girls is tied to the increase in the supply of female teachers, and the increase in the number of educated women is likely to bring with it an extension of the educational system for girls, since few other careers are open to women with a higher education.

In recent years, attitudes to the education of girls have changed rapidly in many developing countries. Because of the inevitable age gap between teacher and pupil, teacher education has become the scarce factor, the bottleneck, the widening of which is the pre-condition for further progress. This is particularly true of the countries where European woman teachers have been returning to their home countries.*

In countries where women have only recently become literate, the younger rather than the older age groups supply the professions (Table 20). Although prejudice usually works against women when both men and women are being considered for a particular kind of job, in this respect the teaching profession is an exception. Women teachers in Arab countries benefit from

---

* The problem is sometimes 'solved' by lowering the standards of education. Two-thirds of the women teachers in Moroccan girl schools in 1960 were 'unqualified', i.e. they were teaching without having had any training as teachers.[10]

the prejudice against girls being exposed to male teachers, and women teachers in the countries under Anglo-Saxon cultural influence benefit from the particular Anglo-Saxon prejudice

Table 20

SEX DISTRIBUTION IN THE PROFESSIONS BY AGE GROUPS

Country:	Percentage of women in total personnel in professional occupations			
	15–24 years	25–34 years	35–44 years	45 years and over
Africa South of the Sahara:				
Ghana	28	17	15	15
Region of Arab influence:				
Turkey	21	22	20	8
Iraq	34	23	17	9
Iran	27		18	14
South and East Asia:				
Thailand	50	38	22	19
Malaya	37	28	22	17
Singapore	50	35	32	24
Philippines	62	58	49	38
Taiwan	44	23	19	12
Hong Kong	58	40	33	23
Korea (South)	55	15	7	10
Latin America:				
Honduras	72	53	50	38
El Salvadore	70	59	52	39
Costa Rica	66	59	53	41
Panama	65	57	56	48
Chile	64	52	47	41
Puerto Rico	68	51	43	43

that men are unsuitable teachers in primary schools. This idea is eagerly propagated by both Americans and Europeans in developing countries. For instance, Maurice Zinkin says in a widely read book about development problems: 'Most Asian primary education is severely handicapped by having to use men, and pay the price of men, for the teaching of the under-tens.'[11] The widespread belief that men are inferior teachers for children helps to explain why there are more women than men in the professions in most Latin American countries and in the Philippines.

Both the Arab and the Anglo-Saxon ideas about the suitable sex of teachers promote the employment of women teachers. But the effects of these conflicting ideas upon the career prospects of women, in terms of promotion, are in sharp contrast. In those countries where women must teach girls and men must teach boys at all stages, women's opportunities are not restricted to teaching in primary schools. They have about an equal chance with men to obtain the better-paid jobs as teachers in secondary schools and as principals of educational establishments. Many private schools in the Arab countries are founded and managed by women.[12] In contrast, where women are held to be more suitable primary teachers than men for both boys and girls, there is a tendency to have male teachers at the higher stages of education and as principals of the schools. Thus, in India the proportion of women teachers is about the same in primary, middle and secondary schools,[13] but in the Philippines we find the American system of fewer and fewer women for the older pupils.[14] This can be seen from the figures below:

Percentage of women among:

	Teachers	Principals
Primary schools	77	22
Secondary schools	57	12
Universities	39	

In some Latin American countries women dominate primary education more than in the Philippines. Over 90 per cent of the pupils training as primary teachers in Brazil are women, and although half of these women make no use of their training later, nearly all the teachers in primary schools are women.[15] Even in Africa, women sometimes dominate primary teaching; in Dahomey in West Africa sometimes described as 'le quartier latin' of Africa, 70 per cent of primary school teachers are women.[16]

It is agreed the world over that women have a major role to play in teaching, although opinions differ as to whom they should teach; girls only, or small children only? No such agreement exists concerning women's role in nursing. In Africa, nursing ranks together with teaching as the most suitable occupation for respectable girls, and the profession of nursing is rapidly changing over from male to female,* but in many parts of Asia parents object to their daughters becoming nurses. In India, the objection is partly because nurses violate caste rules by handling bedpans, and partly because nurses must go out for night work or live outside the family premises, which is considered indecent in many Indian families.[18] Thus, most recruits for Indian nursing schools are low-caste girls or Anglo-Indian girls, which results in a shortage of nurses compared with a surplus of primary teachers in towns.†[19]

THE FEMINIZATION OF CLERICAL JOBS

In industrialized countries, many girls who have been educated beyond the age of 14 take up clerical jobs when they have completed it. In the United States, 7 million women do clerical work and they account for 68 per cent of clerical staffs. Similarly, in other industrialized countries, women account for 60 to 70 per cent of the clerical labour force. Many of these women retire to domestic life after a few years, and this, together with the prejudice against the employment of women in administrative occupations, provides such good promotion prospects for the few young men who do enter the clerical sector, that it does not become completely 'feminized'.

In developing countries, we never find women in the majority in clerical occupations. Latin America comes closest to the predominating pattern in industrialized countries, with one woman to two or three men, while most countries outside the

---

* Among industrial workers in Cape Town in South Africa covered by an investigation, 37 per cent wanted their daughters to become nurses or teachers, a desire which the author of the investigation described as 'not entirely unrealistic', since most African nurses and teachers in the Union are in fact children of African workers and peasants, because no African middle class existed from which *recruitment* for the professions could take place.[17]

† The prejudice against nursing prevails in several other Asian countries. In Pakistan, as in India, there is the same contrast between the way people look upon teaching and nursing as female careers.[20] Burmese girls avoid nursing, leaving this profession to girls from the Karen tribe.[21] In Malaya too, nursing is frowned upon.[22]

Americas have at least ten men to one girl in clerical occupations (Table 18).

Many Latin American countries have reached higher levels of economic development than most developing countries in Asia and Africa, and the wide regional differences in sex distribution within the clerical group partly reflect these differences in

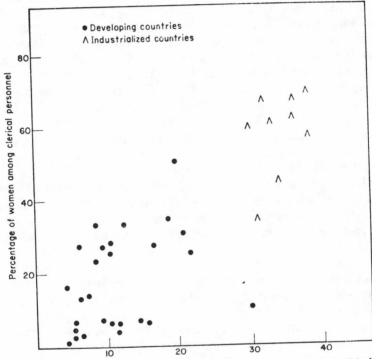

Persons occupied in the modern occupations as percentage of all adults[1]

[1] See Note to Table 3.

Figure 10 Sex Distribution of Clerical Personnel in Countries at Different Stages of Development

the degree of economic development. With economic development, the percentage of women in clerical occupations increases and there is a fair degree of correlation between the stage of economic development reached in a given country and the percentage of women in the clerical sector (Figure 10). Nevertheless,

some poor Latin American countries have a higher proportion of women in clerical occupations than some of the richer
countries in Latin America. This seems to be due to the large
number of girls among the students and the absence of prejudice
against office jobs for young women. Likewise, in Asia and
Africa, we find a high proportion of women clerks in some countries at relatively low stages of development. These are mainly
countries under American influence such as Liberia, Thailand,
the Philippines, Taiwan. American influence and presence in the
Far East has helped to open office doors to women and make
office employment acceptable to them. Nearly half the clerical
staff in Japan consists of women, while the proportion is 10 per
cent in Singapore where there is little American influence to
counteract the Chinese tradition of male clerical staff. The
Europeans, with predominantly female clerical staffs in their
home country stick to local traditional sex patterns in office
recruitment overseas. It was only after independence that the
first few African girls began to appear in African offices.

It has been shown above that, whether the developing countries
are at an earlier or later stage of development, this makes little
difference to the proportion of educated women in the professions.
It has also been shown that very few women get administrative
jobs, and that in most developing countries in Asia and Africa
few women are found in clerical occupations either. Must we
conclude from this that the spread of higher education among
girls simply means that an ever larger number of women receive
higher education just in order to live as highly educated housewives and mothers? Or will there eventually be an overflow of
educated girls into office employment, even in those countries
where clerical occupations were hitherto a male preserve?

This is not an easy question to answer, but we can at least
throw some light on it by considering the situation in different
developing countries where the number of women in office jobs
is relatively low.

We shall first consider the newly independent countries in
Africa south of the Sahara. The desire for rapid Africanization,
combined with the acute shortage of highly educated and trained
persons of both sexes, gives educated African women a unique
opportunity to enter occupations previously almost entirely

male monopolies. A report by the International Labour Organization suggested in 1964 that it will be twenty years before enough African boys and girls are available to fill the occupations which require a university degree, such as doctors, secondary school and university teachers, higher civil service posts, etc.[23] In a recent speech, the Planning Minister of Kenya made this appeal to educated African women: 'The shortage of African high-level and middle-level manpower is already proving a bottle-neck in the Africanization of some sectors. All this amounts to is that women must recognise that there is ample scope for them in many activities of the economy'.*[24]

Similar complaints have been heard in official statements from other African countries with a particularly acute shortage of educated personnel.†

As mentioned above, nursing and teaching seem to be the most cherished occupations for educated girls in Africa. As long as the attractive nursing and teaching jobs are easily obtained by a girl with the required training, there will be little pressure to give the girls access to clerical jobs. Moreover, the number of educated men aspiring to clerical jobs tends to be in excess of the number of clerical jobs available. So it will probably take some time for the clerical profession in Africa to become 'feminized' to any large extent.‡

Turning to the Arab countries of North Africa and Western Asia we find a similar surplus of men for office employment. Indeed, this excess of labour for clerical occupations seems inevitable when the number of children enjoying general school education is increasing by leaps and bounds. As long as only a minority are literate, it is taken for granted that a literate person

* A manpower survey for Kenya published in 1965 foresaw that a serious shortage of women teachers and nurses would also exist in 1970.[25]

† For instance, the governments of Zambia and the Central African Republic, in their replies to a questionnaire by the International Labour Organization, deplored that the women were too conservative and reluctant to utilize the new job opportunities which had become available to them.[26]

‡ It is a widely held opinion in Africa that while more facilities for women's vocational training should be made available in the particular fields of teaching, nursing and domestic science, in spheres other than these three, preference should be given to the adult male worker when vocational training priorities are assessed. This view was accepted at an Interafrican Conference in Lusaka in 1957,[27] and there is little sign of a change of opinion since then.

is entitled to a white collar job. It is not surprising that this attitude tends to survive long after the majority has become literate, until it is finally accepted that ordinary industrial and agricultural jobs are normal occupations for literate persons. In the meantime, literate and educated young men will resent any encroachment by women on white collar employment because this would tend to push the men into jobs hitherto thought to be suitable only for illiterates.*

Thus, the idea of female education and employment in white collar jobs meets with much resistance, and education continues to be disadvantageous in the marriage market.[29] But the departure of French girls has left a vacuum in North African labour markets which provides an incentive for Moslem girls to break with traditions.† When they do so, they generally prefer an office job to employment in a shop or a restaurant because office work entails contact with only a limited group of men in premises to which admittance is restricted.‡[31] Nevertheless, the supply of office girls is lagging behind demand and the main change in North Africa is the replacement of French women by Arab men.

Thus, in many parts of Africa the departure of Europeans has created a shortage of educated personnel which leaves girls free to choose between professional jobs and office jobs, and all can get jobs of the type for which they are trained. In other parts of the world the situation is different. We need go no further than Egypt to find an excess of educated female labour. Forty years ago Egypt was short of educated women as is now the case in Morocco and Kenya. Around 1930 there was such a shortage of female teachers in Egypt and in what is now Jordan that measures were taken to increase their numbers by, for instance, the payment of higher salaries to women teachers than to men.[33] But

* A recent study of attitude to female employment in Morocco concludes that 'if female employment—and particularly employment outside the home—is beginning to be accepted, it must be admitted that it is with much reservation. . . . There are still many obstacles to overcome—both those put forward by the old generation, which remains hostile towards female emancipation, and those caused by the reservations of the young generation: theoretically, these are for female emancipation, but in practice they are afraid of it.'[28]

† In Tunisia, upper class girls are said to be particularly traditional, while lower class girls are less afraid of breaking with traditions.[30]

‡ In Casamanca, at the time of the investigation mentioned above, many girls left the commercial schools before the end of the courses, tempted by attractive job opportunities.[32]

134

this stage was over long ago; today it is difficult for an educated Egyptian girl to find a job, and many have to accept jobs other than the ones for which they were trained.[34]

A third pattern found in India seems to be one of transition from a shortage of women suitable for the 'secluded' type of job earmarked for them, to a shortage of jobs appropriate to educated women who find them as hard to come by as educated men, if not more so. Until recently, there was often an insufficient supply of Indian women for jobs in the public service,[35] so that many openings for white collar female employment were taken up by Anglo-Indian girls. Sometimes, for instance, in the steel town of Jamshedpur, employers had to fall back on girls from tribal communities because educated Hindu girls were reluctant to accept employment.[36]

However, now that so many educated girls seem willing to take white collar jobs, the demand for them falls behind the supply. In 1966 women accounted for 15 per cent of those registered at Indian employment exchanges for white collar jobs such as clerical, sales and related work,[37] while only 2 to 3 per cent of those actually employed in these jobs were women.

THE PULL OF WHITE COLLAR JOBS

There are many more women in white collar jobs in Latin America than in Africa or Asia.* Nevertheless, such jobs are held by only 2 per cent of all adult women; while in industrialized countries, where the clerical sector is both larger and more 'feminized', up to 10 per cent of adult women are in clerical jobs. What is likely to happen if these occupations in Latin America become still more 'feminine', with two-thirds women and one-third men, which is typical of industrialized countries?

The answer to this question seems to be related to the future trend of female employment in professions. In these, the proportion of women in Latin America is markedly *higher* than in

---

* In the comparison between the labour market for white collar jobs in Latin America and in India and Pakistan it must be remembered that Indian and Pakistani girls usually marry at a very early age. In East Bengal most girls are married before the age of fourteen.[38] Thus, the category of educated unmarried girls, which accounts for a large share of white collar employment in Latin America, is virtually non-existent in India and Pakistan.

industrialized countries. In fact, we can see three clearly different patterns of employment of educated women. First is the pattern found in industrialized countries, where the percentage of women in clerical jobs is very high and somewhat lower in the

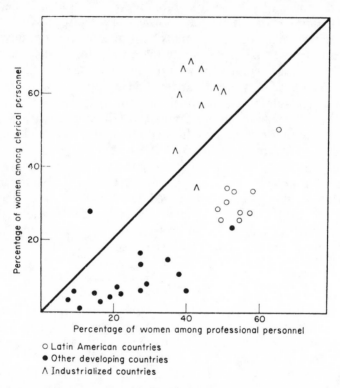

Figure 11 Women in Professional and Clerical Occupations in Developing and Industrialized Countries

professions. Secondly, the pattern in Latin America is of a higher proportion of women in the professions than in clerical jobs. And, thirdly, the pattern characteristic of Asia and Africa shows a smaller proportion of women in both professions and in clerical jobs. A glance at Figure 11 should help to gauge the difference between these three groups of countries, and to dispel any doubt about the statistical significance of the grouping of countries.

136

Let us consider more closely the difference between the group of Latin American countries and that of industrialized countries. Since both professional and clerical jobs are held largely by young educated girls, it is pertinent to ask whether the difference in the pattern of female employment in the two groups of countries can be attributed to women at a certain stage being forced into clerical jobs because the opportunities for entering the professions were limited, or whether it is the result of an expansion in the clerical sector, which draws young women away from professional training and employment.

There can be little doubt that both these forces are at work. During the process of industrialization the proportion of children in the population is declining and this affects the demand for teachers. Moreover, once the goal of primary schooling for all has been achieved, the demand for primary teachers will be growing at a lower rate. Since they account for a very large proportion of professional women in developing countries, these changes in the demand must act as a brake on the total demand for women in the professions, unless this tendency is offset by a growing acceptance of girls in professional jobs hitherto filled more or less exclusively by men.

So much for the pressure on educated women to accept clerical jobs through limited opportunities in the professions. On the supply side, however, it seems plausible to assume that the easy access to clerical jobs in industrialized countries tends to discourage young women from taking the longer training needed for the professions. This pull towards the clerical jobs must be all the stronger because so many women in industrialized countries give up their jobs when they become housewives and mothers, and office work requires a relatively short training.

Until recently the proportion of women in the professions in industrialized countries showed no upward trend.[39] But now the number of young married women in employment seems to be increasing both in the United States and in some other industrialized countries. Moreover, studies comparing the effect on children of working and of non-working mothers have become available; their findings fail to confirm the widespread belief that the employment of mothers of young children adversely affects the next generation.[40]

Perhaps these new developments can be taken as fore-shadowing a change of attitude to the employment of married women with children. If this is so, we shall probably see more girls shunning the low-grade office jobs which offer few opportunities for promotion, and turning their attention to those occupations which require a longer training and give more opportunities for promotion. This change in attitude is likely to appear both in industrialized countries and in developing countries with a high rate of female literacy.

NOTES TO CHAPTER 7

1. ILO *Rev.* 1964, II, 22. 2. Orleans, 145, 160–2, 172. 3. Naigisiki, 153; Clignet, 217; Balandier 1955, 192–3. 4. Fox, 356–7. 5. Cormack, 49, 160–1. 6. Hailey, 1199, 1209. 7. Dodge, 299. 8. Woodsmall 1936, 242. 9. Forget, 158. 10. Forget, 146n. 11. Zinkin, 200. 12. Izzedin, 310. 13. ILO 1963 India, 85. 14. Pecson, 346–7. 15. ILO *Rev.* 1964, II, 171–2. 16. Lefauchaud, 22. 17. van der Horst, 94. 18. Cormack, 5, 160. 19. India Min. of L. Delhi 1964, 31–2; India Pl. C. 1964, 5. 20. Husain 1958, 60, 65. 21. Andrus, 291. 22. Wee, 162. 23. ILO, *Afr. Conf. Report*, 29. 24. Mboya, 17. 25. Mboya, 17. 26. ILO, *Afr. Conf. Report*, 12. 27. CCTA, 30. 28. Nouacer, 191. 29. M'Rabet, 19 *passim*. 30. de Moulety, 154. 31. Forget, 158. 32. Forget, 146n. 33. Woodsmall 1936, 246. 34. Hamamsy, 238–9. 35. Appadorai, 28. 36. Sengupta, 121–3. 37. India Pl. C. 1966, 2. 38. Husain 1956, Vol. I, 79. 39. Farrag, 32. 40. Nye, 191, 210 *passim*.

Chapter 8

Women in the Urban Hierarchy

In Chapters 5 and 6 we discussed the changes which occur when home industries and market trade are replaced by modern forms of industry and trade. It was seen that it was usually the men who were recruited for these modern activities, while women tended to be left behind in the traditional activities. Indeed, in many countries the statistical picture for manpower in industry is one of pronounced differentiation: The modern establishments overwhelmingly favour the employment of men, while women are mostly found in home industries. The inferior position of women in urban development is exacerbated by the strong preference for recruiting men to the clerical and administrative jobs.

When jobs in modern industry, in modern trade, and in offices are held exclusively or overwhelmingly by men, the productivity, attitude and outlook of men and women begin to diverge, just as we found happening when commercial farming replaced subsistence agriculture; men become familiar with modern equipment and learn to adapt themselves to modern ways of life, while women continue in the old ways. Economic progress benefits men as wage earners in the modern sector, while the position of women is left unchanged, and even deteriorates when competition from the growing modern sectors eliminates the traditional enterprises carried on by women. Thus, hand in hand with the cleavage in productivity and in attitudes, an income gap is likely to emerge between men with rising wages in the modern sector and women with unchanged or declining incomes in the shrinking traditional sectors.

And this is not all. If women are hired at all in the modern sector, it is usually for the unskilled, low-wage jobs, men holding the skilled jobs. Thus, the roles assigned to men and women, even in the modern sector, indicate a widening difference between the productivity and earnings of each.

In the modern sector, this pattern of sex roles, with men doing the skilled and supervisory work and women in the unskilled and subservient jobs, so dominates the developing and industrialized countries alike, that it is often regarded as 'natural' by both men and women. It is important to stress, therefore, that this kind of polarization and hierarchization of men's and women's work roles is only found in the modern, urban economy and not usually either in family production for subsistence or in market production in home industries at the village level.

In family production for subsistence, the general rule for the division of labour is for each sex to specialize in a particular type of goods and services, and to have as helpers children and young persons of the same sex as the adult person who is responsible for the production. Thus, in communities where weaving is performed by men, they will be responsible for this work with the help of their young sons, while their wives will do other work, perhaps basket making with their daughters to help them. In communities where women are weavers, they will train their daughters while men and boys may be responsible for other crafts. In other words, a 'horizontal' distribution of work between the sexes is combined with a 'vertical' distribution of work between the adults and the young. This pattern allows both sexes to serve as skilled and supervisory workers when they grow older and more experienced, while members of both sexes work as helpers and apprentices while they are young and inexperienced.

This pattern is usually preserved unchanged at the stage where non-agricultural goods are produced for sale by handicraft or home industry at the village level. A given commodity will be produced by persons of the sex which was traditionally responsible for it within the framework of subsistence production. For instance, women are found producing ready-made dishes, cloth, pots or baskets for sale in communities where this is women's work in the family, and men are found producing these same things for sale in communities where they were traditionally done by the men of the family. At this stage, women often continue to be independent producers and to train younger women in the craft. At a somewhat later stage, though still at the village level, whole families may, as a full-time occupation, specialize in the production for sale of some commodity or in the performance of some service for the general public. Thus it may well happen that all the members of the family take part in the production of a given commodity, and family members of one sex—not necessarily the women—may play the role of helpers for producers of the opposite sex.

It appears, then, that at the stage of home industry for the local market, the division of work assignments and of responsibilities between the sexes is less rigid and predictable than in organized industries of the modern type, because in the home industry differences in skills are related to age rather than to sex. In this pattern, the supervisor is simply a worker who is proficient through long experience, while the helper is either a younger person or one who works only intermittently at a given job and is therefore less experienced. In contrast, modern industry tends to establish a rigid division according to the category of the worker rather than to age. Some workers get a training either at the job or in vocational schools which gives them a permanent qualification for the more difficult and better-paid operations; other workers are recruited as helpers or for simple operations, and, regardless of how long they remain in the industry, they are never allowed to do skilled operations nor promoted to the better-paid jobs; they are classified once and for all as second-class labour, and this is true of men as well as of women. But the important difference in the treatment of the sexes is that while men are recruited to both categories, women are usually recruited only for the unskilled jobs.

SEX DIFFERENTIALS IN INDUSTRIAL SKILLS AND WAGES

Women are very rarely trained as skilled industrial workers in developing countries. In the relatively few cases, mainly in Latin America, where such training is provided for girls, it is frequently in trades with limited prospects for employment.[*][1] The best they can obtain in industry is access to the category of

* The Inter-American Commission of Women, in a report from 1957, concluded that the so-called industrial training of women in Latin America scarcely went beyond needlework.[2]

141

'specialized' workers, that is, women who have received on-the-job training in special operations, but no overall vocational training like apprenticeship on the job or in vocational schools.

This sex pattern of occupations within industry is by no means limited to the developing countries. It is equally true of industrialized countries that skilled work tends to be a preserve of men while women are allowed to best to become 'specialized workers'. This occupational pattern implies the existence of a large sex differential in average earnings in industry; but in developing countries the wage differential between skilled and unskilled work is particularly wide, and, consequently the gap between men's and women's income in industry is more pronounced in developing than in industrialized countries.

It was mentioned in Chapter 6 that a number of developing countries have a statutory prohibition of sex discrimination in the fixing of wages. This rule of equal pay for equal work may sometimes be ignored in practice,[3] but when the rules are adhered to the sex differential in basic wages for ordinary unskilled work are small or non-existent. Sometimes, the equalization of wage rates prevents women being employed in a given enterprise or branch, as mentioned earlier; on other occasions the rules are circumvented, more surreptitiously, by the classification of some specialized and relatively well-paid operations as open to men only, while other specialized—and less well-paid—operations are reserved for women. Where such rules are laid down, more or less formally, the very concept of equal pay for equal work eludes any clear definition.[4] A couple of examples may suffice to illustrate this system of discrimination, which, incidentally, is extensively used in industrialized countries.[5]

In India, the system is officially admitted in a publication by the ministry of labour which concludes: 'In almost all cases, lower wages have been fixed for women workers. The reason is stated to be the difference in the type of work done by the males on the one hand and the females on the other and that there was no violation of the principle of equal remuneration for work of equal value. The extent to which there is full justification for the prevailing differences can be assessed only if there are some scientific procedures devised for an objective job appraisal. There appear to be no such arrangements at present.'[6]

The recruitment and wages policy in developing countries with small sex differentials in basic wages for unskilled work can be illustrated by the industrial wage structure in South Vietnam, where, by 1957, the differences between male and female wages for identical work had nearly disappeared (Table 21). It appears

Table 21

WAGE STRUCTURE IN INDUSTRY IN SOUTH VIETNAM, 1957

Indices: Lowest wage for unskilled men in given industry = 100

| | Women | | Men | | | |
| | general unskilled | 'specialized' | general unskilled | 'specialized' | Skilled work | |
Industry:	work	work	work	work	lowest rate	highest rate
Automobile repairs	88–100		100–122	129–204	139	292
Cinemas		90–122	100–122		154	285
Food manufacture etc.	86–98	95–106	100–115	107–152	113	236
Footwear manufacture		84–111	100–122	156–178	133	479
Pottery	88–112		100–122	122–171	122	244
Public works	94–107	112–121	100–170	130	140	349
Rubber manufacture	91–132		100–182		128	286
Tobacco manufacture	79–98	84–104	100–122	113–141	130	217
Wholesale trade and banking	73		**100**			

that the sex difference in wage rates for unskilled work was rarely more than 10 to 12 per cent, which is much less than is usually found in industrialized countries.

But this is only the outward appearance. By using the category of 'specialized worker', actual earnings for men and women in South Vietnam were made to differ far more than the table seems to show at first sight. This becomes clear when the differential between 'general' and 'specialized' work for women is compared with the same differential for men. The table shows that women doing specialized work were being paid only a small percentage more than women doing general unskilled work and sometimes such specialized work for women was paid even less than unskilled male work in the same industry. By contrast, men were usually paid substantially more for specialized than for general unskilled work.

And this is not all. In most Vietnamese industries a very considerable difference between wages for skilled and for un-skilled work can be seen The skilled workers at the top rates were paid three to four times as much as general unskilled workers, which seems to be fairly typical for developing countries. With such a wage structure the fact that this group of skilled workers is practically closed to women has a serious effect upon the earning capacities of women and is likely to create larger income differentials between male and female industrial workers than in industrial countries with larger sex differentials within the group of unskilled work, but smaller skill differentials. Finally, for the men the edge of the skill differential was blunted by the fact that 'specialized' male workers were paid considerably more than general unskilled male workers. Thus, unskilled men's earning capacity could be substantially improved by training in 'specialized' operations. No corresponding opportunity existed for improving the lot of women workers, since their 'specialized' training would give them only a negligible income advantage over the ordinary unskilled women workers.

Criticism of this system of providing training only for men and leaving all women workers in the low wage categories is usually met, from the employers' side, by the argument that women can be expected to spend a shorter span of years in industry, because most of them are likely to leave around the time of marriage and first childbirth. Available information about the age composition of male and female industrial workers (Table 22) shows that this is true of some developing countries, but by no means of all of them. In Iran, where the textile industry uses a large number of small girls, in Chinese speaking regions and in some Latin American countries, women provide a high percentage of the workers below 15 or below 25 years, and low percentage of the older workers,* but in many other cases the percentage of women workers varies little among the age groups. To explain the tendency for women workers to remain in industrial employment after marriage, reference must be made to the widespread and deeply ingrained prejudice against women's participation in industry. This prejudice produces, typically, a very poor woman for industrial work; one who has a family to support. For such women it is hard to be debarred from the prospect of earning

---

* Part of this difference may be due simply to the fact that the young workers were recruited comparatively recently. If a higher percentage of women is recruited now than previously, this is likely to be reflected in a higher percentage of women among young than among older workers.

higher wages through the acquisition of skill. In countries with a low marriage age, very few young unmarried girls are found in industry. There the women workers are either married women

Table 22

SEX DISTRIBUTION IN INDUSTRIAL OCCUPATIONS BY AGE GROUPS

| Country: | Percentage of women of persons in industrial occupations | | | | |
	10–14 years	15–24 years	23–34 years	35–44 years	45 years and over
Africa South of the Sahara:					
Ghana		32	23	21	25
Mauritius	6	5	4	6	7
Region of Arab influence:					
Sudan	26[a]		13		
Turkey		15	10	11	12
Iraq	7[b]	6	4	4	4
Iran	45	28	20		19
South and East Asia:					
Thailand	58[c]	41	29	27	28
Malaya	38	19	10	10	8
Singapore	44	22	9	10	13
Philippines	71	50	36	38	38
Taiwan	36[d]	26	6	5	3
Hong Kong		42	24	26	27
Korea (South)	42[e]	40	15	11	12
Latin America:					
Honduras	40	24	18	20	22
El Salvadore	43	28	24	22	20
Costa Rica	30	20	13	15	12
Panama	33	14	13	14	13
Chile	19[d]	21	15	15	14
Venezuela		15	13	17	19
Puerto Rico		34[f]	29	23	13

[a] 5 years to puberty.
[b] 5–15 years.
[c] 11–15 years.
[d] 12–15 years.
[e] 13–15 years.
[f] 17–27 years.

145

from families who cannot support themselves on the husband's wages, or widows and deserted women left to fend for themselves and their children.[7] Women workers in these categories are unlikely to give up industrial employment after a few years; they may of course leave the particular establishment that has trained them, but so may the male workers who are given on-the-job training.

Leser has suggested that the effect of wage increases on the labour supply differs according to whether it is given to men or women.[8] A rise in male earnings would normally have the effect of making leisure more attractive and would thus discourage married women from entering the labour market. By contrast, a rise in female earnings replaces leisure by a larger additional income than before for the family as a whole, and would therefore tend to enhance the supply of female labour. Leser concludes that the higher the rate of women's earnings to men's the more favourable are conditions for bringing women into the work force.

Let us consider the typical wage structure in developing countries in the light of Leser's rule. We found that the sex differentials for unskilled work in industry are relatively small, while there are large differentials between wages for skilled work, paid only to men, and the highest wages that women workers can actually obtain. Such a system must encourage the wife of a worker who has a low-paid unskilled job, or is often unemployed, to overcome her prejudice against industrial work (if she has such a prejudice) and look for an industrial job, in order to augment the family income. On the other hand, the wife of a stable and skilled worker will be discouraged from looking for an industrial job. There would be such a wide difference between the maximum income which he and she can earn in industry, that her earnings would add little to the relatively high income of her husband.

In short, the wage system we have been considering, with its lack of promotion for qualified and stable women workers, serves to attract to industrial work the least competent and least reliable women from the poorest and most unstable social groups and to discourage the more competent and stable women belonging to the families of skilled workers. This employment of the women least fitted for industry may be expected to make employers dissatisfied with their female workers and disinclined to recruit women workers who may appear to be more expensive —in terms of wage cost per unit of output—than the lowest-paid category of male workers.

THE HIERARCHY OF RACE AND SEX

In those developing countries where racial or national divisions do not exist, the position of women workers tends to be exclusively that of unskilled labourers at the bottom of the industrial hierarchy. In multi-racial and multi-national societies, the hierarchical pattern is far more complex. Some women will be found in posts, and receive incomes, vastly superior to those enjoyed by men from groups which are regarded as inferior on account of race or nationality.

It is normal in European-owned industrial establishments in developing countries to find a division of labour along both the race and the sex dimension, with European men at the top of the hierarchy, in the most responsible jobs with the highest incomes, and indigenous African or Asian women at the bottom doing the least responsible and lowest-paid jobs. At an intermediate level, men of a third group—Chinese, Indian or Mestizos —are often found in a supervisory capacity, while either they or European women fill the clerical posts.

The hierarchy of industrial earnings in two multi-racial societies, Kenya and the Union of South Africa, is illustrated in Table 23. In Kenya there are three racial groups, Europeans, Asians and Africans. In South Africa, in addition to these three, there is a Mestizo group, the 'coloureds'. In every case, men belonging to a superior group earned more on average than men of the group below in the racial hierarchy.* Similarly, women of a superior group earned more than women of the group below, and men in every case earned more than women of their own group, except for the Africans where the difference was negligible. In all but one case, women of the superior group earned more

* This statement is valid if the group of coloureds in South Africa is assumed to be superior to the group of Asians, which is debatable, as seen from Tables 24 and 25 below.

than men of the group below it, and the earnings of all non-African women were much higher than those of African men.

The hierarchy of earnings reflects the hierarchy in jobs given to persons of a different race and sex. The principle of specialization of labour based on race and sex is widely applied; white men take the administrative jobs, Asian men or white women the clerical jobs, African men and women the unskilled manual jobs.

Table 23

WAGE STRUCTURE IN THE UNION OF SOUTH AFRICA AND IN KENYA

Indices: Lowest-paid racial group of men = 100

	Union of South Africa Average wages of workers in private industry 1949–50		Kenya Average earnings of employees in private industry and commerce 1956	
	women	men	women	men
Racial Group:				
Africans	101	100		100
Asians	133	176	447	623
Coloureds	141	190		
Europeans	215	468	823	1861

Note: In Kenya, European men are a small minority, who only supervise and receive very high wages. In South Africa where the European community is larger, some of its male members are clerks and skilled workers, as shown by Table 24. This explains that differences in average earnings between Europeans and others are much larger in Kenya than in South Africa.

This distribution of the labour force by race and sex in Kenya and South Africa can be seen from Table 24. The table shows people belonging to inferior groups at the top and occupations with the lowest prestige and incomes to the left.

It appears that in Kenya in 1964 half the European male employees in non-agricultural occupations were in administrative jobs and half the European female employees in clerical jobs. On the African side, nearly 80 per cent of the male employees were in the two lowest status groups, while the women were divided between these groups and the professions. In South

Africa, where the European population is much more numerous than in Kenya and the demand for domestic servants is much higher, 87 per cent of the African women and 63 per cent of the coloured women in non-agricultural occupations were domestic

Table 24

OCCUPATIONAL DISTRIBUTION BY SEX AND RACE IN THE UNION OF SOUTH AFRICA AND IN KENYA

Percentages = Numbers of each sex and race group employed in non-agriculturalo ccupations[a] *= 100*

Country, Sex and Race:	Private domestic service	Industry transport, general labour	Trade and other services	Clerical work	Professional work	Administrative work	Total in non-agricultural employment	Percentage distribution of all employed by sex and race
Union of South Africa, 1960:								
Women, African	87	4	4		5		100	*16*
Coloured	63	24	6	2	5		100	*4*
Asian	22	33	24	5	15	1	100	
European	3	9	15	52	19	2	100	*7*
Men, African	9	82	7	1	1		100	*44*
Coloured	4	81	8	3	3	1	100	*6*
Asian	9	46	29	9	4	3	100	*3*
European	1	48	14	18	12	7	100	*19*
Kenya, 1964:								
Women, African	10	45	9	5	31	1	100	*5*
Asian	2	10	10	52	21	4	100	*1*
European	1	5	6	53	24	12	100	*1*
Men, African	6	73	7	5	7	2	100	*81*
Asian		26	19	31	7	17	100	*9*
European		7	5	6	32	50	100	*3*

[a] The figures for Kenya include all employees except in agriculture, those for the Union of South Africa include all active persons excluding agriculture and unknown occupations.

servants. In some South African towns, African women have virtually no alternative to domestic work. For instance it was revealed by a study of the township of Grahamstown that 188 out of 189 African women and 28 out of 38 coloured women in employment were domestic servants.[9]

A labour market organized strictly on race and sex lines is most advantageous to European men and least advantageous to African women who are the least favoured of all the groups. But what of the middle groups? Is the ranking here one of race before sex or sex before race? In other words, is the position of a European woman better than that of an Asian man? And is an Asian woman in a better position than an African man? We can seek an answer to these questions in the two countries under consideration by ranking the various race and sex groups

Table 25

RANKING OF SEX AND RACE GROUPS IN THE UNION OF SOUTH AFRICA AND IN KENYA

	size of income or wage		Ranking with respect to percentage share in low prestige occupation (private domestic service)		percentage share in high prestige occupation (administrative services)		Total ranking points	
Country:	Women	Men	Women	Men	Women	Men	Women	Men
Union of South Africa:								
Africans	2	1	1	4–5	1	3	4	8–9
Coloureds	4	6	2	6	2	4–5	8	16–17
Asians	3	5	3	4–5	4–5	7	10–11	16–17
Europeans	7	8	7	8	6	8	20	24
Kenya	1–2	1–2	1	2	1	2	3–4	5–6
Asians	3	4	3	5	3	5	9	14
Europeans	5	6	4	6	4	6	13	18

The figures in Tables 23 and 24 were used as basis for the ranking above

Note: Figures indicating rank are in direct proportion to income (wage) and to share in high-prestige occupations and in inverse proportion to share in low-prestige occupations.

according to the wages they receive and the percentage of members of each group in administrative occupations and domestic services respectively, i.e. in the occupations with the highest and with the lowest prestige value. The ranking result is shown in Table 25. The ranking order by occupation differs from the order by wages in that it ranks all women lower than Asian men who can find administrative jobs more easily than

European women. In other words, the ranking can be interpreted as an indication that the bias against the admission of women into administrative positions tends to outweigh the desire to preserve them solely for Europeans. On the whole, the racial hierarchy of prestige seems to be more effectively applied to men than to women. This is confirmed by other information; for instance, an enquiry in South African factories revealed that in some of the factories European and coloured women were permitted to do the same work, while men of different race were not allowed to.[10]

In countries where political power has passed into the hands of the group at the lowest rung of the prestige ladder of the labour market, great efforts are being made to change the job hierarchy as fast as members of the majority can be trained for better positions than the unskilled ones to which they were previously entitled. Thus, great opportunities are being opened up for both men and women of the majority group. The latter benefit from the general acceptance of the principle of non-discrimination. Such claims of non-discrimination as equal access to training and equal pay for equal work are symbols of male protest against labour market discrimination by race, but their adoption also marks a step on the road to the elimination of sex discrimination.

We have already commented upon the absence in many developing countries of major sex differentials in basic wages for unskilled work. But in the fields of equal access to jobs in the modern sector and to vocational training, the signs of progress are slender, and when the better jobs previously filled by women from the favoured minority are now taken over by men from the majority groups the result is, on one hand, a mitigation of racial discrimination, and, on the other hand, a reinforcement of sex discrimination.

THE STATUS OF WHITE COLLAR WORKERS

One characteristic feature of labour markets in developing countries is the wide gap between wages of highly trained and skilled persons and of unskilled workers. The presence of this gap is to the disadvantage of women in industry since they belong overwhelmingly to the group of the unskilled. On the other hand, highly trained women, for example teachers and nurses, are benefited by the relatively high wages for such groups. It was mentioned in Chapter 7 that some Arab countries in the early stages of their development had so much difficulty in obtaining enough women teachers to teach the daughters of the higher social groups that women teachers were sometimes paid higher wages than male teachers. This is now past history, but even when women teachers and nurses are paid similar or lower wages than male teachers and nurses they benefit from the higher level of salaries for teachers and nurses compared to those of the male industrial workers.

In 1956–7, the International Labour Office carried out an international comparison between wages paid to staff nurses in hospitals and the wages of male skilled industrial workers.[11] A summary of the statistics collected for the study is given below with a distinction between the ratios of wages in developing and in industrialized countries. It shows the frequency—measured by the number of countries—of different ratios of nurses' wages to wages of skilled carpenters:

	Number of countries with indicated wage ratio:	
Ratio of nurses' to carpenters' wages:	Developing countries	Industrialized countries
Over 1·50	2	1
1·25–1·49	3	
1·00–1·24	1	4
0·75–0·99	1	6
0·50–0·74		4
Below 0·50	3a	3
Total number of countries	10	18

a Wages in the Union of South Africa and the two Rhodesias paid mainly to European personnel.

It seems that the position of nurses in relation to skilled male workers tends to be more favourable to nurses in developing than in industrialized countries. This is just one more indication that the highly trained are in a more favourable position than the less highly trained personnel in developing countries where the effect of skills on wages is strong enough to outweigh the effect of any element of sex discrimination in wages. In industrialized countries it is the other way round; the tendency for men to be better paid than women is pronounced, whereas the effect on wages of differences in training is comparatively weak in industrialized countries. The low wages paid to nurses in industrialized countries give rise to acute shortages, which are sometimes met by the employment of nurses from developing countries. In the industrialized countries the money wages are higher for nurses than in their own countries, although they may seem low in comparison with male labour in industry. Thus, even on the female side we find a 'brain drain', i.e. the migration of highly trained manpower from developing to more developed countries.

In towns where very few women work outside their own household, teachers and nurses play a dominant role in the female labour market. Thus, in most Arab countries more than 20 per cent of all women in non-agricultural occupations are in the professions. A similar picture is found in multi-racial communities with very limited job opportunities for women of the inferior racial groups. For instance, women in the professions account for 30 per cent of all African women employees in Kenya. Although these percentages are high, they do not fully convey the importance of the professional women in developing countries with few women in urban employment. The significance of this group of professional women is seen when one considers that virtually all other women gainfully employed in labour markets of this type are illiterate persons doing unskilled manual work or petty trading. Public opinion—including opinion within the group of professional women—tends to forget the existence of these broad but inarticulate groups of working women. Teachers and nurses are the only active women who count, and therefore the status of women in the labour market may be thought, mistakenly, to be higher in countries with few active women than in more economically developed countries where the low-grade office girl or the unskilled female shop assistant typify the working woman.

In industrialized countries, and in Latin America, public

153

opinion is accustomed to think of self-supporting women as assistants to more highly qualified male workers and supervisors. By contrast, in countries where it is thought to be indecent for women to work under the supervision of men not belonging to their own family, educated women work in 'semi-secluded' but more independent jobs in the professions and this bestows a high status on educated women workers. Thus it seems less surprising that the first two governments to be presided over by a woman prime minister were not in countries with a high degree of female participation in the labour market, but in two Asian countries with highly secluded labour markets, where upper-class women are in the professions only, and men have not become accustomed to viewing the role of educated women as that of a less qualified assistant to a male supervisor.

In the early stages of economic development, when office work is carried out only by men, both professional and clerical work benefits from the relatively high wages which are paid for work which requires skills and education. Later on, when secondary education or commercial schools become more widespread, differentials in wages for skill and education are sharply reduced, and, concurrently, women begin to take over clerical jobs in low categories, while men hold on to the supervisory and other more highly qualified jobs. At that stage, job opportunities for educated women widen and this is likely to improve the status of middle-class women within the family, since they are better able to support themselves if their husbands desert them or treat them badly. But the status of women in the family and the status of women in the labour market are two different things. The woman's status in the family may improve while her status in the labour market deteriorates; this is likely to happen to middle class women at this stage when they are offered low-grade office jobs while high status jobs continue to be a male prerogative.

NOTES TO CHAPTER 8

1. Giri, 389–90. 2. ILO *Rev.* 1964, II, 173. 3. Suwondo, 338. 4. Singh, 63. 5. Guilbert *passim.* 6. India Min. of L. Delhi 1964, 45. 7. Ryan, 24; Gadgil, 19. 8. Leser, 106. 9. Irving 1958, No. 1, 22 and Irving 1958, No. 2, 10. 10. van der Horst, 4, 24. 11. Kruse, 497.

PART III

From Village to Town

Chapter 9

The Lure of the Towns

In recent times, a large number of villagers in most developing countries have moved to town. This often involves a move straight from a life more primitive than village life in Europe in the Middle Ages, to a big town with city lights, cinemas, urban traffic and modern shops. This sudden and radical change in conditions and outlook is more extreme than it was in the recent or past rural-urban migration of industrialized countries.

When men and women, just by moving some hundred or so miles, telescope a technological revolution which has taken mankind centuries to evolve, tremendous psychic strain is unavoidable. Sociologists and social psychologists have observed the social and psychic disturbances among newly arrived immigrant families in towns in developing countries. This problem, which seems to be particularly acute in towns with a scarcity of women, is described by a British sociologist who has studied the situation in 'men's towns' in Africa: 'Normal economic opportunities for women are restricted or illicit. Men tend to leave their wives in the country. There is a tremendous demand for the sexual services of the scarce women in town. Irresistible pressure carries the latter into irregular liaisons, brewing and petty trade, which seem at first to offer even to the poorest woman emancipation from male-dominated tribal social systems.' The result is said to be: 'general lack of respect for urban women as a whole, preference for marrying country girls, and so perpetuation of the whole cycle'.[1] It is generally agreed to be undesirable for families to split up with men living in the town and women and children in the countryside. This implies that there is a choice between two alternatives: the aim must be either

157

to inhibit as far as possible the growth of towns and let the whole family stay on in the countryside, or else to find a way to establish a more complete integration of the women into the urban milieu.

It is perhaps understandable that sociologists and others, moved by the human tragedies which follow in the wake of rural-urban migrations, often endorse the first solution and condemn the migration as such. But this standpoint, if accepted, would be tantamount to abandoning the hope of economic development. In all countries with a high income level the bulk of the population lives in urban centres and, conversely, in low-income countries the majority invariably live in rural areas. The change-over from the latter to the former type of economy is impossible unless, during a long period of transition, large numbers give up a rural existence to embrace a new life in town. Rural-urban migration is certainly not a sufficient factor in itself for economic development but it is one of the indispensable conditions and, where no rural-urban migration takes place, there can be very little, if any, economic development. Therefore, the second solution is the only one with a realistic approach to the problem.

Before we deal with the problem of how to achieve a more complete integration of new migrant families in the towns where they settle, we must first see how the change from a primitive subsistence economy in the village to what is most often a slum existence in a modern or semi-modern town has affected the activities of the migrants. This is a dramatic change not only for those family members who must change from farmer to urban wage labourer, but also for those women who are and remain occupied solely in domestic duties. The more primitive the village life they left behind, the bigger the change, because families in very primitive villages produce nearly all they need within the family, whereas urban families must purchase most of the commodities they need.

Even in the most primitive community, human beings must perform a wide range of activities in order to subsist. They must produce or collect food of various kinds, carry it home and prepare it; they must provide themselves with houses or some other kind of shelter adapted to the climate; they must produce or collect containers for the transport and preparation of food, weapons, simple tools and various other necessities. And few are the communities which do not produce some kind of clothing for protection or ornament, and some ceremonial or luxury goods or services.

Nowadays very few communities, even in the most backward regions, live exclusively in a subsistence economy, without exchange between families within the community and with other communities. But in sparsely populated regions of Africa, Asia and Latin America many communities still exist where by far the larger part of the goods and services needed are produced within the confines of the individual family. In these communities, only such things as salt, weapons and simple tools, together with ceremonial services, are acquired, more or less casually, from other households, against money or in barter.

At a somewhat more advanced stage, the exchange within the local community or with other communities is more regular and is based upon specialization in the production of goods or services for sale in addition to the production of most of the family's own requirements. With further development, production for sale becomes increasingly important and more and more subsistence activities are replaced by the purchase of products against money earned in specialized production or by wage labour for other producers. In highly industrialized communities, nearly all goods and services are produced for sale and acquired for money. Men have given up all subsistence activities other than hobbies like gardening, fishing or minor improvements to the family dwelling. However, even in highly industrialized communities, a large proportion of the women continue to devote their time exclusively to subsistence activities like domestic work within their own household.

A family staying on in a rural area can proceed gradually, step by step, from subsistence production for the family's own needs to specialized production for a market. Farm families may continue to produce their own food but may also begin to grow some cash crops for exchange against some of the non-agricultural products which were hitherto produced by male or female members of the farm family. But for migrating families, the abandonment of subsistence production is sudden, occurring

159

precisely when the family gives up farming to move to a town which offers employment other than agriculture.

In developing countries, the movement from village to town profoundly changes the whole existence of a family; not only must it change its economic occupation, but also its way of life. Many of the goods and services provided by subsistence activities in the village are replaced by purchases in town. These sometimes swallow a large part of the family income, leaving little or nothing for the purchase of goods and services which the family had hoped to obtain in town. The disappointment at not achieving the expected higher standard of living adds to the stress occasioned by a new way of life.

The rest of this chapter deals with subsistence production and its effects on the family economy in villages and towns. The following chapter discusses the changes in economic activity which occur when families transfer from rural to urban areas, and the effect of these on the family economy. Chapter 11 is devoted to a discussion of the broader effects of these changes on the economy and its growth potential, and, finally, Chapter 12 reviews the change in the position and status of women which accompany transformations in a developing economy.

THE VALUE OF SUBSISTENCE PRODUCTION

Incomes in developing countries may be conveniently classified into three groups: (*a*) Income in money earned by the sale of products and services or by work for money wages and salaries, (*b*) Incomes in kind earned by barter of the family's goods and services or by work for wages in kind, (*c*) Incomes in kind consisting of the goods produced and the services provided for the family's own needs.

In industrialized countries, domestic work done by housewives in their own household is the most important item in the last-named income group. It is a generally accepted convention that neither statistics of national income nor tax authorities regard domestic activities in terms of income, and therefore persons with no activity other than domestic work in their own homes are not regarded as belonging to the labour force. In addition to the housewives' 'income', income groups (*b*) and (*c*) include board and lodging received in kind by some employees and 'autoconsumption' of food in farmers' families. These items account for a very small part of total income in industrialized countries, and, therefore, money income differs very little from total income except for the services of housewives.

In developing countries, production and collection for barter, wages in kind, and production for family use play a much larger role than in industrialized countries. Hence, money income is much lower than total income, and the more backward the country the wider the difference. In official estimates of national income in the least economically developed African countries like Upper Volta and the Republic of Niger, money income accounts for about one-third of total income as against 75 per cent in Kenya, where the stage of development is relatively advanced by African standards.[2] However, the conventional method for estimating incomes in kind in developing countries considerably under-estimates the size of such incomes; for instance, the estimate of production in Kenya mentioned above includes estimates of incomes in kind in the form of food, drinking water and forest products, and of owner-constructed dwellings. But it makes no allowance for non-agricultural products and services produced for self consumption or for barter. These are often important items in rural areas where money incomes are low and where women continue to produce many of the goods used in the household.

We may get an impression of the real importance of subsistence activities from a study of 1,200 households in the Bantu areas of South Africa.[3] That study was based upon rather a broad definition of income, including not only (1) money income and (2) the kinds of subsistence income conventionally included in national income estimates, but also (3) a number of additional items of subsistence income. This investigation was thus unusually complete, and the domestic services of housewives appear to be the only major item omitted. The main results of the study are reproduced in Table 26. It appears that money income accounted for only one third of total income in these areas. This consisted mainly of wages and salaries paid to government employees and money remittances from other areas in the Union where a large proportion of the male Bantus were working for wages and were sending money home to family members left in the villages. Subsistence income, estimated by the conventional method (column 2 in the table), accounted for 13 per cent of total income and nearly all of this was food, produced mainly by the women, Thus, the two items usually

Table 26

MONEY AND SUBSISTENCE INCOME IN BANTU AREAS OF THE UNION OF SOUTH AFRICA

Percentage of total income

Source of Income:	Income in money	Subsistence income according to conventional method of estimation	Subsistence income not recorded in conventional estimation	Total
Agriculture, fishing, forestry	4	13	33	50
Crafts and industry			5	5
Commerce	1		2	3
Other private services	3		15	18
Government	8			8
Remittance of wages and pensions from non-Bantu areas of the Union	16			16
Total	32	13	55	100

recorded in official statistics together accounted for no more than 45 per cent of total income, while items usually omitted in income statistics (column 3) accounted for 55 per cent of total income. The omission would of course have been larger still if domestic services of housewives had been included.*

The group of incomes usually omitted, but included in this Bantu study, was made up largely of food items obtained by collecting and hunting, of output of home crafts such as clothing, footwear, sleeping and sitting mats, baskets, clay pots, calabashes, pipes, fuel collected by the women, funeral services,

* In Malawi African rural household services are estimated to be 23 per cent of gross domestic produce.[4]

hair cuts, entertainment, and traditional administrative and medical services. Moreover, it includes the value of the pounding, husking and grinding of foodstuffs and the slaughtering of animals. These are fairly important activities which usually escape reckoning in national income estimates when food is recorded at farm gate prices and not at local retail prices for crudely processed foods.

In cases where subsistence production and services are left out or understated in estimates of national income, the effect is to widen the apparent income gap between more and less developed countries, both when the comparison is between developing countries, and when incomes of developing countries are compared with incomes in the rich countries. This, incidentally, can help to explain why developing countries take little interest in a revision of the conventional system of accounting. A working party of African national income experts decided not to recommend the inclusion of estimates for subsistence activities other than food and rent of dwellings with the rather unconvincing argument that this procedure would 'inflate' the national product.[5] However, this decision of the expert group may not have been wise, for the present system of under-reporting subsistence activities not only makes the underdeveloped countries seem poorer than they really are, in comparison to more developed countries, but it also makes their rate of economic growth appear in a more favourable light than the facts warrant, since economic development entails a gradual replacement of the omitted subsistence activities by the creation of income in the non-subsistence sector which is recorded more correctly.

Now, the subsistence activities usually omitted in the statistics of production and incomes are largely women's work. We have already discussed the predominance of women in agricultural production and particularly in food production for family use in many parts of the world. Add to this the processing of the food before cooking, i.e. the grinding, husking, pounding of grains and other basic foods for family consumption, which is virtually always done by women; the fetching of water and fuel for the household is also women's work; women usually collect most of the vegetable food, and they take part, together with men, in both crafts and house construction and in most other subsistence activities, the hunting of large animals and tree felling being the only major exceptions.

It is not always realized how very time-consuming is this crude processing of basic foods, such as the pounding or grinding of cereals, the preparation of yams and tapioca, and the brewing of beer. According to an estimate made in the Congo, the household processing of tapioca and maize took four times as long as all the work hours spent on the cultivation of these subsistence crops.[6] Some enquiries made in other parts of Africa showed that women spend on average one hour per family meal in preparing the basic grain or root before cooking can begin.[7] Of course, the time spent in such operations varies widely with the type of basic crop and the equipment used in the household. In Mexico, grinding of grain by hand took 4 to 6 hours a day per family, and, therefore, the coming of mills brought a very considerable saving of labour.[8]

Not surprisingly, women often revolt against these low productivity tasks. In this Mexican case, when the grain mill was first introduced, the men found that the machine-made flour had an inferior taste, and the first mill had to close down. In the end the men gave way and a new mill which opened two years later was more successful.[9] In other regions, women insist on using bought rice or flour wheat instead of the traditional home-processed foodstuffs. In many developing countries this has led to the replacement of nationally produced by imported foodstuffs.

In dry regions, for instance in the Arab Belt, the daily walks to fetch fuel and water often cover long distances and take up more of the village women's time than their agricultural activities. In Africa, these tasks add much to a work programme which is usually already filled up by work in the fields. In a district of Tanzania, some women must go three miles to fetch fuel wood and in the dry season they may have to walk ten miles to find water.[10] Even when distances are short, much work is needed to meet the demands for water.*

* One study revealed that three women in a family had the joint task of fetching an average of 110 litres a day in eleven trips, half for the household and half for the animals.[11] Another and more comprehensive study covered all the

The burden laid on the women by these tasks varies both with the climate and with population density. A dense population can better afford some rural investment in wells for drinking water and mills for the processing of locally produced cereals than can a sparse population. But women in densely populated regions may have to go long distances to find fuel wood and may prefer to use dung as fuel. In many regions of Africa, so sparse is the population that rural investment in a water supply and mills is uneconomic; this lays a crushing burden of daily work upon the women. One report speaks of African women 'sitting about hungry with millet in their granaries and relish to be found in the bush', because hey were too tired to do all the jobs needed for preparing the meal. These women normally took three hours to prepare a meal.[13] Another African study from a region where many women combine agricultural work, wage labour and domestic work, mentions that women, in order to cope with their work, must feed their children as quickly as possible. They practise a system of forcible feeding with an assistant holding the child's hands and feet.[14]

Work hours spent by African farmers, their wives and other adult family members on non-agricultural activities are shown in Table 27. If these figures are typical, African women, in addition to their agricultural work, would be spending some 20 to 30 hours per week on domestic and other non-agricultural tasks.

It is clear from the information given above that the domestic tasks which African women have to do are of a quite different type from the domestic work performed by housewives in industrialized communities. The latter use their time mainly in cleaning the house and taking care of the children, in addition to purchasing and cooking food. Rural African women, who are also doing a great deal of work in the fields, cannot spend much time on cleaning the house and caring for the children. They must limit their domestic activity mainly to the tasks mentioned above: the processing of food, the brewing of beer, the fetching

---

local transport within one village territory. This transport was made by head loads, predominantly by the women, over a maximum distance of less than one mile. The task amounted to no less than 722 ton-kilometres per year for forty households. Water carrying accounted for more than one-third, the rest was fuel, tapioca and other crops, and some building materials.[12]

of fuel and water. The lighter task of supervising the infants is often left to girls in the age group 6 to 11 years.[15]

The non-agricultural work done by African men is mainly wage labour (usually outside the village), hunting, and house construction, although in some communities some of the domestic tasks, such as washing clothes, ironing, or sweeping the premises are performed by men.[16] In densely populated regions with little opportunity for hunting, wage labour is the main supplementary source of income for male subsistence farmers

Table 27

HOURS OF NON-AGRICULTURAL WORK PERFORMED BY MEMBERS OF AFRICAN CULTIVATOR FAMILIES

Average hours worked per week

Country in which sample villages are located:	Women				Men				
	Domestic work	Wage labour and trade	Other non-agricultural work	All non-agricultural work	Fishing and hunting	House-building	Wage labour and trade	Other non-agricultural work	All non-agricultural work
Dahomey	32	9		41	11	3	1		15
Nigeria	14			27		1			4
Central African Republic A	20		4	24	5	3	1	4	13
B	18	1	2	21	4	7	1	4	16
C	13	1	6	20	13	4	1	9	27
Uganda	21		2	23		4	2	1	7
Kenya	24	3		27					

and sometimes for their wives too. In India, for instance, wage labour accounts for most of the time spent by men in occupations other than farming. But even in a relatively densely populated country like India the rural people in some sparsely populated regions garner a large part of their subsistence from gathering food and from hunting, and they produce many non-agricultural goods for family use. These items are usually either left out or greatly understated in statistics of production and income, with the result that regional income differentials become a misleading guide to regional differences in levels of living.

In India, as in Africa, most of the grain produced for subsistence is hand-processed by the women. The spread of mills for processing was deliberately retarded by government action in order to protect employment in hand-operated mills.[17] But now Indian women are showing unwillingness to continue with the tiresome task of processing food by hand, and those who can afford it tend to change over to the consumption of food which is less difficult to prepare, such as processed rice and wheat flour. As a result, the production of some traditional crops is declining.

SUBSISTENCE ACTIVITIES IN URBAN AREAS

The usual tendency to understate the importance of subsistence activities in rural areas has been discussed at some length in the preceding section. It is obviously a question of importance in the comparison between rural and urban levels of living. Many of the needs which are satisfied by subsistence activities in rural areas must be purchased out of money incomes by town populations in the same country. Therefore, if the subsistence activities are understated in any country, the rural-urban differential of income levels is *ipso facto* overstated.

When economic development takes place in a given country and villagers begin to purchase products and services which were hitherto produced within the family, many of the young family members will migrate from the village temporarily, or permanently, in order to earn money incomes in those parts of the country where the money economy has already penetrated. The spread of cash expenditure by the rural population is enhanced when the migrants return with their savings or send home a part of their earnings to support family members left in the migrants' native villages.

However, the change in the village economy produced in this way is small compared with the sudden change which happens to the migrant when he or she—practically from one day to another—is transformed from a subsistence producer to a wage earner. If the women stay behind, the men must find ways to pay in cash for the services which their women were hitherto performing as part of the division of labour within the family. If the women migrate with them, the men must nevertheless find ways to pay for many of the services which would have been performed by the wives, had the family stayed in the village, simply because town conditions prevent the women from contributing to the support of the family by the village type of subsistence activities.

167

In fact, the urban surroundings make it impossible for the migrant and his wife to carry on any of the usual subsistence activities, except that the wife will still be doing the cooking.

In town, food production and collection by the migrant or his wife and children must be replaced by the purchase of food, and this food is purchased in a semi-processed form, eliminating much of the time-consuming work of processing which in the village was done by women.

Neither wood and dung for fuel nor the usual materials for home crafts and for owner-construction of dwelling are available in the town. The urban women usually have to walk shorter distances to get water than the village women, though sometimes she must wait in a queue before she can tap the water. In many towns, the places where water can be tapped are so few and far between, or the quality of the water supply is so bad, that the sale of water is a full-time occupation for a considerable number of people of either sex.[18]

The need to pay for urban accommodation is among the worst of the changes following migration. Even the space to put up a hut may need to be paid for, and the price of real urban dwellings swallow a large part of the incomes of urban workers, while nearly all villagers in most developing countries live in owner-constructed houses or huts made of local materials which are more or less freely available. In Latin American countries, rent and other housing expenditure usually takes over 10 per cent of the wage packet of urban workers,[19] but in many cases they have to pay a much higher proportion of their income in rent.*

* A survey made in the South African town of Grahamstown gave the results reproduced below.[20] African households located in community-controlled housing facilities of two to four rooms each were distributed by the proportion of rent in total income as shown below:

Percentage distribution of households
in the sample

Rent less than 10 per cent of income	1·5
Rent 10 to 20 per cent of income	29
Rent 20 to 30 per cent of income	30
Rent 30 to 40 per cent of income	21
Rent over 40 per cent of income	19
Total	100

Likewise, the leisure activities which are part of village life cannot be found in the towns. Hunting is not only a source of highly valued food, but also the most cherished leisure activity for male villagers (although we counted it as work in Table 27 above). The same is often true of fishing, gathering fruit, and even of brewing beer and felling trees. In towns, such activities must be replaced by visits to cinemas or bars which cost money instead of providing income in kind in addition to the pleasure of the activity.

Visits to cinemas and consumption of stimulants are the main luxuries for urban workers. Stimulants account for a significant share of the budgets in all developing countries. To be sure, the excessive use of stimulants is also a feature of village life in many developing countries. But in the miserable slum existence of townlife, there is a much stronger urge to seek consolation from stimulants. A survey of immigrant workers in Bombay showed that these used no less than 15 per cent of their total income on tea, tobacco, the cinema and other luxuries, the latter group including drink, gambling and the services of prostitutes.[22]

The greatly enjoyed leisure activity of paying visits to relatives may not be possible for migrants, partly because of travel costs and partly because even visiting costs money in town. In the village, visitors, if they stay for some time, may take part in any productive activity that happens to be going on. In town, by contrast, visits by relatives from the home village are a charge on the host family. And the acceptance of this burden is not just an ostentation or a special kindness but a social necessity for the urban family which may some day need to fall back upon the support of its village friends. For the same reason, many urban budgets contain gifts sent to relatives in the villages, even when these relatives are better off than the urban family.

Less than 2 per cent of the families spent less than 10 per cent of their income on rent while 19 per cent spent more than 40 per cent of their income to pay rent. It is worth noting that the housing schemes where these people were located is situated three miles from the centre of Grahamstown. The bread-winner in the family therefore has to choose between walking 6 miles every day or using a further 10 per cent of his wages for bus fares to and from work.[21]

It is no wonder that migrants try to mitigate the transition from auto-consumption in the village to the highly monetized urban patterns of expenditure. In the big towns of many under-developed countries, a large number of under-fed goats bear witness to the efforts made to carry on some subsistence activities in the new surroundings. Women take long walks to adjacent areas where they can find some fodder for the goats or grow a few vegetables; many continue to 'collect' food by visiting more wealthy co-citizens to get left-overs; the collection of waste materials for house construction replaces the collection of building materials in forests and bush. The attempt to continue the owner-construction of dwellings results in the erection of miserable huts and sheds scattered among ordinary houses or massed in special slum areas, so that those districts inhabited by the migrants acquire a sordid and desolate character. Likewise, fuel collection is continued in a new form; women and girls collect animal droppings from the streets or ransack rubbish dumps in search of suitable material.

Although the construction of his hut or other primitive shelter is economically important to the migrant because it saves the payment of rent for a proper urban dwelling, apart from this, the subsistence activities are unlikely to add much to the family income, and only the poorest families would gain more than a negligible addition. It is different, of course, when the immigrants have regular fields on the outskirts of the town where they can grow their own food and can thus more genuinely combine village and town life.[23]

A rural family in a developing country, which produces its own food and earns its money income by the sale of cash crops or by wage labour, can afford to spend nearly all its money income on the purchase of industrial consumer goods. These goods are cheaper in town than in the village and village people are likely to believe that the town is a place where a given money wage can command more goods than in the village. But the opposite is true, since food is much more expensive in towns than in villages. It has been suggested that this tendency of the villager to evaluate his gains more in relation to the price of manufactured goods than to the price of food, is an important part of the attraction of the towns with their apparently high wages.[24] Moreover, the villager is likely to suffer from the same tendency to under-estimate the value of subsistence activities, as we found prevailed among statisticians.

When a cultivator family or a labourer family, used to pro-ducing its own food in the village, migrates to town, attracted by the apparently high money wage, it soon discovers that nearly all their wages go in acquiring the products with which their sub-sistence activities in the village had previously provided them. Statistics of family budgets from urban areas in developing countries show that on average the town family spends between one-half and two-thirds and sometimes much more of their income in purchasing food and fuel and in paying the rent of their dwelling.[25] In a typical case, these are the three main items which the family had been acquiring by its own labour in the village. Moreover, the family may need to spend more on clothing and to pay for transport to and from work, an item which may sometimes swallow as much as 10 per cent of the family income for urban workers.[26] Therefore, money wages need to be very much higher in town than in the village, if villagers are to avoid a decline in living standards when they migrate to town with their family.

The ability of the villagers to judge the purchasing power of the wages they can hope to earn in the town, depends to some extent on the degree of monetization they have reached in their own villages. In areas where cash crops are important, as in parts of Ghana, the Ivory Coast and Nigeria, the cultivators are accustomed to purchasing a considerable amount of their food. They are less likely, therefore, to disregard the prices they will have to pay for food if they migrate to towns. In regions where some rich villagers have built urban styles of home all the villagers are more likely to be aware of the cost of housing in towns.

In developing countries, average money wages may be several times higher in towns than in rural areas, but such averages include wages of skilled workers and wages in modern enter-prises which do not usually recruit people coming fresh from the village. Money wages for the types of job which immigrants are likely to obtain—in the construction industry, in public works or in more traditional industries—are often less than twice the wages paid in villages and sometimes little higher than rural wages.[27] Migrants who get such jobs may be worse off than in their home villages because they must pay for the goods and services which they or their wives contributed for family use in the village.

Statistics of consumer expenditure usually show that urban workers devote a smaller share of their budget to food than do rural workers. This observation is often taken as an indication that the urban worker's budget is less strained than the rural worker's. However, it should be clear from the preceding discussion that this is an unwarranted assumption; the smaller proportion of the urban budget used for food simply reflects the fact that so many necessary items must be paid for in the town which are acquired in subsistence activities in the village. It is even likely that in many thinly populated developing countries with good opportunities for hunting, fishing and the gathering of fruit, villagers live on a much better diet than do unskilled urban labourers and their families.*

As seen above, in developing countries the activities of women are radically changed when they move from rural to urban areas, because most of the subsistence activities which they perform in rural areas cannot be carried on in urban surroundings. Therefore, the range of domestic tasks which women can do in town is much narrower than it is in the village, and domestic activities require fewer hours. Hence, women are left with more time for non-domestic activities than they had in their home village, even in regions where they were not doing much farm work. Moreover, the need to pay money for goods and services which in the village was delivered in kind by the women puts the family budget under strain and creates the need for the women to contribute to the family's money income. In the following chapter, we shall compare the economic activities of women in

---

* This may be the case also in some regions with little access to 'free food' in the villages but low urban wages. For instance, a survey of persons in East Pakistan who had changed from agricultural to non-agricultural employment revealed that most of them found that their food consumption standards had deteriorated after the occupational change. Consumption of stimulants and soap had increased, but that of animal food, fruit and vegetables had declined.[28] Likewise, a study of consumption levels in El Salvador showed poorer nutrition among new immigrants to towns than among the village population in their home villages.[29]

rural and urban areas in an attempt to determine the conditions required for a new balance between the contributions of the two sexes to family income.

NOTES TO CHAPTER 9

1. Southall 1961, 56.   2. Leroux 1963, 4, 75; *Kenya Econ. Survey* 1967, 6. 3. Reynders, 233–64.   4. Dean, 15.   5. UN. ECA., *Rep. Subst. Tr.*, 3–4. 6. Soyer-Poskin, 145.   7. Richards 1939, 103–4; *Wills Small-scale*, 13. 8. Lewis, O., 99.   9. Lewis, O., 108.   10. Jellicoe, 14.   11. de la Rivière, 52.   12. Guet, Vol. II, 129–31.   13. Richards 1939, 104–5. 14. Ominde, 3.   15. Ominde, 6.   16. Georges, 27; Richards 1939, 102; Earthy, 22.   17. India Pl. C. 1955, 46–8.   18. Forget, 147; Galetti, 32. 19. ILO *Yearbook* 1967, 687–8.   20. Irving 1958, No. 2, 20.   21. Irving 1958, No. 2, 10–11, 28.   22. Prabhu, 102.   23. Galetti, 492–3.   24. Balandier 1955, 79.   25. ILO *Yearbook* 1967, 687–90.   26. Irving 1958, No. 2, 10–11, 28; Samaj, 128.   27. Usher, 441; Kay, 24; *Indian Labour Yearbook* 1965, 64–9.   28. Husain 1956, Vol. I, 350.   29. Beaujeu, 12.

Chapter 10

Urban Job Opportunities for Women

We have been viewing economic development as a gradual movement of the population from village to town, accompanied by a fundamental change in the domestic activities of women. But economic development can also be seen as a gradual movement of the population from agricultural to non-agricultural occupations. It is important for a correct understanding of the process of economic development and its implications for the status of women to bear in mind that these two major shifts—the geographical migration from village to town and the occupational migration from agricultural to non-agricultural activities—are just two different manifestations of the same process of change.

It is well known that a reduction in the proportion of the population engaged in agriculture goes hand-in-hand with economic development. The economic level reached by a given country is often measured simply in terms of the proportion of its people engaged in agriculture. This proportion varies from nearly all the adult population in Africa to 5 to 10 per cent of adults, or still less, in highly industrialized countries. But it is often overlooked that the reduction in agriculture's share of the population is only one particularly obvious example of a more general feature of economic development; it is true of many more activities than farming that in primitive communities they are practised virtually within every family. From this point of view, economic development is tantamount to progress towards a more intricate specialization and division of labour outside the individual household. For instance, in primitive communities virtually all adults take part in house-building and in the production of some non-agricultural consumer goods and primitive

174

tools. At a higher stage of economic development each of these activities becomes the specialized occupation of some members of the community.

We have seen that the economic activities of rural women vary widely from region to region. In some parts of the world, notably in Africa and South East Asia, women perform a large part of the agricultural work, in addition to their domestic duties. In other parts of the world, primarily in Latin America and in Arab countries, women work little in the fields. Another important distinction is that between regions where rural women take part in a wide range of non-agricultural activities, such as trade, home industries, construction work and services, and, on the other hand, regions where women generally stay away from such work and limit their activities to domestic duties, supplemented by some farm work in peak periods, the care of hens and such like.

A woman who has been working only in the fields and in the household is in a difficult position when she migrates to a town. She can take an industrial job only if she is prepared—and able—to change both her place of residence and her occupation. In other words, she would have to accept a completely new way of life involving her in social relationships with strangers. On the other hand, a woman who has previously worked in some non-agricultural job in her home village, may be able to carry on with this when she reaches town, and even if she has to change her actual job, she will still not have to learn to adapt herself to unaccustomed contacts with people outside the family, for she will already be used to this if she was engaged on trade or other services in the village. Even if she was a home industry worker she can still avoid external contacts by leaving the sale of products and the purchase of materials to male members of the family.

Thus, the activity pattern of immigrant women in the town is determined primarily by the customary pattern of female employment in the village, and especially by the extent to which women participate in non-agricultural activities in the village. Therefore, we must now summarize our findings concerning female activities in these non-agricultural occupations at village level. For brevity, we shall refer to this sphere as the bazaar and service occupations so as to distinguish it from agriculture on the one hand and from modern occupations on the other.

THE TWO STEPS IN ECONOMIC DEVELOPMENT

When subsistence activities are replaced by specialized production, and traders appear in the villages, not only men, but sometimes women engage in such activities. In many countries, market trade, home industries, and domestic and other services have become important fields of employment for women. In some parts of the world a large number of rural women work in mines, in construction; they carry headloads and load railway waggons.

We may distinguish a regional pattern in these activities. Trade plays an important part in the position of women in many parts of Africa, where the majority of both rural and urban women engage in market trade on a smaller or larger scale, and paid domestic service is an important female occupation in both rural and urban areas of Latin America. Likewise, women's participation in home industries is far more widespread in some regions than in others. All the bazaar and service occupations, as here defined, account in some Arab countries for only one to two per cent of all adult women. By contrast, 25 and 20 per cent of all adult women in Jamaica and Ghana respectively take part in these activities (Table 28). In both these countries

Table 28

WOMEN IN BAZAAR AND SERVICE OCCUPATIONS AND IN MODERN OCCUPATIONS

Country:	Women in bazaar and service occupations	Women in modern occupations	Percentage of women among personnel in:	
	as percentage of all adult women		bazaar and service occupations	modern occupations
Africa South of the Sahara:				
Sierra Leone	4	1	19	10
Liberia	2	1	15	8
Ghana	21	1	54	9
Mauritius	6	4	25	11

Region of Arab influence:				
Morocco	4	2	19	15
United Arab Republic	2	1	9	6
Turkey	1	2	8	12
Syria	1	1	7	7
Iraq	1	1	6	5
Iran	4	4	18	15
Pakistan	3		9	3
South and East Asia:				
India	5	1	26	9
Ceylon	4	4	17	14
Burma	a	a	34[a]	22[b]
Thailand	9	3	47	26
Cambodia	7	1	35	11
Malaya	4	3	17	12
Singapore	11	9	23	13
Philippines	10	5	44	29
Hong Kong	5	21	20	26
Korea (South)	4	1	25	9
Latin America:				
Honduras	9	4	54	25
El Salvador	12	6	59	25
Nicaragua	15	5	56	25
Costa Rica	9	8	42	25
Panama	13	10	42	31
Colombia	12	6	46	25
Ecuador	11	4	41	21
Chile	13	8	43	22
Venezuela	11	8	32	22
Cuba	6	8	28	19
Jamaica	25	10	68	29
Dominican Republic	6	4	39	20
Puerto Rico	8	13	24	30

[a] No information is available.
[b] In urban areas only.

Note: Bazaar and service occupations include own-account workers and family aids in industry and trade, and all personnel in transport, domestic and other service occupations. Modern occupations include employees in industry and trade and all personnel in clerical, administrative and professional occupations.

there are more women than men in bazaar and service occupations, and in a number of other developing countries, in Latin America as well as in Africa and South East Asia, women account for 40 to 50 per cent, or even more, of the total labour force in these occupations.

When a country is moving from a primitive to a more advanced stage of economic evolution, bazaar and service occupations play the peculiar role of an intermediate step between agriculture and the modern occupations. During the first phases of this process, the bazaar and service sector is slowly on the increase and may come to employ 15 to 20 per cent or even more, of all adults, while the proportion of adults working in the agricultural sector is slowly diminishing. Sooner or later, the bazaar and service sector will begin to feel competition not only from imports but also from a growing modern sector.

Thus, two successive steps in economic development can be seen; in the first step, subsistence activities for family use are replaced by commercial production for sale and small scale market trade and services. In the second step, this type of activity is replaced by employment in modern factories, offices, modern shops and modern service industries.

During the first stage of transformation, many boys and girls from cultivator families, instead of following in their parents' footsteps, take to work in bazaar and service occupations. At a later stage of development, perhaps after several generations, the next step is taken, the step from these occupations to the modern sector.

Enterprises of the modern sector are situated almost exclusively in urban areas,* and the agricultural sector, of course, in the rural areas. But in between these is the sector identified here as the bazaar and service occupations which are localized partly in rural and partly in urban areas. Therefore, people in rural areas have a choice between changing their occupation when they migrate to a town or before they move to it, as indicated by Figure 12. In Figure A a family gives up agriculture and moves to town to work in the bazaar and service sector, while in Figure

---

* It does happen sometimes that a large modern industry is set up in a rural area, but usually this has the effect of attracting so many subsidiary activities to the area that it rapidly becomes urbanized.

B a family first moves from agriculture to the bazaar and service sector in the village, and only at a later stage do they move to the town where they continue to work in the same occupations.

When development is rapid, a considerable number may move directly from subsistence agriculture to employment in

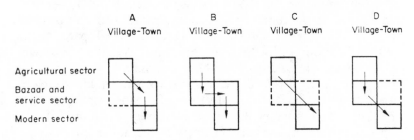

| A | B | C | D |
| Village-Town | Village-Town | Village-Town | Village-Town |

Agricultural sector

Bazaar and service sector

Modern sector

Figure 12 Occupational Change and Rural-Urban Migration in Developing Countries

the modern sector without a temporary stop-over in the bazaar and service sector (Figure 12 C). Normally, however, employers in the modern sector prefer to recruit people who were previously employed in the bazaar and service sector, or their children (Figure 12 A, B and D), thus vacating the less attractive jobs in the bazaar and service occupations for new entrants who come direct from the agricultural sector. An Indonesian study showed that 67 per cent of women migrants recruited for industrial jobs in Djakarta came from employment in village industries,[1] and a survey of female factory workers in Ceylon showed that nearly all of them (87 per cent) were daughters of persons with non-agricultural occupations.[2] Latin American and Indian investigations of the fate of male and female rural-urban migrants show that most of the men in Latin America and both men and women in India got jobs as helpers in traditional construction activities.[3]

THE IMPACT OF TRADITION AND OF IMPORTED CULTURE PATTERNS

We have seen in previous chapters that, in the early phases of development, jobs in modern occupations are given almost

179

exclusively to men, the small modern sector in developing countries usually employing only 5 to 15 per cent of women. Of course, this is largely explained by the low literacy rate of women in many countries in these early stages of economic development. A comparison with industrialized countries shows their sex distribution within the modern sector to be around 30 per cent women and 70 per cent men. This is an almost invariable proportion which holds for industrialized countries in all parts of the world, including North American and Western European countries, as well as Japan and New Zealand.

There is thus a distinct correlation between the stage of development, as expressed by the relative size of the modern sector, and the proportion of women in that modern sector (Figure 13). But this correlation is far from perfect,* for the figure shows that a number of developing countries have a high proportion of women in their modern sector although these countries are still at a low stage of development as shown by the relative size of the modern sector. Three Central American republics (Honduras, El Salvador and Nicaragua) and two countries in South East Asia (Thailand and the Philippines) have 25 to 30 per cent women in the modern sector, although this sector accounts for only 7 to 12 per cent of all adults.

It is not difficult to provide explanation for the high level of female employment in occupations in some countries at a low stage of development: these particular countries all have the characteristic feature in common that the proportion of women in bazaar and service occupations is over 40 per cent (Figure 14).

On the other hand, in all the countries in the realm of Arab, Chinese or Hindu culture, where the idea of the seclusion of women is only slowly losing its grip even in those towns where modern enterprises are located, the female work share in modern occupations is very low. It is from 5 to 7 per cent in Egypt, Syria and Iraq, 3 per cent in Pakistan and 9 per cent in India. Even in a modern Chinese town like Singapore, women account

* No clear trend emerged from an attempt to measure changes over time in the percentage of women among the personnel employed in modern occupations in developing countries. But the lack of a conclusive result may be due to difficulties in eliminating the effects of census re-classification. It is to be hoped that the 1970 censuses for developing countries will provide us with more certain information about the trends in female employment in the modern sector.

for only 13 per cent of the labour force in modern occupations, and 80 per cent of adult women take no part in economic activity. This low rate of female participation in the modern sector is consistent with the traditional Chinese pattern of employment.

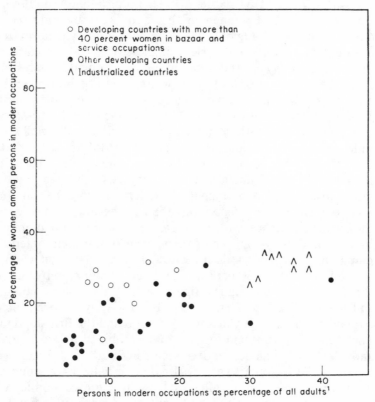

Figure 13   Sex Distribution in Modern Occupations in Countries at Different Stages of Development

It seems that China had no more than 11 per cent women in non-agricultural employment in the 1950s,[4] and as late as 1958 the proportion of women among workers and employees in the modern sector in China was no more than 15 per cent.[5] This was after the 'big leap' in Chinese wage employment, from 25 million in 1957 to 45 million in 1958, which was largely a transfer of male own-account workers to the category of wage labour, while the proportion of women among them rose only from 13 to 15 per cent. Around 1960, the proportion of women in modern occupations in Thailand, Burma and the Philippines was higher than in China and Singapore.

It was mentioned in Chapter 6 that in both Indonesia and India the employment of women in the manufacturing industry is more common in regions where female employment in the traditional trades and industries is highest. The Malay countries, Indonesia, Malaysia and the Philippines, provide interesting examples of how the position of women may be influenced by different conquering peoples in a region with a common background of indigenous culture. Malay women are by tradition active and the adoption of the Moslem religion did not send Indonesian women and the women of Malaya indoors to domesticity.[6] Nevertheless, the Moslem religion, together with British and Dutch influence, has contributed to the creation of a much lower female participation pattern in both bazaar and service and modern occupations than in the Philippines where the Spanish influence, which attracted some women into domestic life, was later outweighed by American encouragement of female employment in the modern sector.[7] The result is that women account for around 30 per cent of modern-sector employment in the Philippines, the highest figure for any developing country outside the Western Hemisphere, but for only 12 per cent in Malaya where a large Chinese population and the British preference for the recruitment of men have combined to produce the most 'male dominated' modern sector in South East Asia.

Also in Latin America and Africa, female patterns of economic behaviour have been influenced by foreign economic and cultural pressures. In the Central American republics, American influence has been much stronger than the Spanish, and, as already mentioned, these countries to-day have a higher proportion of women in their small modern sectors than the much more economically developed countries in South America and the Carribean which were under the cultural influence of Spain and other European countries. In Africa, few women are found in the modern sector in any part of the continent. Bazaar and service occupations on the other hand show a much higher proportion of women in those parts of West Africa where climate discouraged large European settlements, and where the Moslem religion failed to penetrate, than is found in either South, East or North Africa.

THE PATTERN OF MIGRATION AND OF FEMALE WORK

We have seen above that the wide differences in female activity rates in the bazaar and service occupations are linked to a variety of cultural influences and traditions. We have found, moreover, that female activity rates in the bazaar and service sector exerts influence on female activity rates in the modern sector (Figure 14).

Bazaar and Service Occupations

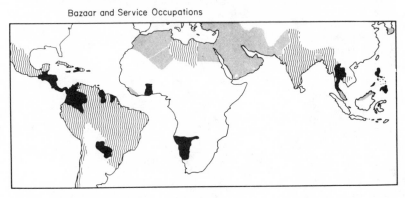

Modern Occupations

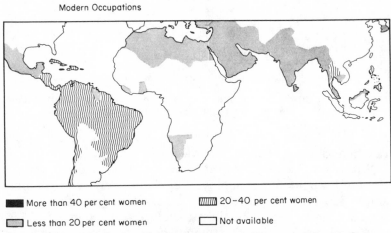

■ More than 40 per cent women   ▨ 20–40 per cent women

▨ Less than 20 per cent women   ☐ Not available

Figure 14   Sex Distribution of the Labour Force in Bazaar and Service Occupations and in Modern Occupations

But it seems to be a general rule in all developing countries, both those with high and those with low female activity rates, that men are quicker than women to change over from traditional to modern type occupations. In virtually all the developing countries covered by the present investigation we find more women in the bazaar and service sector than in the modern sector, as can be seen from Figures 14 and 15. In addition, we find in

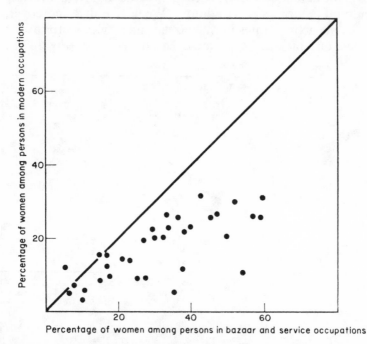

Figure 15 Sex Distribution in Modern Occupations Compared to Sex Distribution in Bazaar and Service Occupations

many developing countries a much higher female participation rate in agriculture than in the modern sector.

With economic development comes a proportional increase in the total labour force employed in the modern sector, while employment in agriculture and in some of the bazaar and service occupations declines, sometimes even in absolute numbers. This structural shift in the economy may have the effect of reducing women's share in the total labour force, because they may fail to find employment in the modern sector sufficiently rapidly to compensate for the relative or absolute decline of those sectors which employ a high proportion of women. When economic development induces a large number of men to change from agricultural, bazaar and service employment to modern sector employment, the accompanying movement of families from rural to urban areas may cut their wives off from employment in agriculture or bazaar and service occupations without giving them enough opportunity for employment in the still small modern sector, mostly staffed by men. In such cases, the overall percentage of economically active women will decline as a result of the structural change in the economy, even though the proportion of women working in the modern sector may be increasing while that of women employed in other sectors remains unchanged.*[8]

Now, as seen in Chapter 9, a woman's domestic tasks change considerably when a family migrates from village to town, because she can no longer perform many of the duties which she did formerly in the village for family consumption. Therefore, a woman who in her rural home did little or no work beyond domestic tasks has much less to do in the town unless she can and will make up for this by taking up some economic activity outside the household. Opportunities for outside work, however, are unlikely to be available. Indeed, we have just found that women's participation in economic activities outside the domestic sphere is likely to decline rather than increase after migration to town.

It is obviously a hard strain on a family budget when migration has the effect of reducing both the income earning capacity of the female family members and their contribution in kind to family income. When that happens the family is likely to be worse off in town than it used to be in the village, even in cases where the townward migration enables the male family members substantially to increase their incomes. In such cases, there will still be disillusion among the migrants despite the husband's

* This stage of a decreasing proportion of active women in the adult population may not end before the modern sector has become so large compared to the other sectors that the positive changes in female employment in this sector can offset the negative effect on female employment of the structural change in the economy.

wage improvement, and tension is likely to arise between the male and female members of the migrant families, because the men become more economically burdened, while the women enjoy unaccustomed leisure—or suffer from unaccustomed idleness.

The problem of adaptation to town life is worst in those countries where women are most active in the village and least active in the towns, while migration is much less of a problem in countries where, after migration, women can compensate for their smaller contribution in kind to family income with a larger contribution in money earned from working in the bazaar and service sector or in the modern sector. Since in developing countries female activity rates differ widely both in the villages and in the towns, patterns of migration and the social situations arising from migration also differ widely, depending upon the types of female activity predominating in a given country or region.

The problem can be illustrated by the schematic presentation below, which identifies four major regions of the under-developed world, each of them representing a characteristic pattern of female activity rates before and after migration.

Female activity rates in village	Female activity rates in town	Country groups
Low	Low	Arab countries
Low	High	Latin American countries
High	High	South East Asian countries
High	Low	Africa and India

It goes without saying that this grouping of countries into four broad regions is a simplification of a somewhat complex pattern.

Some comments on each of these four regions are now called for.

THE ARAB AND THE LATIN AMERICAN PATTERNS

As mentioned, there are two parts of the world where rural women are primarily engaged in domestic activities; one is the Latin American countries, where Spanish and other European influence was strong, and the other, countries in North Africa and West Asia under Arab influence. In these regions, three interdependent factors have combined to make it possible to lighten the burden of work outside the household done by the farmer's wife: the existence of a large class of landless labourers; an agricultural system which allows most of the farming operations to be done with animal draught power: and a cultural tradition which favours women's confinement within the domestic sphere.

Now, if women's contribution to the family income is fairly similar in the rural areas of these two regions, the same is by no means true in the towns. In most Arab countries, no more than some 5 per cent of urban women carry on any economic activity; the remaining 95 per cent of adult women do little more than cooking the daily meals and taking care of children. In contrast, in Latin American towns between 25 and 33 per cent of adult women have some kind of job, be it in the modern or in the traditional sector (Table 29). This is very little different from activity rates for urban women in industrialized countries.

We can now explain why sex patterns of migration in Latin America are radically different from those in developing countries in other continents. In Latin America, young rural women are attracted to the towns because they offer them better employment opportunities than the rural areas. Poor farmers send their daughters to town to become domestic servants, because they are not needed at home if the mother does little more than domestic duties. Moreover, there is little agricultural work for them to do, except in regions where female labour is needed for plucking the principal crop. In town, on the other hand, women find many employment opportunities ranging from domestic service for the daughters of poor farmers, to clerical jobs for the educated daughters from better-off farm families. As a result the flow of women from the countryside to the towns is larger than that of men.

Owing to this high rate of rural-urban migration of young girls, Latin American towns, in sharp contrast to other towns in developing countries, have a higher proportion of women that the rural areas. This peculiar feature of urban development

187

in Latin America thus reflects the special role played by women in Latin American agriculture. In Africa, for instance, women need their daughters from around 10 years old until marriage to take care of household duties and the younger children while

Table 29

WOMEN'S ACTIVITIES IN VILLAGE AND TOWN

Percentage distribution of adult women by activity groups

| | All Rural Areas | | | | All Urban Areas | | |
| | | Other economic | Domestic | | Economic | Domestic | |
Country:	Agriculture	activities	activities	Total	activities	activities	Total
Africa South of the Sahara:							
Ghana	38	28	34	100	54	46	100
Dahomey	17	57	26	100	66	34	100
Region of Arab influence:							
Morocco	6	2	92	100	18	82	100
Jordan	24	3	73	100			100
South and East Asia:							
India	44	8	48	100	17	83	100
Ceylon			78	100	13	87	100
Burma				100	31	69	100
Thailand				100	42	58	100
Indonesia	35	11	54	100	24	76	100
Philippines	18	15	67	100	32	68	100
Latin America:							
El Salvador			90	100	33	67	100
Costa Rica	1	8	91	100	30	70	100
Venezuela	3	7	90	100	26	74	100
Dominican Republic	3	16	81	100	29	71	100

Note: The comparability of the figures may be somewhat distorted because of differences in the extent to which part time activities are included, this affects particularly the percentages for rural areas. See also note to Table 3.

they themselves work in the fields. In Latin America, rural women do less work in the fields, and thus have more time for domestic duties and less need of help from their young daughters. It is therefore economically advantageous for a poor rural family in Latin America to send the young girls to town as domestic servants, even if they get little beyond board and lodging.

THE SOUTH EAST ASIAN PATTERN

The two different patterns of female activity in rural and urban areas which we have just described, are characterized in the case of the 'Arab pattern' by low female activity in both village and town, and in the case of the 'Spanish-American pattern'* by low activity in the village and high activity in towns. Both these patterns contrast sharply with the South East Asian patterns of high female activity in both village and town.

In South East Asia, women take a large share of the agricultural work and, in addition, they handle rural trade in foodstuffs and work in home industries and services. But women in this region are also extremely active in the towns. For instance, in the urban areas of Thailand, more than 40 per cent of the adult women have jobs, and the same is true of one-third of adult urban women in Burma. In Indonesia, 25 per cent of adult urban women have jobs, a unique figure for a Moslem country (Table 29).

The range of employment opportunities open to urban women in the countries of South East Asia is unusually wide and both the traditional and the modern sector have high levels of female employment (Table 28). Owing to the favourable job opportunities for women in the towns, Burmese men who migrate to town usually bring their wives with them. In colonial times, it was primarily the women who took industrial jobs in British enterprises where they worked alongside Indian male workers who had non-working wives.[9] In this unusual pattern of multi-racial employment, the Burmese women played a role similar to that of tribal and low-caste women in India who work as labourers together with Indian farmers, while these farmers' wives do mostly domestic work. But there are important differences. The husbands of the female agricultural labourers in India usually do the same wage labour as their women, while Burmese men, at least in the colonial period, considered wage labour as suitable only for women.

In South East Asia, as in Spanish Latin America, the money earnings of women in town compensate for the fact that the migrant woman's contribution in kind to the family income is necessarily smaller in the town than it was in the village. They sometimes earn more than the husband, who is said to resent this.[10]

Women in South East Asia are full-time participants in

* This expression is meant as a contradiction to the 'Indian-American' and the 'Negro-American' patterns.

economic activities in rural areas, no less than in the town. The most important change in the work burden when a South East Asian family moves from the village to town is that the husband may need to work longer hours than he is accustomed to, while most women continue to do a very full day's work both before and after migration.

THE AFRICAN PATTERN

It was seen in previous chapters that, besides South East Asia, Africa South of the Sahara is the other major region of female farming and trading. It is interesting that these two regions, which resemble each other in the pattern of female employment not only in agriculture but also in the bazaar and service sector, contrast sharply in their employment of women in the modern sector. In South East Asia, women have penetrated into the modern sector to an extent which, when the low stage of economic development in these countries is taken into account, must be considered large. In Africa, by contrast, the modern sector is virtually a male preserve. The main exception is the employment of white and 'coloured' women in South Africa, but even there the Bantu girls are not found in the modern sector, although their rate of literacy is higher than female literacy in most other African countries. Even in West Africa, with high female participation in trade and relatively high rate of female literacy, by African standards, very few women are employed in the modern sector.

It is obvious that in countries of female trading, the absence of women from white collar jobs cannot be due to resistance against their working outside the home, as it is in the Arab countries. But in Africa we find another objection to female employment for a wage: African men loathe the idea of their wives or daughters working under the authority of a foreign man, as was mentioned in Chapter 6. They seem to prefer women to work on their own account in bazaar and service occupations rather than in the modern sector where they are likely to be dependent on a man outside their family. This attitude, together with the desire, shared with men in other continents, to reserve for themselves the much-desired jobs in the modern sector, keeps the women out of that sector, even in those African countries where women's literacy rate is fairly high.

Let us now consider the effects of the low female participation in urban employment in Africa and in India. In rural areas African women are kept very busy doing usually at least a half of the work in agriculture and, in addition, contributing to the family income in kind by many types of activity possible only in sparsely populated rural areas and quite impossible in towns. Compared to this high rate of female activity in the village, the modern sector in the towns—industries, shops and offices—employs few, if any, women, and relatively few are occupied in home industries. The main employment opportunities in urban areas are in small scale trade, and this sector seems to be so overcrowded that the earnings of most women must be extremely small. In some of the regions with a large European population, African women are employed mostly in domestic service. In the Union of South Africa, African women account for about 15 per cent of the persons engaged in non-agricultural activities, and of these relatively few active women more than 85 per cent are domestic servants, as already mentioned.

In short, the migration from village to town entails for the African woman the exchange of a life of toil for a life of leisure. For the African man, who usually works shorter hours in the village than women (Table 30) migration to town means longer hours and stricter work discipline. As mentioned, tension must arise within the family when, after migration, one spouse has much more leisure and the other much more work than they are accustomed to.[11] Moreover, this tension increases when the husband finds himself in the unaccustomed role of the sole family breadwinner.[12]

It is hardly surprising that there should be a widespread desire among African women to exchange a village life of hard toil for an urban life of leisure.[13] But, equally understandably, their menfolk are often unwilling to accept the doubling of their customary burden of work. Therefore they often leave their wives and children in the village when they migrate to towns, and, although colonial restrictions on female migration usually disappear with the advent of independence, most towns in Africa South of the Sahara continue to be predominantly male towns, while villages have a large surplus of women. The excess of men in the towns together with the limited employment opportunities there for women entice married women into prostitution. This is of course a further incentive for men to leave their wives in the village, where unmarried men are rare and where women are under the control of elder family members.[14]

Table 30

AVERAGE WEEKLY HOURS WORKED BY WOMEN AND MEN IN RURAL AREAS

		Women			Men
Country in which sample villages are located:		All economic activities	Domestic activities	Total work	Total work
Dahomey		11	32	43	39
Nigeria		16	14	30	25
Cameroon		13	16	29	29
Central African Republic	A	19	20	39	28
	B	23	18	41	29
	C	17	13	30	39
Uganda		29	21	50	23
Kenya		26	24	50	
India		31	34	65	
Philippines		8	53	61	41

The African pattern of a higher female activity rate in the countryside than in towns is equally characteristic of several parts of Asia, including both India and Ceylon. In Indian towns, only 17 per cent of adult women have any gainful activity beyond work in the household, which, incidentally, includes the extremely time consuming cooking of traditional dishes (Table 29). But this average includes small towns with a great deal of female employment in home industries, and in the big Indian cities the female activity rate is even lower.*

In India, as in Africa, a low female activity rate in the towns creates a pattern of male migration with a considerable surplus of men in many towns and cities.[16]

---

* The proportion of women in employment in large Indian cities has been steadily declining over the last half century.[15]

Because the combination of a high female participation rate in agriculture and a low rate in towns is more frequent in India and Africa than elsewhere, these are the regions where we are most likely to see economic development accompanied by a decline in the proportion of the adult population belonging to the national labour force. The implications of this are not limited to the effects on the welfare of individual families discussed above. The decline in the proportion of adults in the labour force has equally important implications for the attainable rate of economic growth. The following chapter is devoted to these aspects of the problem.

NOTES TO CHAPTER 10

1. Inst. E.R. Djakarta, 254–5.　2. Ryan, 9.　3. Deshmukh, 190–1; UN. ECLA., *Urb. Lat. Am.*, 141–2.　4. Eckstein, 169.　5. Orleans, 160–2. 6. Suwondo, 337ff.; Aziz, 42–4.　7. Fox, 352–3.　8. Penniment, Vol. IV, 320; Sinha, Vol. IV, 337.　9. Andrus, 264, 269–71.　10. Gregory, 151; Fox, 355–6.　11. Leblanc, 56 *passim.*; Izzet, 311.　12. Forthomme, 43–5; Winter, 39; Baeck, 167.　13. Watson, 45.　14. Sofer, 619.　15. Nath Sep. 1965, 1411.　16. Prabhu, 80.

Chapter 11

The Unemployment Scare

Low rates of work participation for women tend to depress urban family incomes in many developing countries. This problem, which we identified in the preceding chapter, is felt most acutely among immigrants to towns in countries where women contribute most to family incomes in the rural setting, by their participation in agricultural production and by their domestic activities. Such a combination, we saw, is frequently found on the African continent. Indeed, sociological literature on Africa abounds in descriptions of the strains and stresses created by the change in men's and women's roles after migration to town. But the problem is no less important in India where the low-caste women's activity rates contrast sharply in the village and in town.

Some economists from developing countries have pointed to the need for higher urban work participation rates for women, from the point of view of both economic and social development.[1] But the opposite view is far more widespread: it is argued that the advantage to some families by more employment of women would be offset by a corresponding loss for other families whose bread winner would lose his job if more women were given employment.

This view has been propounded with great energy at all international conferences dealing with women's work. A delegate to the ILO Conference of 1964 described a draft resolution from the women's Committee as 'the result of excited and often stormy verbal exchanges in the Committee'. He continued by saying that 'I firmly believe that it is a serious error of judgment for developing countries to ascribe high action priority to plans for encouraging women to enter the market, especially women with family responsibilities, when those same countries do not have or cannot create sufficient jobs for their male populations. In this connection, this reply from one of the African developing countries is relevant: "This problem (meaning the problem of absorbing married women with family responsibilities into the market) does not exist for us, because we have a serious problem of unemployment among men".' [2]

The same question was in the foreground of the discussions at three international conferences in the following year. In one of these, the Indian delegate, Mrs Lakshmi Menon made a plea that 'developing countries could not afford to deprive themselves of the contribution of their women' but other delegates suggested that 'in certain countries women seeking employment should not lose sight of the fact that underemployment and unemployment were still a feature of their national life'.[3] The discussions at the African meeting of the ILO in 1964 showed considerable disagreement. Some delegates took a pessimistic view of future employment possibilities. They recommended that women's employment should be very carefully considered, and suggested that there might be need for giving priority to men in the employment market, while other delegates thought that Africa's development in all spheres required the contribution of its woman power as well as its manpower.[4]

The 1965 World Population Conference of the United Nations echoed the disagreement about the problem of employment of women in the face of existing unemployment for men. Again the idea was voiced that the provision of employment opportunities for women must await the general expansion of job opportunities, while only a minority regretted the tendency 'to view increases in manpower as a liability'.[5]

Many spokesmen for female emancipation in developing countries seem to accept the idea that women's work is a threat to economic development. For instance, Romila Tharpar, writing about the history of female emancipation in Southern Asia, states that 'one belief held widely in Asia is that if women are educated they will want employment and that this will merely raise the present high rate of unemployment. The long term effect of raising the whole standard of a people by providing parents who are educated and conscious of their responsibility

195

is often completely overlooked.'[6] Clearly, the author is unaware that the statement she quotes about women's employment merely raising the present rate of unemployment is far from being a unanimously agreed dogma among economists dealing with development problems. However, having accepted the premise she is pushed into the inconsistent standpoint of recommending a thorough education for girls, while at the same time implicitly recommending the girls not to try to use their education for its proper purpose. Once the premise is accepted that in the first instance only men can contribute to economic development, it seems illogical not to give them priority for higher education during that period.

But let us look more carefully at this premise. It is closely related to the idea that large-scale unemployment is unavoidable in developing countries, because large numbers of villagers are edged away from their homes by lack of employment or lack of land to cultivate. This stream of migrants is supposed to be too large for the additional employment which can be provided in the towns where they arrive. Therefore some must go idle and hence the suggestion that it is better for women to leave the available jobs to men, rather than to compete for them and thus contribute to bidding down the level of wages, as happened, for instance, in England during the industrial revolution, when the British towns were swelled by migrants who had been driven away from their rural homes.

But neither the rural nor the urban scene in developing countries of today resemble that of Britain during the industrial revolution. Only in exceptional cases do villagers migrate because the only alternative is sheer starvation. Usually they have some land or employment at least in the busy agricultural season, but they prefer to migrate either to earn more or to find more attractive surroundings in the towns. Since they can always return to the village and the life at subsistence level offered there, migrants in developing countries are not prepared to work—and to let their wives and children work—12 hours a day in order to earn wages which are barely sufficient for the family's subsistence. Urban wages in developing countries may be extremely low compared to wages in industrialized countries, but they are earned in a 40- to 48-hour week, and wages for adult men are usually sufficient to support non-working wives and children. And in towns of high unemployment, we often find that many of the unemployed are not miserable immigrants from over-crowded villages, but literate persons from not so poor families who prefer to be unemployed for a time, supported by relatives and friends, rather than accept work usually done by illiterates only.

In countries where the typical unemployed person is a migrant for whom there is an alternative job of productive work in the village—were he to return to it, or had he never left it—the opening up of the labour market to women is not the same thing as shifting unavoidable unemployment from women to men. On the contrary, the provision of work for women could be a means of raising the total available male and female employment in that country, provided that measures are taken to limit the stream of rural-urban migration.

EMPLOYMENT OPPORTUNITIES IN RURAL AREAS

The protests against competition from women in the labour markets of developing countries are directed against their competition for ordinary unskilled jobs in industry as well as against the admission of educated women to office jobs. These are urban types of job. In the rural areas, on the other hand, the complaint is that educated women are unwilling to accept jobs as teachers, nurses, social workers, etc., either because of their family attachments in town or because of a general desire to live in towns.[7] Only rarely is women's agricultural work mentioned in this context, and no wonder since women's agricultural work is needed in the peak season when labour is short, a normal feature of virtually all developing countries.

If this is so, the usual reasoning of those who object to the employment of women in developing countries is clearly fallacious. They fail to realize that unemployment in rural areas exists only for part of the year. They mistake this seasonal unemployment for an overall labour surplus and suggest that if anybody has to be unemployed it is better that it should be women. In other words, they presume that if some urban jobs were given to urban women instead of male immigrants, the agricultural sector would be unable to employ those men.

197

The truth is, however, that in nearly all developing countries the agricultural sector could absorb much more labour with little, if any, decline in annual wages or incomes, provided that more labour-intensive systems of agriculture were adopted, whereby employment could be secured for a larger part of the year.*

Even in densely populated developing countries scope is offered for additional agricultural employment by bringing dry land, which is cultivated yearly or every second year, under irrigation, thus making it possible to take two or more crops per year. In more thinly populated developing countries more agricultural employment can be provided by replacing systems of shifting cultivation with more labour intensive farming systems, or by the construction of roads and other rural infra-structure investment, whereby new areas can be opened up for cultivation.

In view of these possible ways of creating more employment in agriculture, the employment of women in urban occupations should be seen not as a measure which deprives men of employment, but one which provides more hands for the agriculture in that country, thus making it possible either to improve food supplies to the towns and reduce food imports or to increase agricultural exports. We must therefore look more closely into what would happen in rural areas if some men were prevented from migrating to the towns because urban women were given access to urban jobs.

Let us begin by making a distinction between sparsely populated regions with agricultural systems which allow all members of the local village community to take land under cultivation, and more densely populated regions where land is privately owned and some members of the rural communities must work for a wage. In most of Africa South of the Sahara, the typical system of land tenure allows free access to land for all members of the village community. Villagers who migrate to town from such regions do so because they hope to obtain a better income, to live in urban surroundings, to save money to pay a bride price upon return to the village, to find jobs which they consider more suitable for literate persons than farming, to avoid the hard

* The problems which are briefly touched upon here provide the central theme of the present author's book on *The Conditions of Agricultural Growth.*

manual work of agriculture, to escape tribal discipline, etc. Their departure means that less land is cultivated each year than would have been cultivated had they stayed at home.[8] Thus the departure of the migrants tends to reduce the food available for the towns or for export and in some cases the migration makes the country dependent on food aid. In regions with this 'African type' of agriculture it might often be good for the economy of the country if more young villagers stayed at home and more urban jobs were filled by urban women.

In regions with an 'Asian type' of agriculture, i.e. with individual ownership of land and a large number of agricultural workers, these latter are often attracted to town by wage differentials or other real or imaginary advantages, with a result that agricultural production is held below the level it would have attained had they stayed.[9] Often wage labourers leave because the seasons when they can easily find work are so short that they receive only a low annual income. Here again, a change to a more intensive system of agriculture with, for example, the irrigation of some of the land, might be a more desirable solution than the departure of the labourers, which may leave agriculture short handed in the busy season.

There are cases, to be sure, where agricultural labourers or cultivators leave the village for the town because of famine and lack of work due to a harvest failure. The best policy would then be to facilitate their early return to the villages by measures which can help to avoid a similar catastrophe in the future. Recent experience in India, in the Bihar famine, suggests that this tragedy happened because the upkeep and expansion of irrigation facilities had been neglected, and this neglect seems to have been the main cause not only of the famine, but also of the prevailing seasonal under-employment in the rural areas.

It is recognized by leading experts on manpower problems in India that 'at peak agricultural seasons, migration of agricultural workers to other areas would have an unfavourable impact on production. This fact proves that a certain percentage of the under-employed is functionally necessary in the agricultural sector, as it represents "labour-in-waiting" for the peak season activities.'[10] But it is generally agreed among agricultural experts that such 'labour-in-waiting' need not be kept under-employed but can be given employment for a much larger proportion of the year by suitable agricultural intensification. If there is no use for additional labour in the towns, agricultural development is a better cure for rural under-employment than restrictive attitudes to urban female employment in order to make room in the urban labour market for redundant migrants.

Employment opportunities in agriculture were overlooked by most governments immediately after independence; economic development was often thought of as almost synonymous with the development of industry. As a result, public investment in agriculture was neglected, and little encouragement was given to private investment and additional employment in agriculture.*

That stage of one-sided emphasis on urban development has now passed, and governments in most developing countries are considering how they can best exploit the potential for agricultural expansion. Usually this will require considerable additional manpower in agriculture and related rural activities,[12] since few developing countries can afford to rely entirely or mainly on the capital-intensive methods for the expansion of agriculture which are in use in the industrialized countries. Therefore the rate of increase of labour productivity in agriculture cannot be expected to be as high as the rate at which food production must increase. This is tantamount to saying that the agricultural labour force must continue to increase in most developing countries, in contrast to industrialized countries where the numbers engaged in agriculture are declining year by year.

Thus, it is not desirable—even if it were possible—for male urban employment to expand so rapidly that it absorbs the whole of the male population increase in rural areas. Therefore, increasing female participation in urban labour markets may often help to keep rural-urban migration within bounds in the interest of rural development.

* An official Indian report, issued as late as 1959 regretted that in planning for the second five-year plan 'all we could do was to provide only 80 per cent of the new entrants with employment opportunities in the non-agricultural sector'.[11]

THE URBAN LABOUR MARKET

In all the cases where agriculture offers employment opportunities at least for some months each year, villagers will hesitate to emigrate unless they have a reasonable chance of obtaining employment with the usual conditions in a neighbouring or more distant town. But if for some reason the chances of getting urban employment improve, an additional inflow of migrants is likely. An observer of urban labour markets in Zambia described the situation by saying that 'those seeking work are only the vanguard of a much larger body of potential migrants who would flock to the towns if there were reasonable chances of obtaining paid employment'.[13] This is characteristic not only of Zambia, but of most other developing countries. Town life seems so attractive to young people from the villages that they take the chance of going to town as soon as employment opportunities become available.

Studies of internal migration in many countries have shown that frequent communication between migrants and their relatives back home in the village is a main factor determining the direction and size of further migration. The flow of migration is stimulated whenever villagers learn from emigrant co-villagers about improved employment opportunities in a given town. Conversely, the flow is restrained by bad news and by the spectacle of disappointed villagers returning because they found no employment with conditions they had hoped for.

When the unemployed are ineligible for a dole, they can stay in a town only if they have relatives, co-villagers or others who are willing to support them. Therefore, in some parts of the world we find relatively low unemployment in those quarters of the towns that are crowded with immigrants. A study of migrants into Bombay showed that only 4 per cent were unemployed at the time of the investigation, about two-thirds said they had experienced no difficulty in finding a job, and more than one-third had found a job within a month of arrival.[14] A similar study in Delhi showed that 60 per cent had found a job within three months of arrival, but one-third of the migrants had visited more than fifteen towns before they finally found a job in Delhi.[15] A study of the slum areas of Buenos Aires revealed that a majority

201

of migrants found work within a fortnight of their arrival; the unemployment rate among newly arrived migrants was only 2 to 3 per cent; and no less than 21 per cent of the migrant women were gainfully employed, which was a higher rate of activity than that found for the city-born population living in slums.[16]

These low rates of unemployment suggest that people without possible means of support if unemployed hesitate to move to town unless employment opportunities are good, and that many leave again for their home village or for another town when they fail to find employment. In India, there seems to be a good deal of such 'floating migration' between towns, and many disappointed seekers after urban employment return to their villages.[17]

In such an open labour market, with migrants arriving in larger or smaller numbers depending on the prospects for getting a job, a restriction on the recruitment of women would be likely to have the same effect as any other improvement would have on the employment situation for men, and would thus attract more male migrants. That is to say, the men already living in the town would have less competition from women living in the town or from female migrants, but more competition from male migrants. Conversely, if vacancies in towns were filled by urban women hitherto occupied only with domestic activities in their own home, the result would be to deter male migrants, and the net flow of migration would tend to diminish. In a typical case where those who gave up their plans for migration would be employed at least for part of the year in a village, total activity and output would increase because the activity of urban women would also increase.

However, in some countries mainly in Africa, but also in some non-African countries,[18] young people from rural families need not wait in the villages until suitable employment opportunities turn up in a neighbouring town. They can move in and join a queue of unemployed waiting for jobs to turn up, because they can find relatives or friends in the town who are willing and able to support them during the waiting period. In African towns mutual support and cohesion among family members is legendary, as it is among members of the same tribe and in immigrant groups from a given village. Young migrants may keep afloat for years while unemployed, and it is therefore relatively easy in

Africa to realize the dream of escaping from the dreariness of the village to the 'modern' life in town.

In the colonial period, restrictions on entry to towns confined the young people to the village, unless they could secure employment in mines and plantations. This system is still in force in South Africa, but in the independent African countries such restrictions on rural-urban migrations have been lifted, and young men—and some young women—take a chance on hanging on in the towns while unemployed, supported by relatives and others, in the hope that sooner or later they will be able to obtain regular employment in the modern sector. This crowd of young people on the waiting list for employment in factories or in service trades, together with the people who give them financial support, make up the pressure group which, on the one hand, insists on additional employment being created in the towns, and, on the other hand, claims that urban jobs should be reserved for men. But in most cases it is preferable from the point of view of economic progress that they should go back to their villages, while more urban women should be employed in urban jobs.

EDUCATION AS A CAUSE OF UNEMPLOYMENT

Of course, to be unemployed in towns for a long period is easier for young men and women from better-off rural families than for young persons from the lowest strata of the rural hierarchy, and it is easier still for children of relatively well-off urban families. But these rural and urban children from middle class families are the ones who have been to school and have had the benefits of higher education. It is understandable, therefore, that unemployment rates are much higher among educated youth and persons from not-so-poor families than among poor migrants.

A sample survey of unemployed in Puerto Rico showed that the average income of the families to which the unemployed belonged was above the general average.[19] These people could afford to be unemployed and wait for a good job to turn up, while the slum dwellers without connections had either to accept any job in sight, or else return to their village, as already mentioned. This kind of selection produces a pattern of unemployment with low rates for illiterates from poor families, while young persons from better-off families, in a typical case, enjoy education up to a relatively advanced level, after which they remain unemployed for a comparatively long period because they are ambitious about the type of job they are prepared to accept.

In India, the differences in unemployment rates as between illiterates and the educated are strikingly large. A sample survey of urban unemployment in the middle of the 1950s recorded unemployment in large towns as being 11 per cent among graduates, 8 per cent among other literates and 6 per cent among illiterates.[20] Five years later, the tendency for urban unemployment to be concentrated on the educated youth seemed to have become much more pronounced. The new sample showed that among young men between 16 and 21 who had at least completed high school no less than 24 per cent were unemployed, as against only 3 per cent for the illiterates in the same age group.[21] In Calcutta, an investigation of 7,000 applicants for jobs requiring matriculation showed that 81 per cent of the applicants had never had a job and that more than half of these had been unemployed for over two years.[22]

It seems inevitable that unemployment among people with a certain level of education should be high in periods when the average level of education attained by young people is increasing rapidly. As long as only a small minority are literates, or have reached some level of education, this minority can aspire to attractive jobs and refuse to accept less desirable jobs. When many more reach the educational level which was previously a monopoly for a small minority, most of them must accept jobs which were not previously acceptable to people with that degree of education, or else they will be unemployed. This is due to the simple fact that the number of non-manual jobs available is likely to increase more slowly than the number of educated persons available to fill them. But this fact is not easily accepted by those concerned. In countries where literacy is the general rule, literate persons take it for granted that most of them get manual jobs, but in countries where literacy is increasing rapidly, although is not yet general, literate young persons will prefer to remain unemployed for long periods, if they can afford it, rather than to take jobs which were traditionally held by persons with no or less education than they themselves. In fact, such people may be regarded as voluntarily unemployed,* since many employers of manual labour would recruit educated people in preference to the uneducated or poorly educated. If the literates and other educated unemployed were to accept the type of job they disapprove of, they would prevent a corresponding number of rural migrants with less or no education from obtaining urban employment, and the likely result would be a smaller flow of migrants to the towns.

Naturally, the least qualified persons among the educated male youth, who spend years looking in vain for the type of job they had hoped to obtain as a result of their education, are hostile to the idea of having their job opportunities further reduced by the entrance of educated girls in the labour market. In some cases, their reaction is to oppose female education, but in most developing countries there is by now a widespread acceptance of female education among educated men. Therefore, the opposition of the unfortunate job seekers is not to the education of girls, but to the employment of educated girls. They join the older generation in its claim that the purpose of the education of girls should be to develop their personalities and make them better mothers and housewives, and that no married women should be gainfully employed. But practise does not always conform to this theory. It seems that men often maintain this standpoint only until they themselves have married an educated girl and discover how hard it is to keep up the desired standard of living for the family without help from her.†

* In countries where no dole is paid to unemployed persons, no sharp line of demarcation can be drawn between voluntary and involuntarily unemployed persons. A manpower survey of urban areas in Thailand showed that one-third of the unemployed men and half the unemployed women were persons who had never had a job, had never actively looked for one, but said they were thinking of looking for work.[23] Such persons may accept particularly attractive jobs which they happen to hear about, but they will not apply for jobs which they find less appealing.

† In both Bombay and Delhi, the desire for employment is widespread among married educated women. According to sample studies made in 1964, 48 per cent of married educated women in Bombay and 44 per cent in Delhi were either employed or looking for work. Forty per cent of those Delhi women who did not work or seek work abstained because of family duties, the other 60 per cent because they (or their relatives) disapproved of women working outside the home or because they found their family income sufficient.[24]

In a period of rapidly spreading education for both boys and girls, the problems cannot be solved by giving the boys illusions about the advantages a certain amount of education will give them in the labour market, while girls are told that they must not aspire to a career even though they have attained a high educational level. It seems better that both boys and girls should learn to use their education in gainful employment, but not to expect the wage premium for education to be as high as it was when education was less widespread and carried more prestige than it does now in those countries where there is no particular shortage of educated persons.

THE COST OF URBANIZATION

The above argument was based on the assumption that if some men were unable to get jobs because more women were filling them, then the men should if possible be given employment in rural areas where the demand for labour was supposed to be more flexible than in the towns where the unemployed were living. However, a higher rate of employment for urban women may be an advantage for the economy as a whole, even in cases where it gives rise, not to additional employment in the village, but to agricultural work-sharing without any positive effect on output. The reason for this is the pronounced difference in nearly all developing countries in the ways in which rural and urban infra-structure investment is brought about.

In most villages, people provide the infra-structure they need, or most of it, by their own efforts, without burdening public investment budgets. Villagers in developing countries usually build their own houses of local materials, supply themselves with water, light and fuel, arrange their own local transport by carrying headloads or use donkeys or carts. In towns, by contrast, public investment budgets are burdened by investment costs to provide migrant families with dwellings, light, water, sanitation, schools, hospitals, etc.

Because of this difference in the means of providing investment, the need for public investment in developing countries is more closely related to the growth of the urban population than to the growth of the total population of the country. It is for this reason that a policy which restrains the townward movement of people can help to reduce the burden of investment in infra-structure.

In Africa, for example, population in the twenty-eight largest cities increased by no less than 5 per cent annually in the period from 1948 to 1960. This is, of course, a far higher rate of increase than that for the total population in Africa,[25] and it is this rate of urban growth, rather than the overall growth rate of population, that entails a great demand for capital investment.[26] In a country where the village population is largely self-sufficient, capital requirements will be larger if the towns grow quickly by immigration while the rural population is constant, than if over-all population growth is more rapid, but the rate of growth of towns is smaller.

The problem of economizing on urban infra-structure has been tackled in different ways. One method, widely used in colonial days, consisted in recruiting only the men and preventing their families from joining them in the place where they were to work. The men could then be housed cheaply in dormitories, and the investment needed to accommodate this additional manpower could be kept to a minimum. Another way to save on urban infra-structure was followed in the Soviet Union: entry into towns was rigorously restricted and urban dwelling space was strictly rationed; but women, instead of being kept away from the towns, were drawn into employment whenever possible. In this way, the necessary infra-structure investment *per earner* was kept to the minimum, and it was not necessary to split up families.

The desire to save investment in urban infra-structure is one of the arguments invoked for setting up industries in villages. But such village industries are often unsuccessful precisely because of the lack of infra-structure in rural areas. It is worth stressing, therefore, that industries can also be set up in towns, without a need for additional urban infra-structure, provided that these industries recruit their labour force among urban women who would otherwise have been confined to domestic duties. If men alone are recruited to new industries and if these men are immigrants to the town, the employment of one person requires investment not only in the establishment in which he is employed, but also in all the infra-structure needed to accommodate him and his family. If employment is provided for both men and women from immigrant families, this investment for infra-structure will be lower per person employed, and if employment is given only to hitherto idle wives and daughters of the families already living in the towns, little additional infra-structure will be needed.

A town which utilizes to the full the work capacity of both its male and female inhabitants by giving priority in employment to people already living in the town, may gain on two counts: by a lower requirement of investment in infra-structure per person employed and by higher tax proceeds and personal savings than would be forthcoming if the urban families had fewer earners per family. It is fairly obvious that the ability to save is greater for one family with two earners than for two families of the same size and with only one breadwinner in each. Families with two earners may be able to pay the cost of their own housing while families belonging to the same social group but with only one earner, must live in slums, unless they can get hold of a subsidized dwelling. One-earner families may be unable to pay any local taxes to cover investment in infra-structure, while two-earner families have a higher capacity for paying taxes.

An employment policy which induces women to accept employment instead of staying at home is likely to result in restricting somewhat the growth of urban areas by holding down the birth rate. Although little direct evidence is available,[27] it is generally assumed that working women produce fewer children than they would if they were non-working, partly because they may marry at a later age and partly because they may be more inclined to practise birth control.[28] If this is so, poor countries can reduce the burden of supporting both non-working children and non-working women by encouraging urban women to look for employment, instead of reserving the urban jobs for men.

THE STRATEGY OF DEVELOPMENT PLANNING

One important condition for the rapid growth of agricultural production and rural incomes in developing countries is that the most able of the young villagers, especially the literates, must be prevented from migrating to town and instead must become the spearhead of progress in the village.[29] Therefore, the whole idea of restricting the urban employment of women in order to make room for this rural elite in the towns is out of tune with the present strategy of development planning. The new and more dynamic approach is, through a policy of rural modernization, to attach young literate villagers to their home villages, instead of drawing them to the towns by urban employment creating policies. It is in harmony with this approach to encourage women in the towns to seek gainful employment, which, as already stressed, would have the twofold effect of economizing on investment in urban infra-structure, and of eliciting more private savings in the towns.

When the problem of women's employment in the urban areas is viewed in this light, as an integrated part of an over-all plan for rural and urban expansion, the African and Indian pattern of employment of women appears as an impediment to progress. The transfer of male man-power from the agriculture and other rural occupations to the modern urban sector raises the productivity of the male labour which is transferred. But at the same time, rural-urban migration in Africa and India has the effect of reducing the average number of earners per family, because the activity rates of women are lowered by the transfer from village to town. On other words, part or all of the improvement in productivity which is obtained by the transfer of male manpower is offset by the decline of total activity per family; hence, the transfer leaves the average family with little or no increase in income, and therefore of capacity to pay taxes and to save on their own account.

A comparison of this pattern of development, typical of Africa and India, with the typical Latin American pattern, makes the latter appear to be more conducive to economic growth. When a Latin American family moves from a rural to an urban area, an increase of productivity per male worker is compounded with an increase of female activity rates to produce a notable increase in the average income per family, and, therefore, an increase in savings for further growth.

NOTES TO CHAPTER 11

1. Lewis, W. A., 116–17; Nath Sep. 1965, 1412. 2. ILO 48 session, 468–9.
3. UN. *Sem. Part. Wom.* 1966, 8–9.   4. ILO *Afr. Conf. Report*, 82–3.

5. UN. *Pop. Conf.*, Vol. I, 231.   6. Tharpar, 493.   7. ILO India, 89.
8. Boutillier 1962, 106; Balandier 1955, 40–5; Kay, 22–3; d'Aby, 53–4.
9. Gourou, 6; Lopez, 237; Hansen, 385, 393–4; Weulersse, 174; Som, 144.
10. Datar, 4; See also Som, 144.   11. India Min. of L. 1959, Ch. 3, 18.
12. India Pl. C. 1964, 4.   13. Kay, 23.   14. Prabhu, 62.   15. Deshmukh,
185, 189.   16. Germany, 220, 228.   17. Bose Sydney 1967, 606.   18. UN.
ECLA., *Urb. Lat. Am.*, 131.   19. Elizago, Vol. IV, 267.   20. ILO *Rev.* 1962,
Vol. II, 376.   21. Olin, 315.   22. India W. Bengal 1959, 19–20.   23. Thailand
Report of the Labour Force Survey Bangkok 1963, 25.   24. Ramachandran,
Ranaday.   25. UN. ECA., *Urb. Trop. Afr.*, 9.   26. UN. ECLA.,
Urb. Lat. Am., 136.   27. UN. Pop. Conf., Vol. I, 221–2; Gendell, Vol. IV,
283–7; Gutkind, 150ff.   28. Colver, 383–4; Jaffe, 62–3; Bose Bangkok
1967, 49.   29. India Min. of L. 1959, Ch. 3, 20; ILO *Afr. Conf. Record*,
85; ILO *Rev.* 1963, Vol. I, 186–7.

Chapter 12

The Design of Female Education

In the most widely read book about labour conditions in India, the problem of women workers is summarized as follows: 'If the number of women employed in industry is small, it does not reflect any reluctance of the Indian women to take to vocations in industry; but it is only because industrialization in India has not progressed far and there yet remains millions of men to be provided with work. In women, a vast manpower potential, both willing and eager to work, is existing and when the time comes for rapid industrialization, their services could be well drafted.'[1]

The first idea propounded in the above quotation is that industrialization must reach a certain stage before the employment of women in the modern sector can really begin. This line of reasoning was controverted in the preceding chapter, where we reached the opposite conclusion: that the recruitment of women to the modern sector helps to accelerate the growth of the economy beyond the rate attainable by the use of male labour alone.

What are we to think of the other main idea in the quotation, i.e. that 'a vast manpower potential' of women stands ready to be drawn into employment the moment this appears to be desirable? On closer inspection, this idea seems as questionable as the first one. It is of course true that there are now more women applicants for industrial jobs on many Indian labour exchange registers than there are vacancies to be filled, but there is little doubt that if the demand for women workers were to increase markedly, a point would soon be reached where the supply of willing and qualified women would be deficient.

In India, as in most other developing countries, women's

attitudes to work outside the household are changing slowly. Women teachers are now considered respectable in nearly all developing countries; the nursing profession is respected in many developing countries—but *not* in India; women typists and clerks are accepted in Latin America and are beginning to be accepted in some developing countries in Asia. But, as yet, the idea of women in the role of industrial worker is frowned upon by respectable women in most developing countries—including India. Since women have access, at best, only to unskilled and low-paid industrial jobs, industrial employment has no prestige value for women who aspire to a career, and the earning capacity of women workers is not high enough to compensate for the social stigma attached to women's industrial work. Therefore a change of policy, aiming at a better utilization of the labour potential of urban women, would need to be combined with policy measures designed to make industrial jobs attractive to young literate urban women, instead of a refuge for lonely and destitute widows and for deserted wives, who are unable to support themselves in ways which are considered acceptable.

But women's way to employment in the modern sector is barred not only by women's prejudices, but also by their lack of proper qualifications. It is true that literacy, formerly an exception, is now becoming the rule among urban girls in nearly all developing countries, but owing to the enduring prejudice against female employment urban girls are rarely given the type of education which would qualify them for employment in the modern sector. Apart from the major exception of commercial schools for girls in Latin America, very few opportunities for training girls exist in developing countries. At the same time, facilities for the vocational training of boys are increasing rapidly in nearly all these countries. It would seem, therefore, that in most of the developing countries outside Latin America the qualifications gap between male and female labour is becoming increasingly wider.

THE PRODUCTIVITY OF FEMALE LABOUR

In primitive communities, the difference in productivity between male and female labour is not very large, as was explained in previous chapters. Both men and women produce goods and services for family use only. Although most men have the advantage of superior physical strength, at this stage neither men nor women can benefit from specialization. All those who work, be it men or women, must spread their activity over many fields in order to cover the various needs of the family.

A major difference between male and female productivity begins to develop when men become specialized producers of some agricultural or non-agricultural goods or services while all or most women continue to produce a variety of traditional products and services for family use. The specialized producer can devote much more time to training in his particular craft than can a subsistence producer with a variety of jobs to do, and, furthermore, a specialized producer working for a wider market can afford to acquire better tools and other equipment than can a subsistence producer. Only very recently, and then only in highly industrialized countries, have a significant number of subsistence producers in such communities—i.e. the housewives—begun to apply anything but the most primitive types of equipment to their work. In developing countries, the men who work in the modern sector handle much more advanced equipment than the women, who perform household duties or use home-made tools for their home-made industrial products.

As long as the specialized worker in agriculture or crafts is trained within the family, the difference in male and female productivity remains relatively small, since the girls are given some training by their mothers in household and other duties. But the gap in productivity between the two sexes widens considerably at the stage when boys get some systematic training in schools or in workshops, while girls continue to be taught only by their mothers. At a later stage, when girls also go to school, the gap is reduced so far as literacy and other school subjects are concerned, but another gap then emerges because an increasing number of boys receive vocational training while virtually all the girls continue to receive only the traditional initiation into their roles as housewives and mothers. Even within the ordinary schools there is a significant difference in the teaching of the two sexes. The school will normally seek to stimulate the boys' interest in subjects that are useful in the labour market, while the interest of the girls is directed towards subjects of little or no vocational relevance. Last, but no least, nearly all the parents teach their boys and girls that boys are superior to girls and that they alone can show initiative and accept positions of responsibility.

Employment in the modern sector requires not only formal training, but also a certain attitude to work which may best be described as the capacity to work regularly and attentively. This attitude is not easily acquired by people who are accustomed to come and go, to work and rest as they please. Those who work within the confines of the family are not likely to acquire this attitude unless their position is so precarious that they are forced into working harder and longer in order to subsist. It is well known that people who are accustomed to hard work in intensive agriculture are more able to adapt themselves to other types of work than are people accustomed to the more leisurely rhythm of work in shifting cultivation. Within the framework of shifting cultivation, women usually work harder than the male family members, as previously shown. Hence, employers of African labour sometimes find that women workers are highly efficient industrial workers, because their habit of hard work makes up for their lower level of general knowledge and formal training.[2] However, this is only an exception to the general rule that the labour productivity of women in developing countries is inferior to that of male workers from the same community, because women have a lower level of education and training.[3]

THE ESCAPE FROM COMPETITION

It was suggested above that the difference between female labour productivity and that of men is due to differences in education. But there are of course other approaches to the question of a sex differential in labour productivity, ranging from denial of its existence to the consideration that it is the result of an over-all and innate superiority of male over female.

The idea that women are by nature inferior workers is widespread in developing as well as in industrialized countries.[4] This prejudice is usually mitigated to some extent by the assumption that in certain occupations women are more efficient than men. We have already mentioned as an example the widespread prejudice against men as teachers of small children. This type of prejudice is likely to result in a selection of applicants for various occupations which then provides a spurious confirmation of the prejudice. For instance, if it is generally agreed that women are superior teachers but inferior to men in nearly all other occupations, teaching will attract many able women but few able men. The inevitable result of this kind of selection combined with the general prejudice about female inferiority is to reinforce the conviction about the innate differences in the abilities of the two sexes.

In communities where girls are taught by their parents that they are inferior to boys and where boys receive a training which makes them more qualified than girls for employment in the modern sector, it is inevitable that women who enter the labour market will suffer from a deep insecurity and feeling of inferiority. It is not surprising, therefore, that they seek security by sticking to certain occupations which are supposed to be suitable for women, while only a small minority want to enter into open competition with men in the fields which by general consensus among men as well as women are considered as less suitable for women. Therefore, the flocking of women to certain occupations would seem to be primarily due to their own desire to be employed in supposedly 'feminine' professions while men's fear of accepting women in the 'masculine' occupations may be a less important factor.

At a conference about women's role in developing countries, Carr-Saunders warned against attaching 'too much importance to education of women for a narrow range of tasks, especially for the office skills of typing and shorthand. I sometimes think that in this we can trace a remnant of the old idea of what is proper for women; if they must be employed, it is thought that they should find employment only in special tasks. . . . They should not be confined to particular skills.'[5] In the same vein, W. Arthur Lewis has warned against telling the women 'that if they work outside their homes they may only be domestic servants or typists or crowded into some other narrow range of jobs.'[6]

But these are not the only voices. Other scholars invite women in developing countries to abstain from intrusion into men's spheres in the labour market. A European anthropologist, addressing a conference of women in South Asia, praised women's movements in the area which 'follow less the Western concept of *mechanical equality* among the sexes (which is a practical Utopia) than that of certain *preferential rights* for women, in order to establish ultimate harmony and co-operation between both sexes.'*[7] Unfortunately, the demand for preferential rights, instead of 'mechanical' equality, cannot fail to appeal to women who are in the process of breaking out of the secluded sphere of home subsistence production on to the threshold of a labour market where they feel like inferior and often unwelcome intruders. In fact, women workers usually prefer the existing system of confining women to special jobs reserved for them in industries and offices.

Crowding women within a narrow range of jobs in industries and offices comes, in the first instance, from decisions by the employers. In the academic field, on the other hand, it is the result of the girls' free choice. When girls are first admitted to universities, they always seem to gather in the arts faculties. Later they reluctantly enter first the medical faculty and then related branches like pharmacy and bio-chemistry. These preferences suggest that the girls accept the tradition that women should deal with children and sick persons and leave the abstract or technical branches to the men.

Many Indian universities have now reached the stage where women are overcrowding the arts faculties and social faculties, while in the medical faculty women are still in a minority.[8] In this respect, the Philippines are ahead of India: in 1960–1, 285 women and three men passed professional government examinations in pharmacy.[9] In Thailand, the number of women medical students was formally restricted in order to prevent the medical profession from becoming predominantly female.[10]

As economic development gets under way, women tend increasingly to enter the non-agricultural labour market. This growing number of young women cannot indefinitely be accommodated in the occupations which were first considered to be

* Italics as in original.

appropriate for women. As a result, women spill over into other occupations, entering reluctantly at first but with increasing enthusiasm as the new occupations become more 'feminine'. The effect of this is similar to the well-known phenomenon of 'tipping' in the market for urban dwellings in multi-racial communities where each race huddles in special quarters and 'white' districts are only reluctantly opened to and entered by 'coloured'.[11] After an occupation is invaded by the sex considered inferior a stage is reached when it is deserted by the sex which considers itself superior, just as an urban quarter invaded by 'coloured' is deserted by its white inhabitants when the 'density' of 'coloured' has reached a certain level. In both cases, prejudice is reinforced by economic considerations: a suddenly increased supply of labour for a given occupation exerts a downward pressure on wages, just as the sudden entry of a new group of tenants tends to raise the level of rent. In both cases, the superior group—sex or race—finds the occupation or locality less attractive and tends to leave the field open to the inferior sex (or race). The downward pressure on male wages in occupations invaded by women would not occur if women could avoid flocking to a few occupations and were welcome in, and trained for, the whole range of economic activities.

In countries with a tradition of female seclusion, there is of course a great deal of force in the appeal to women to repudiate 'mechanical equality' and instead to strive for a special position in the labour market. In India, for instance, pathetic attempts are made to find special fields for women, sheltered from male competition. The authoress of a book about the employment of Indian women reviews the possibilities of employing women in the transport industry and says hopefully: 'In Calcutta a few trams are reserved exclusively for women during office hours, and the conductors of these trams may one day be women.'[12] Similarly, the authoress of an article about the prospects for the Indian woman in 1975 mentions an "important banking company which has done pioneering work in employing women staff and in providing special banking facilities to women. It has All Women's Banks in many urban areas staffed entirely by women.'[13] Such suggestions might be considered harmless and curious attempts to gain an advantage from the remaining examples of the seclusion of women, were it not that they contradict and weaken women's demand for general access on equal terms to the labour market. It is significant, in this connection, that an official commission, reporting on women workers, should find it relevant to state that 'there are no particular jobs which can be better performed by women in the industrial field', and that one of the authoresses mentioned above should quote this statement without comment.[14]

An investigation of opinions held by Indian women studying at American universities revealed that even they were in favour of special functions for women. They keenly denied any wish to compete for the functions traditionally performed by men: 'Hindu women today, in fact, do not see the struggle for "equal rights" as the competitive demand for the *same* function as those performed by men. They demand only the recognition and honour due to their role (though it is true they are entering politics and professions, feeling that they are needed in them). It is, still, a non-competitive society.'[15] Another girl student said: 'Our custom is to have the husband support the family . . . I know that in this system the wife has very little opportunity to work outside the home and make full use of her capacities. But this arrangement keeps the harmony in the family. Both husband and wife are rulers in two different fields.'[16]

These Indian girls were studying at an American university in the 1950s which Betty Friedan has described as the period of 'mystification of women' where many American college girls could be quoted for similar statements.[17] But if these views were perhaps influenced by what the Indian girls thought would be well received in the host country, they are at least worth quoting for the light they throw on the influence of western sociological theories on the elite of the developing countries.

In some countries where the tradition of the seclusion of women is strongly entrenched, the preference for 'secluded trades' and special jobs for women combines with the fear of male unemployment to produce an extremely effective barrier against the opening of the general labour market to women. The Moroccan study quoted in previous chapters mentions that even women workers in Morocco think that women with an earning husband should refrain from ordinary employment as unskilled labourers, while teachers and nurses are more accept-able because 'they fill functions in which men would have difficulty in replacing them'.[18]

In countries with a tradition of female trading, women are more inclined to enter the general labour market and less keen on having special rights. From Thailand come complaints that Western influence adversely affects the position of women there by making sharper distinctions between the sexes than has traditionally existed in that country. The people from the West have brought scouting for boys, needlework for girls, special hospitals for women, public toilets separated by sex. 'All help now to emphasize a person's sex.'[19] Like the Thai women, the Burmese women were in some ways much freer than is usual for Asian or European women, and Margaret Mead reproaches Western administrators for having failed to take into account the self-dependent role of Burmese women.[20]

From Africa, too, come complaints that European ideas have a bad influence upon the position of women. Missionaries, Catholic as well as Protestant, are blamed for having taught the girls little more than domestic skills and for having 'more or less encouraged a stay-at-home policy of the urban women on moral grounds'.[21] Traditionally, African women have more freedom to move around and earn money than most Asian women, but, nevertheless, their traditional status is one of subordination to men. The secretariat report to the Inter-African Conference in Lusaka in 1957 summarized the position of African women as follows: 'It is a crude generalization, but perhaps it needs to be said, that African society is a male society, in which women have a defined place and role; the place is subordinate and the role is to carry the routine daily burdens of life.'[22]

When the tribal bonds begin to weaken, African men try to preserve their position of authority over women by substitut-ing 'a justification of western inspiration for the justification by tribal custom'. In other words, they claim authority and obedience on the grounds of women's educational deficiencies and not because of tribal rights.[23] Likewise, many African men object to women having careers because it will make the urban woman economically independent and unwilling to submit to male authority.[24] In cases where the lack of qualified manpower causes educated African women to be employed in white collar jobs, it seems to be generally accepted that they must be employed in low grade jobs, while the men move up to the more responsible jobs. The ILO Report on African Women, quoted earlier, states that 'with the advancement of Africans to higher posts which used in a number of African countries to be held by Europeans, new openings are available to men and women alike', but it continues as follows: 'Men now set their sights higher, and instead of regarding a job in an office or a job in a factory as their goal, they feel they can aim at something better and do not oppose the employment of women in the posts which they formerly considered to be the exclusive field of men. . . . General experience suggests that the higher men can go, the more opportunities will be offered to women in the lower grades.'[25] This idea of women's role in the labour market is probably shared by most men in industrialized countries, but it is rarely set forth with such frankness as in this text which is meant as a benevolent encouragement to African women looking for a job.

TRAINING FOR THE MODERN SECTOR

As long as girls remain under the twofold handicap of a family education which suppresses their self-confidence and of training facilities in schools and elsewhere which are inferior to those given to boys, they are bound to be inferior workers who contribute little to the national product despite their hard toil in many traditional tasks of low productivity. Although much lip-service has been given to the importance of women in the future and the need to give them better training, progress in this field seems to be very slow. The emphasis is still on a training which fits them only for subsistence production in their own households by teaching them better cooking, better child care, sewing and embroidery. Such subjects take up much of the time in many rural and urban primary schools, and the courses offered to girls and women under programmes of community development and rural extension are devoted largely to them. Even at university level, much of the teacher training of women is in fact a training for the role as instructor in home economics and similar subjects. It would be foolish to deny the importance in developing countries of more enlightened methods of cooking, more hygienic methods of child care, and so forth, nevertheless there is a danger that the striving towards making more efficient housewives will make us forget or condone the utterly feeble efforts to improve women's professional efficiency outside the secluded professions of teaching and nursing.

Some developing countries in addition to this domestic training have programmes for training women in crafts and home industries. Where women live in seclusion, to teach them a craft which they can do at home may be the only possible first step towards bringing them into the labour market. Thus, training in hand spinning in India, and in embroidery in Tunisia, may help towards the eventual abandonment of seclusion.[26] But the effect of offering this kind of training to women who do not live in seclusion may be to drag them into low-productivity jobs rather than to help them to find more productive and remunerative employment. Indeed, the training in crafts and home industries is frequently offered to women as a sort of compensation for the refusal to give them jobs in the modern sector and as a deliberate method of reducing the number of women competing with men for employment in the modern sector. Sometimes women insist on being taught sewing and similar crafts so as to avoid wage labour in agriculture or manufacturing industries.[27]

Apart from the training for low-productivity activities in crafts and subsistence production, few facilities for women's training are offered in developing countries.[28] There are many commercial schools in Latin America, and a few in Asia and Africa. In the field of industrial training, a fair number of courses for girls are given in Latin America, although they lead mainly to work with rather limited employment prospects.[29] Some schools of this kind exist in Asia and practically none in Africa.* Finally, there are a few agricultural courses in some African countries, but none apparently in other continents.

This is a striking omission considering the prominent role women play in the agricultural labour force of many developing countries. Although the school curriculum for boys does include theoretical and practical courses in modern farming principles

---

* In South Africa, women are excluded from the technical and vocational schools open to Africans.[30]

and techniques in some countries, this kind of instruction, which is meant to counteract the school leavers' flight from agriculture, is not given to the girls. Instead, they have courses in nutrition, cooking, child care and other domestic subjects.[31] Similarly, it is usual in adult training programmes to teach agricultural subjects only to men, and domestic subjects to the women.

Sometimes men come out in direct opposition to the training of women in agriculture. A report on the agricultural training of women in the Central African Republic mentions that 'the men, particularly the young ones, seem to fear that training of women would be synonymous with emancipation of women and lead either to immorality or to a too great independence of the family authority.[32] Similarly, men's dread of women acquiring skills is apparent in a report about community development in Tanzania: 'It was considered important not to isolate the women too much for the purpose of learning new skills, and so create the possible impression of imparting to them an exclusive mystique. Otherwise, as past experience in rural areas had shown, husbands sometimes grew suspicious that the fearful prospect of female emancipation was being subtly introduced in order to undermine their traditional masculine authority.'[33]

The community development programmes and extension services vary widely in different countries in their emphasis or lack of emphasis on agricultural training for women. The Indian community development programme for women is designed to obtain their participation in social service activities, but so far the problem of their agricultural training does not seem to have been considered.[34] In many African countries, on the other hand, this problem is under discussion, and in some cases community development organizations or extension services are already teaching improved agricultural methods to women.*[35]

* In some African countries, the admission of women to intermediate and higher-level agricultural training is being facilitated to some extent. In colonial times, there were women instructors in East Africa.[36] More recently, the Agricultural Education Commission of Kenya suggested that by 1980 20 per cent of places in intermediate-level agricultural training institutions would have to be reserved for women. At present, none of these institutions can accommodate women, and qualified woman applicants are turned down.[37] Likewise, in Malawi qualified girls are refused admission to the Agricultural College because there is no special accommodation for them. But in this country there seems to be no intention to create accommodation for girls at a later stage (as in Kenya) for

A NEW PATTERN FOR THE FUTURE?

It is difficult to foresee what will come out of the efforts to provide a future for educated women in the agricultural sector. In most countries, rural women will no doubt be concerned primarily with industries processing food and other materials of agricultural origin, with rural trade and the increasing number of rural service occupations which will appear as the villages begin to modernize. It was shown in Chapter 10 that it is desirable to provide opportunities for non-agricultural work to women living in rural areas, because women migrants with some experience of non-agricultural work in their home village tend to adapt more easily to working in the towns to which they migrate. However, the primary motive of providing work for rural women —in agriculture or in non-agricultural occupations—is of course to obtain their immediate help in increasing production in the rural areas and to make sure that an improvement in men's earning power in agriculture is not offset, to an appreciable extent, by a decline in women's work participation and hence in women's earning power.

Another reason for providing attractive work opportunities for educated rural girls—in agriculture or in non-agricultural village activities—is that if such opportunities do not exist, enterprising young girls will migrate to town before marrying or will press their husbands to migrate. Therefore a policy designed to encourage the young male villager to help in the task of modernizing the rural scene has a better chance of success if it includes possibilities for the educated girl to find attractive employment in the village.

It is often pointed out that with the education of rural youth, boys as well as girls, comes the risk that the young people will refuse to stay on in the village, under the customary authority of village elders. This is a very real risk, but one which has to be

'it was felt that to appoint women agricultural officers when there was a high rate of unemployment among men, would be unpopular'.[38] In Egypt, women are accepted for high-level training in agriculture, but women who had passed their civil service examination were turned down when they applied for employment with the Ministry of Agriculture because 'the nature of the work available was not suitable for women'. As a result, the government had to call on employers not to refuse employment to women who had passed the civil service examinations.[39]

accepted, for without education in rural areas there can be no economic uplift. Conflict seems unavoidable between the traditional village community and the young generation of both sexes. The literate young people naturally want to assert some influence in the village and they tend to leave the village if their attempts are unsuccessful. In countries where it is easy for an enterprising village girl who runs away to a neighbouring town to find either a husband or a job, neglect in catering for rural girls can only jeopardize the attempts at rural uplift.

Another important factor is the advent of birth control. The spread of official propaganda for birth control cannot fail to have far-reaching effects in communities where the prestige of a woman was traditionally measured by the number of children she was able to produce. If the rearing of a numerous family is no longer to be considered as a virtue, profound changes in the educational system for girls become necessary. Both rural and urban girls must be given other ideals and other ways of asserting themselves, both in their own eyes and in relation to the male members of their community. One means of achieving this is to improve education and vocational training facilities for girls, and to encourage the girls to make use of the opportunities for careers both in rural modernization and in the modern urban sector.

In the past, because a young woman's ambition to have a career would normally conflict with the desire to rear a large family, public opinion in European countries and the United States was opposed to the idea of gainful employment for married women. Consequently, a rise in urban incomes usually reduced the proportion of married women who pursued activities other than those of a wife and mother. We shall probably not see a repeat of this pattern in the countries which become industrialized in the remaining decades of this century. As public propaganda for family limitation gradually becomes more widespread and persuasive, we shall expect to see married women in developing countries being encouraged to seek employment outside the home as a means of limiting the number of births.

Another major difference in the lot of women today and yesterday and the women of tomorrow is a result of the mechanization of much of their domestic work.

In the early days of European industrialization, a great deal of labour was required to cater for the domestic needs of every family, but now, with the advent of modern domestic equipment and processed food, women can look forward to caring for their households with a fraction of the hours of work previously needed. The effect of these technical changes is now becoming apparent in the employment trends for women in industrialized countries. There can be little doubt that before long similar trends will be seen in the urban sector of many developing countries. With fewer children and lighter domestic duties, the work pattern for married women in developing countries will probably be radically different from the one seen during earlier periods of industrialization when most married women stayed at home. It follows that in the future, when a large proportion of women may have jobs, it becomes an important task to devise new educational and training programmes, which can help to reduce the productivity gap between male and female labour, thus fitting women to their new way of life.

NOTES TO CHAPTER 12

1. Giri, 375.　　2. Wells, 102–3; Xydias, 288.　　3. UN., Comm. Status of Wom. 1968, 36.　　4. Evans-Pritchard, 54–5.　　5. Carr-Saunders, 513. 6. Lewis, W. A., 116.　7. Ehrenfels, 44.　8. Karve, 120–1; Sengupta, 225. 9. Fox, 356.　　10. Ward, 39.　　11. Becker, 58–62.　　12. Sengupta, 211. 13. Karve, 124.　　14. Sengupta, 283.　　15. Cormack, 34.　　16. Cormack, 126.　17. Friedan, 138ff.　18. Forget, 162.　19. Hanks, 447.　20. Mead 1958, 43.　21. Comhaire-Sylvain, 54; Baker, 77; Simons, 268–9.　22. CCTA, 123.　　23. Leblanc, 281.　　24. CCTA, 141; Kaberry, 146.　　25. ILO, *Afr. Conf. Report*, 14.　　26. Das, 42, de Moulety, 153.　　27. Jean, 41–2; Sengupta, 223.　　28. UN., Comm. Status of Wom. Res. Adv. of Wom., 23, 51–5. 29. ILO *Rev.* 1964, II, 172–3.　30. Simons, 275.　31. Boismenu, 12; Van Glinstra, 266.　32. Boismenu, 7.　33. Reeves, 67–8.　34. India Min. of L. 1964, 23.　35. UN., Comm. Status of Wom. Part. Comm. Dev. 1967, 55; de la Rivière, 9ff.; Kenya Agr. Education Comm. 33, 87–8. 36. Hailey, 894.　37. Kenya Agr. Education Comm., 71–2.　38. UN. ECA., 1967. Wom. E. Afr., 20.　　39. UN. ECA., Wom. N. Afr., 22.

Appendix—Tables 31–46

Table 31

SIZE AND OCCUPATIONAL DISTRIBUTION OF THE FEMALE LABOUR FORCE IN SIERRA LEONE, 1963

Occupation:	Women occupied in given group as percentage of all adult women in the country[a]			Percentage of women among:		
	Employees	Employers, own-account workers and family aids	Total	Employees	Employers, own-account workers and family aids	Total
1. Agriculture[b]		41·9	41·9	5	43	42
2. Industry and construction	0·1	0·8	0·9	2	15	9
3. Mining, transport			0·1	1	1	1
4. Trade	0·1	3·0	3·1	26	48	47
5. Clerical work	0·1		0·2	16	18	16
6. Administration				9		9
7. Professions	0·3	0·1	0·4	29	23	27
8. Private domestic services }	0·1			4	33	6
9. Other services			0·1		8	8
10. Unspecified[c]		0·3	0·3			
11. All economically active	0·9	46·2	47·1	6	39	36

a The number of adult women (i.e. women of 15 years and over) was 0·7 million or 51 per cent of all adults.
b Including animal husbandry, hunting, fishing and forestry.
c Including unemployed persons.

Table 32

SIZE AND OCCUPATIONAL DISTRIBUTION OF THE FEMALE LABOUR FORCE IN LIBERIA, 1962

Occupation:	Women occupied in given group as percentage of all adult women in the country[a]			Percentage of women among:		
	Employees	Employers, own-account workers and family aids	Total	Employees	Employers, own-account workers and family aids	Total
1. Agriculture[b]	0·3	41·7	42·0	4	46	43
2. Industry and construction	0·1	0·2	0·4	2	8	3
3. Mining, transport	0·1		0·1	2	6	3
4. Trade	0·1	1·1	1·2	13	40	35
5. Clerical work	0·2		0·2	13		13
6. Administration	0·1		0·1	9		9
7. Professions	0·5	0·1	0·6	27	26	27
8. Private domestic services ⎫ 9. Other services ⎭	0·2	0·1	0·3	7	49	13
10. Unspecified	0·1	0·1	0·2	7	31	11
11. All economically active	1·6	43·4	45·1	6	45	36

[a] The number of adult women (i.e. women of 15 years and over) was 0·3 million or 52 per cent of all adults.
[b] Including animal husbandry, hunting, fishing and forestry.

Table 33

SIZE AND OCCUPATIONAL DISTRIBUTION OF THE FEMALE LABOUR FORCE IN GHANA, 1960

Occupation:	Women occupied in given group as percentage of all adult women in the country[a]			Percentage of women among:		
	Employees	Employers, own-account workers and family aids	Total	Employees	Employers, own-account workers and family aids	Total
1. Agriculture[b]	0·4	30·9	31·3	6	40	37
2. Industry and construction	0·3	5·2	5·5	3	39	26
3. Mining, transport	0·1	0·1	0·2	3	5	4
4. Trade	0·2	14·8	15·0	24	83	80
5. Clerical work	0·2		0·2	7	7	7
6. Administration				3	3	3
7. Professions	0·5	0·1	0·6	19	21	20
8. Private domestic services ⎱ 9. Other services	0·3	0·6	0·9	15	60	29
10. Unspecified[c]		3·0	3·0		33	33
11. All economically active	2·0	54·6	56·6	7	45	38

[a] The number of adult women (i.e. women of 15 years and over) was 1·8 million or 49 per cent of all adults.
[b] Including animal husbandry, hunting, fishing and forestry.
[c] Including unemployed persons.

Table 34

SIZE AND OCCUPATIONAL DISTRIBUTION OF THE FEMALE LABOUR FORCE IN MAURITIUS, 1962

Occupation:	Women occupied in given group as percentage of all adult women in the country[a]			Percentage of women among:		
	Employees	Employers, own-account workers and family aids	Total	Employees	Employers, own-account workers and family aids	Total
1. Agriculture[b]	6·6	0·7	7·3	20	12	19
2. Industry and construction	1·1	0·5	1·6	4	9	5
3. Mining, transport	0·1		0·1	2		2
4. Trade	0·2	0·4	0·7	8	8	8
5. Clerical work	0·7		0·8	24	21	24
6. Administration				4		4
7. Professions	1·7	0·3	2·0	40	54	42
8. Private domestic services ⎫	5·2	0·3	5·5	57	28	54
9. Other services[c] ⎭						
10. Unspecified					5	5
11. All economically active	15·6	2·3	17·9	24	11	18

[a] The number of adult women (i.e. women of 15 years and over) was 0·2 million or 50 per cent of all adults.
[b] Including animal husbandry, hunting, fishing and forestry.
[c] Including military personnel.

Table 35

SIZE AND OCCUPATIONAL DISTRIBUTION OF THE FEMALE LABOUR FORCE IN MOROCCO, 1960

Occupation:	Women occupied in given group as percentage of all adult women in the country[a]			Percentage of women among:		
	Employees	Employers, own-account workers and family aids	Total	Employees	Employers, own-account workers and family aids	Total
1. Agriculture[b]	0·5	5·0	5·5	5	11	10
2. Industry and construction	0·8	1·7	2·4	15	25	20
3. Mining, transport				1		1
4. Trade	0·1	0·1	0·2	12	3	4
5. Clerical work	0·4		0·4	27	13	27
6. Administration				2	1	1
7. Professions	0·4		0·4	14	11	13
8. Private domestic services	1·8		1·8	86		86
9. Other services	0·2	0·1	0·3	5	10	7
10. Unspecified	0·3	0·1	0·4	8	1	4
11. All economically active	4·5	7·0	11·5	13	11	12

a The number of adult women (i.e. women of 15 years and over) was 3·3 million or 51 per cent of all adults.
b Including animal husbandry, hunting, fishing and forestry.

Table 36

SIZE AND OCCUPATIONAL DISTRIBUTION OF THE FEMALE LABOUR FORCE IN THE UNITED ARAB REPUBLIC, 1960

Occupation:	Women occupied in given group as percentage of all adult women in the country[a]			Percentage of women among:		
	Employees	Employers, own-account workers and family aids	Total	Employees	Employers, own-account workers and family aids	Total
1. Agriculture[b]	0·8	1·0	1·7	4	3	4
2. Industry and construction	0·3	0·2	0·5	2	7	4
3. Mining, transport				1		6
4. Trade		0·4	0·4	3	6	5
5. Clerical work } 6. Administration	0·2		0·2	5	2	22
7. Professions	0·6		0·6	23	5	53
8. Private domestic services	1·1		1·1	53		2
9. Other services	0·1		0·1	2	3	22
10. Unspecified[c]		0·4	0·5	6	27	6
11. All economically active	3·2	2·0	5·2	7	5	

[a] The number of adult women (i.e. women of 15 years and over) was 7·5 million or 51 per cent of all adults.
[b] Including animal husbandry, hunting, fishing and forestry, see note to Table 3.
[c] Including unemployed persons.

Table 37

SIZE AND OCCUPATIONAL DISTRIBUTION OF THE FEMALE LABOUR FORCE IN TURKEY, 1965

Occupation:	Women occupied in given group as percentage of all adult women in the country[a]			Percentage of women among:		
	Employees	Employers, own-account workers and family aids	Total	Employees	Employers, own-account workers and family aids	Total
1. Agriculture[b]	1·1	52·4	53·5	23	51	50
2. Industry and construction	0·8	0·8	1·6	10	18	13
3. Mining, transport			0·1	2	1	1
4. Trade		0·1	0·1	2	1	1
5. Clerical work ⎫	0·5		0·5	15	2	12
6. Administration ⎭						
7. Professions	0·6		0·7	22	12	21
8. Private domestic services	0·3		0·3	12	12	12
9. Other services			0·1	4	2	3
10. Unspecified	0·1		0·1	1	1	1
11. All economically active	3·4	53·4	56·8	10	46	38

a The number of adult women (i.e. women of 15 years and over) was 9·1 million or 50 per cent of all adults.
b Including animal husbandry, hunting, fishing and forestry.

Table 38

SIZE AND OCCUPATIONAL DISTRIBUTION OF THE FEMALE LABOUR FORCE IN SYRIA, 1960

Occupation:	Women occupied in given group as percentage of all adult women in the country[a]			Percentage of women among:		
	Employees	Employers, own-account workers and family aids	Total	Employees	Employers, own-account workers and family aids	Total
1. Agriculture[b]	1·2	2·0	3·2	8	8	8
2. Industry and construction	0·7	0·5	1·3	6	14	7
3. Mining, transport				1		1
4. Trade				1		1
5. Clerical work	0·2		0·2	6	1	6
6. Administration				7	2	4
7. Professions	0·5		0·5	29	14	27
8. Private domestic services	0·1		0·1	17		17
9. Other services	0·4		0·5	15	8	14
10. Unspecified	0·1		0·1	2	35	3
11. All economically active	3·2	2·7	5·9	7	9	7

[a] The number of adult women (i.e. women of 15 years and over) was 1·2 million or 50 per cent of all adults.
[b] Including animal husbandry, hunting, fishing and forestry.

Table 39

SIZE AND OCCUPATIONAL DISTRIBUTION OF THE FEMALE LABOUR FORCE IN IRAQ, 1957

Occupation:	Women occupied in given group as percentage of all adult women in the country[a]			Percentage of women among:		
	Employees	Employers, own-account workers and family aids	Total	Employees	Employers, own-account workers and family aids	Total
1. Agriculture[b]	0·2	0·7	0·9	2	2	2
2. Industry and construction	0·4	0·4	0·7	4	7	5
3. Mining, transport						
4. Trade		0·1	0·1	2	2	2
5. Clerical work				5	2	5
6. Administration	0·1		0·2	2	4	2
7. Professions	0·4	0·1	0·5	22	15	21
8. Private domestic services	0·4		0·4	49		49
9. Other services		0·1	0·1		7	2
10. Unspecified						
11. All economically active[c]	1·6	1·3	2·9	4	3	3

a The number of adult women (i.e. women of 15 years and over) was 1·8 million or 51 per cent of all adults.
b Including animal husbandry, hunting, fishing and forestry.
c Excluding persons with unknown occupation.

Table 40

SIZE AND OCCUPATIONAL DISTRIBUTION OF THE FEMALE LABOUR FORCE IN IRAN, 1956

Occupation:	Women occupied in given group as percentage of all adult women in the country[a]			Percentage of women among:		
	Employees	Employers, own-account workers and family aids	Total	Employees	Employers, own-account workers and family aids	Total
1. Agriculture[b]	0·7	2·2	2·9	4	5	5
2. Industry and construction	3·0	2·1	5·1	18	36	23
3. Mining, transport	0·1		0·1	2	1	2
4. Trade		0·1	0·1	3	1	2
5. Clerical work	0·1		0·1	5	1	4
6. Administration				3	3	3
7. Professions	0·3		0·3	23	9	19
8. Private domestic services ⎱						
9. Other services ⎰	2·0		2·0	27	3	24
10. Unspecified				1	1	1
11. All economically active	6·2	4·4	10·7	12	7	9

[a] The number of adult women (i.e. women of 15 years and over) was 5·4 million or 49 per cent of all adults.
[b] Including animal husbandry, hunting, fishing and forestry.

Table 41

SIZE AND OCCUPATIONAL DISTRIBUTION OF THE FEMALE LABOUR FORCE IN PAKISTAN, 1961

	Women occupied in given group as percentage of all adult women in the country[a]			Percentage of women among:		
Occupation:	Employees	Employers, own-account workers and family aids	Total	Employees	Employers, own-account workers and family aids	Total
1. Agriculture[b]	0·7	13·0	13·7	6	16	14
2. Industry and construction	0·1	1·1	1·2	2	12	9
3. Mining, transport						
4. Trade		0·1	0·1	1	2	2
5. Clerical work				1	1	1
6. Administration						
7. Professions	0·1	0·1	0·2	9	11	10
8. Private domestic services }	0·4	0·2	0·7	16	13	15
9. Other services						
10. Unspecified[c]		0·1	0·1	3	10	9
11. All economically active	1·4	14·6	16·0	5	14	12

[a] The number of adult women (i.e. women of 15 years and over) was 23·5 million or 47 per cent of all adults.
[b] Including animal husbandry, hunting, fishing and forestry.
[c] Including unemployed persons

Table 42

SIZE AND OCCUPATIONAL DISTRIBUTION OF THE FEMALE LABOUR FORCE IN INDIA, 1961

Occupation:	Women occupied in given group as percentage of all adult women in the country[a]			Percentage of women among:		
	Employees[b]	Employers,[b] own-account workers and family aids	Total	Employees[b]	Employers,[b] own-account workers and family aids	Total
1. Agriculture[c]	11·8	27·3	39·1	44	33	36
2. Industry and construction	0·6	3·3	3·9	12	35	27
3. Mining, transport	0·1		0·1	7	4	6
4. Trade		0·6	0·6	3	13	11
5. Clerical work	0·1		0·1	3		3
6. Administration				3		3
7. Professions	0·3	0·1	0·4	15	20	16
8. Private domestic services	0·4		0·4	36		36
9. Other services		0·7	0·7		26	21
10. Unspecified[d]	0·4	1·7	2·1	27	28	28
11. All economically active	13·8	33·8	47·5	31	32	32

[a] The number of adult women (i.e. women of 15 years and over) was 125·2 million or 48 per cent of all adults.
[b] The distribution between employees and others was done by estimate in some cases.
[c] Including animal husbandry, hunting, fishing and forestry.
[d] Most of the persons included in this group are casual workers in rural areas.

237

Table 43

SIZE AND OCCUPATIONAL DISTRIBUTION OF THE FEMALE LABOUR FORCE IN CEYLON, 1963

Occupation:	Women occupied in given group as percentage of all adult women in the country[a]			Percentage of women among:		
	Employees	Employers, own-account workers and family aids	Total	Employees	Employers, own-account workers and family aids	Total
1. Agriculture[b]	12·2	1·9	14·1	40	7	25
2. Industry and construction	2·0	1·0	3·0	11	27	14
3. Mining, transport	0·1		0·1	2		2
4. Trade	0·1	0·3	0·4	3	8	6
5. Clerical work	0·2		0·2	6	6	6
6. Administration				3	4	3
7. Professions	1·9		1·9	43	8	39
8. Private domestic services }						
9. Other services[c] }	1·9	0·2	2·1	26	14	24
10. Unspecified[d]		2·7	2·8	12	27	26
11. All economically active	18·4	6·2	24·7	26	13	21

[a] The number of adult women (i.e. women of 15 years and over) was 2·9 million or 47 per cent of all adults.
[b] Including animal husbandry, hunting, fishing and forestry.
[c] Including military personnel.
[d] Including unemployed persons.

Table 44

SIZE AND OCCUPATIONAL DISTRIBUTION OF THE FEMALE LABOUR FORCE IN URBAN AREAS OF BURMA, 1953[a]

Occupation:	Women occupied in given group as percentage of all adult women in urban areas[b]			Percentage of women among:		
	Employees	Employers, own-account workers and family aids	Total	Employees	Employers, own-account workers and family aids	Total
1. Agriculture[c]	0·8	1·8	2·6	20	22	22
2. Industry and construction	6·4	2·7	9·1	29	36	31
3. Mining, transport	0·1		0·1	1	1	1
4. Trade	0·4	13·5	13·9	12	52	47
5. Clerical work }	0·5	0·5	0·9	6	18	9
6. Administration }						
7. Professions	0·8	0·2	1·0	28	15	24
8. Private domestic services }	2·4	0·1	2·5	16	7	15
9. Other services }						
10. Unspecified	0·7	0·7	0·7	1	18	13
11. All economically active	11·4	19·4	30·8	19	37	27

[a] The data refer to 252 towns i.e. nearly all urban areas.
[b] The number of adult women (i.e. women of 15 years and over) was 1·0 million or 49 per cent of all adults.
[c] Including animal husbandry, hunting, fishing and forestry.

239

Table 45

SIZE AND OCCUPATIONAL DISTRIBUTION OF THE FEMALE LABOUR FORCE IN
THAILAND, 1960

Occupation:	Women occupied in given group as percentage of all adult women in the country[a]			Percentage of women among:		
	Employees	Employers, own-account workers and family aids	Total	Employees	Employers, own-account workers and family aids	Total
1. Agriculture[b]	1·6	75·3	76·9	35	51	51
2. Industry and construction	2·1	1·5	3·6	27	47	33
3. Mining, transport	0·1	0·1	0·2	4	13	8
4. Trade	0·2	5·3	5·4	22	58	56
5. Clerical work	0·3		0·3	13	36	14
6. Administration				5	15	9
7. Professions	0·7	0·1	0·8	34	32	34
8. Private domestic services	0·6		0·6	78		78
9. Other services	0·2	0·8	1·0	16	53	35
10. Unspecified		0·5	0·5	3	41	25
11. All economically active	5·8	83·5	89·3	27	51	48

[a] The number of adult women (i.e. women of 15 years and over) was 7·5 million or 50 per cent of all adults.
[b] Including animal husbandry, hunting, fishing and forestry.

Table 46

SIZE AND OCCUPATIONAL DISTRIBUTION OF THE FEMALE LABOUR FORCE IN CAMBODIA, 1962

Occupation:	Women occupied in given group as percentage of all adult women in the country[a]			Percentage of women among:		
	Employees	Employers, own-account workers and family aids	Total	Employees	Employers, own-account workers and family aids	Total
1. Agriculture[b]	0·6	55·5	56·1	24	46	46
2. Industry and construction	0·5	1·0	1·5	14	36	23
3. Mining, transport	0·1		0·1	2	5	4
4. Trade	0·1	3·7	3·8	16	49	46
5. Clerical work			0·1	6		6
6. Administration				5	21	12
7. Professions	0·4		0·4	9	21	9
8. Private domestic services }	1·7	0·1	1·8	27	25	26
9. Other services						
10. Unspecified	0·1	0·9	1·0	21	44	41
11. All economically active	3·4	61·3	64·7	18	46	42

[a] The number of adult women (i.e. women of 15 years and over) was 1·6 million or 50 per cent of all adults.
[b] Including animal husbandry, hunting, fishing and forestry.

Table 47

SIZE AND OCCUPATIONAL DISTRIBUTION OF THE FEMALE LABOUR FORCE IN MALAYA, 1957

Occupation:	Women occupied in given group as percentage of all adult women in the country[a]			Percentage of women among:		
	Employees	Employers, own-account workers and family aids	Total	Employees	Employers, own-account workers and family aids	Total
1. Agricultural[b]	11·8	11·6	23·5	39	29	33
2. Industry and construction	1·8	0·5	2·4	11	17	12
3. Mining, transport	0·2	0·1	0·3	6	9	6
4. Trade	0·1	0·9	1·1	3	14	10
5. Clerical work	0·3		0·3	7	4	7
6. Administration				3	2	2
7. Professions	1·0	0·1	1·1	29	24	28
8. Private domestic services	1·3		1·3	98		98
9. Other services	0·7	0·2	0·9	12	14	12
10. Unspecified[c]	0·1	0·4	0·5	5	17	11
11. All economically active	17·5	13·8	31·3	24	25	24

a The number of adult women (i.e. women of 15 years and over) was 3·0 million or 48 per cent of all adults.
b Including animal husbandry, hunting, fishing and forestry.
c Including military personnel and unemployed persons.

Table 48

SIZE AND OCCUPATIONAL DISTRIBUTION OF THE FEMALE LABOUR FORCE IN SINGAPORE, 1957

	Women occupied in given group as percentage of all adult women in the colony[a]			Percentage of women among:		
Occupation:	Employees	Employers, own-account workers and family aids	Total	Employees	Employers, own-account workers and family aids	Total
1. Agriculture[b]	0·3	2·3	2·6	13	33	27
2. Industry and construction	4·6	0·9	5·5	14	20	14
3. Mining, transport	0·2		0·2	2		2
4. Trade	0·4	1·9	2·2	5	13	10
5. Clerical work	1·3		1·3	10		10
6. Administration	0·1		0·1	4	3	4
7. Professions	2·0	0·1	2·2	38	23	37
8. Private domestic services } 9. Other services }	7·3	0·6	7·9	44	27	42
10. Unspecified[c]		0·6	0·6	18	27	13
11. All economically active	16·2	6·4	22·5	18	19	18

a The number of adult women (i.e. women of 15 years and over) was 0·4 million or 46 per cent of all adults.
b Including animal husbandry, hunting, fishing and forestry.
c Including military personnel and unemployed persons.

Table 49

SIZE AND OCCUPATIONAL DISTRIBUTION OF THE FEMALE LABOUR FORCE IN PHILIPPINES, 1960

Occupation:	Women occupied in given group as percentage of all adult women in the country[a]			Percentage of women among:		
	Employees	Employers, own-account workers and family aids	Total	Employees	Employers, own-account workers and family aids	Total
1. Agriculture[b]	0·9	9·6	10·5	12	15	15
2. Industry and construction	1·6	4·5	6·0	20	68	42
3. Mining, transport			0·1	2	2	2
4. Trade	0·7	2·7	3·4	41	54	51
5. Clerical work	0·5	0·6	0·6	23	43	23
6. Administration		0·1	0·1	7	28	14
7. Professions	1·5	0·1	1·6	53	33	51
8. Private domestic services } 9. Other services	4·0	0·4	4·4	67	62	66
10. Unspecified[c]		3·2	3·2	2	39	36
11. All economically active	9·3	20·5	29·8	29	24	26

[a] The number of adult women (i.e. women of 15 years and over) was 7·3 million or 50 per cent of all adults.
[b] Including animal husbandry, hunting, fishing and forestry. See note to Table 3.
[c] Including unemployed persons.

Table 50

SIZE AND OCCUPATIONAL DISTRIBUTION OF THE FEMALE LABOUR FORCE IN HONG KONG, 1966

Occupation:	Women occupied in given group as percentage of all adult women in the colony[a]			Percentage of women among:		
	Employees	Employers, own-account workers and family aids	Total	Employees	Employers, own-account workers and family aids	Total
1. Agriculture[b]	0·3	2·3	2·7	25	43	39
2. Industry and construction	20·3	2·5	22·8	41	27	39
3. Mining, transport	0·1	0·2	0·3	2	25	5
4. Trade	3·0	0·5	3·5	18	57	21
5. Clerical work						
6. Administration	0·1	0·4	0·5	6	8	7
7. Professions	2·7	0·4	3·1	48	40	47
8. Private domestic services	7·5	0·3	7·8	37	26	37
9. Other services						
10. Unspecified[c]	0·9	1·6	2·5	27	34	32
11. All economically active	34·9	8·3	43·2	34	29	33

[a] The number of adult women (i.e. women of 15 years and over) was 1·1 million or 50 per cent of all adults.
[b] Including animal husbandry, hunting, fishing and forestry.
[c] Including military personnel and unemployed persons.

Table 51

SIZE AND OCCUPATIONAL DISTRIBUTION OF THE FEMALE LABOUR FORCE IN THE REPUBLIC OF KOREA, 1955

Occupation:	Women occupied in given group as percentage of all adult women in the country[a]			Percentage of women among:		
	Employees	Employers, own-account workers and family aids	Total	Employees	Employers, own-account workers and family aids	Total
1. Agriculture[b]	0·3	44·6	44·9	10	46	45
2. Industry and construction	0·3	0·9	1·3	11	15	13
3. Mining, transport				2	3	3
4. Trade	0·1	1·6	1·6	15	30	29
5. Clerical work	0·2		0·2	5	12	5
6. Administration				1	8	3
7. Professions	0·2	0·1	0·3	13	16	14
8. Private domestic services ⎫						
9. Other services ⎭	1·1	0·2	1·3	49	47	48
10. Unspecified						
11. All economically active	2·9	47·4	49·6	14	43	40

a The number of adult women (i.e. women of 15 years and over) was 6·5 million or 51 per cent of all adults.
b Including animal husbandry, hunting, fishing and forestry.

Table 52

SIZE AND OCCUPATIONAL DISTRIBUTION OF THE FEMALE LABOUR FORCE IN HONDURAS, 1961

Occupation:	Women occupied in given group as percentage of all adult women in the country[a]			Percentage of women among:		
	Employees	Employers, own-account workers and family aids	Total	Employees	Employers, own-account workers and family aids	Total
1. Agriculture[b]	0·1	0·4	0·6	6	1	1
2. Industry and construction	0·7	1·8	2·5	9	46	22
3. Mining, transport						
4. Trade	0·5	1·1	1·6	37	35	36
5. Clerical work	0·8		0·8	33	45	33
6. Administration			0·1	8	21	11
7. Professions	1·6		1·6	61	19	57
8. Private domestic services ⎫	6·0	0·4	6·4	73	64	72
9. Other services ⎭						
10. Unspecified[c]		1·0	1·0	2	19	16
11. All economically active	9·8	4·8	14·6	22	7	13

[a] The number of adult women (i.e. women of 15 years and over) was 0·5 million or 51 per cent of all adults.
[b] Including animal husbandry, hunting, fishing and forestry.
[c] Including unemployed persons.

Table 53

SIZE AND OCCUPATIONAL DISTRIBUTION OF THE FEMALE LABOUR FORCE IN EL SALVADORE, 1961

Occupation:	Women occupied in given group as percentage of all adult women in the country[a]			Percentage of women among		
	Employees	Employers, own-account workers and family aids	Total	Employees	Employers, own-account workers and family aids	Total
1. Agriculture[b]	1·8	0·2	2·0	4	1	3
2. Industry and construction	2·3	2·4	4·7	16	48	24
3. Mining, transport						
4. Trade	0·7	2·4	3·1	47	57	54
5. Clerical work	0·9		1·0	32	58	33
6. Administration	0·2		0·2	17	15	17
7. Professions	1·4	0·1	1·5	57	24	52
8. Private domestic services	4·6		4·6	97		97
9. Other services	2·4	0·3	2·7	57	61	57
10. Unspecified	0·1	0,1	0·2	9	15	11
11. All economically active	14·3	5·6	20·0	19	16	18

[a] The number of adult women (i.e. women of 15 years and over) was 0·7 million or 52 per cent of all adults.
[b] Including animal husbandry, hunting, fishing and forestry.

Table 54

SIZE AND OCCUPATIONAL DISTRIBUTION OF THE FEMALE LABOUR FORCE IN NICARAGUA, 1963

Occupation:	Women occupied in given group as percentage of all adult women in the country[a]			Percentage of women among:		
	Employees	Employers, own-account workers and family aids	Total	Employees	Employers, own-account workers and family aids	Total
1. Agriculture[b]	1·1	1·8	2·9	3	5	4
2. Industry and construction	1·4	2·9	4·3	14	48	26
3. Mining, transport						
4. Trade	0·7	3·4	4·1	54	61	59
5. Clerical work	1·1		1·1	25	44	25
6. Administration				7	14	11
7. Professions	1·3	0·2	1·6	61	31	53
8. Private domestic services ⎫	8·2	0·8	9·0	73	64	72
9. Other services ⎭						
10. Unspecified	0·1	0·1	0·1	10	59	32
11. All economically active	13·9	9·2	23·1	21	18	20

a The number of adult women (i.e. women of 15 years and over) was 0·4 million or 52 per cent of all adults.
b Including animal husbandry, hunting, fishing and forestry.

Table 55

SIZE AND OCCUPATIONAL DISTRIBUTION OF THE FEMALE LABOUR FORCE IN COSTA RICA, 1963

	Women occupied in given group as percentage of all adult women in the country[a]			Percentage of women among:		
Occupation:	Employees	Employers, own-account workers and family aids	Total	Employees	Employers, own-account workers and family aids	Total
1. Agriculture[b]	0·7	0·2	0·9	2	1	2
2. Industry and construction	1·9	1·0	2·9	13	27	16
3. Mining, transport						
4. Trade	1·1	0·5	1·6	25	12	19
5. Clerical work	1·6		1·6	27	23	27
6. Administration	0·1	0·1	0·2	6	16	11
7. Professions	3·1	0·1	3·3	59	26	56
8. Private domestic services	5·9		5·9	100		100
9. Other services	1·3	0·2	1·5	31	37	31
10. Unspecified	0·3	0·2	0·4	11	6	8
11. All economically active	15·9	2·3	18·2	22	6	16

a The number of adult women (i.e. women of 15 years and over) was 0·4 million or 51 per cent of all adults.
b Including animal husbandry, hunting, fishing and forestry.

Table 56

SIZE AND OCCUPATIONAL DISTRIBUTION OF THE FEMALE LABOUR FORCE IN PANAMA, 1960

Occupation:	Women occupied in given group as percentage of all adult women in the country[a]			Percentage of women among:		
	Employees	Employers, own-account workers and family aids	Total	Employees	Employers, own-account workers and family aids	Total
1. Agriculture[b]	0·1	1·4	1·5	2	3	3
2. Industry and construction	1·1	1·4	2·5	9	21	14
3. Mining, transport						
4. Trade	1·1	1·0	2·1	36	29	32
5. Clerical work }	3·5	0·7	4·2	43	31	41
6. Administration }						
7. Professions	3·0	0·3	3·2	60	34	56
8. Private domestic services }	7·6	2·5	10·2	65	72	67
9. Other services }						
10. Unspecified[c]	0·2	1·6	1·8	19	40	36
11. All economically active	16·6	8·9	25·5	33	13	21

a The number of adult women (i.e. women of 15 years and over) was 0·3 million or 49 per cent of all adults.
b Including animal husbandry, hunting, fishing and forestry.
c Including military personnel and unemployed persons.

Table 57

SIZE AND OCCUPATIONAL DISTRIBUTION OF THE FEMALE LABOUR FORCE IN COLUMBIA, 1964

Occupation:	Women occupied in given group as percentage of all adult women in the country[a]			Percentage of women among:		
	Employees	Employers, own-account workers and family aids	Total	Employees	Employers, own-account workers and family aids	Total
1. Agriculture[b]	0·6	1·6	2·2	3	6	4
2. Industry and construction	1·5	2·2	3·7	13	33	20
3. Mining, transport		0·2	0·3	2	17	7
4. Trade	0·7	0·8	1·5	31	22	26
5. Clerical work	1·7		1·7	36	20	36
6. Administration	0·2	0·3	0·4	12	17	15
7. Professions	1·8	0·2	2·0	54	19	47
8. Private domestic services	7·1		7·1	94		94
9. Other services	1·1	0·6	1·7	35	55	40
10. Unspecified[c]	0·4	0·2	0·6	16	18	16
11. All economically active	15·2	6·1	21·3	25	13	20

[a] The number of adult women (i.e. women of 15 years and over) was 4·8 million or 51 per cent of all adults.
[b] Including animal husbandry, hunting, fishing and forestry. See note to Table 3.
[c] Including military personnel.

Table 58

SIZE AND OCCUPATIONAL DISTRIBUTION OF THE FEMALE LABOUR FORCE IN ECUADOR, 1962

Occupation:	Women occupied in given group as percentage of all adult women in the country[a]			Percentage of women among:		
	Employees	Employers, own-account workers and family aids	Total	Employees	Employers, own-account workers and family aids	Total
1. Agriculture[b]	1·1	2·1	3·2	4	5	5
2. Industry and construction	1·2	4·2	5·3	10	39	24
3. Mining, transport						
4. Trade	0·4	1·2	1·6	29	22	23
5. Clerical work	1·0		1·1	28	52	28
6. Administration				6	8	7
7. Professions	1·4	0·3	1·8	51	35	47
8. Private domestic services						
9. Other services	5·1	0·4	5·6	72	41	68
10. Unspecified	0·1	0·2	0·3	5	9	8
11. All economically active	10·3	8·5	18·8	19	14	16

[a] The number of adult women (i.e. women of 15 years and over) was 1·3 million or 51 per cent of all adults.
[b] Including animal husbandry, hunting, fishing and forestry.

253

Table 59

SIZE AND OCCUPATIONAL DISTRIBUTION OF THE FEMALE LABOUR FORCE IN CHILE, 1960

Occupation:	Women occupied in given group as percentage of all adult women in the country[a]			Percentage of women among:		
	Employees	Employers, own-account workers and family aids	Total	Employees	Employers, own-account workers and family aids	Total
1. Agriculture[b]	0·5	0·6	1·0	2	6	4
2. Industry and construction	2·8	1·7	4·5	12	35	16
3. Mining, transport					1	
4. Trade	0·7	1·3	2·0	30	26	27
5. Clerical work	2·1	0·1	2·1	30	32	30
6. Administration		0·3	0·3	7	20	17
7. Professions	2·4	0·2	2·5	53	25	50
8. Private domestic services	7·9		7·9	92		92
9. Other services	1·3	0·7	2·0	29	71	36
10. Unspecified[c]		0·8	0·9	2	20	13
11. All economically active	17·6	5·6	23·2	23	21	22

[a] The number of adult women (i.e. women of 15 years and over) was 2·3 million or 52 per cent of all adults.
[b] Including animal husbandry, hunting, fishing and forestry.
[c] Including military personnel.

Table 60

SIZE AND OCCUPATIONAL DISTRIBUTION OF THE FEMALE LABOUR FORCE IN VENEZUELA, 1961

Occupation:	Women occupied in given group as percentage of all adult women in the country[a]			Percentage of women among:		
	Employees	Employers, own-account workers and family aids	Total	Employees	Employers, own-account workers and family aids	Total
1. Agriculture[b]	0·3	0·9	1·3	3	4	3
2. Industry and construction	1·5	2·0	3·5	9	34	15
3. Mining, transport	0·1		0·1	2	1	2
4. Trade	0·5	0·5	1·0	12	7	9
5. Clerical work	2·6		2·6	34	18	34
6. Administration		0·1	0·2	5	15	11
7. Professions	2·9	0·2	3·2	53	30	50
8. Private domestic services	5·2		5·2	94		94
9. Other services[c]	1·9	1·2	3·1	32	74	42
10. Unspecified[d]	0·4	0·4	0·7	7	17	10
11. All economically active	15·4	5·5	21·0	22	12	18

[a] The number of adult women (i.e. women of 15 years and over) was 2·0 million or 49 per cent of all adults.
[b] Including animal husbandry, hunting, fishing and forestry.
[c] Including military personnel.
[d] Including unemployed persons.

Table 61

SIZE AND OCCUPATIONAL DISTRIBUTION OF THE FEMALE LABOUR FORCE IN CUBA, 1953

Occupation:	Women occupied in given group as percentage of all adult women in the country[a]			Percentage of women among:		
	Employees	Employers, own-account workers and family aids	Total	Employees	Employers, own-account workers and family aids	Total
1. Agriculture[b]	0·5	0·2	0·7	2	1	1
2. Industry and construction	2·8	0·6	3·4	14	15	14
3. Mining, transport	0·1		0·1	1	1	1
4. Trade	0·6		0·6	11	5	10
5. Clerical work	1·9	0·1	2·0	26	14	25
6. Administration	0·1	0·2	0·3	9	4	5
7. Professions	2·0	0·3	2·3	54	29	48
8. Private domestic services } 9. Other services	4·6	0·3	4·9	58	30	55
10. Unspecified				2	1	2
11. All economically active	12·5	1·7	14·2	16	6	13

a The number of adult women (i.e. women of 15 years and over) was 1·8 million or 48 per cent of all adults.
b Including animal husbandry, hunting, fishing and forestry.

Table 62

SIZE AND OCCUPATIONAL DISTRIBUTION OF THE FEMALE LABOUR FORCE IN JAMAICA, 1960

	Women occupied in given group as percentage of all adult women in the country[a]			Percentage of women among:		
Occupation:	Employees	Employers, own-account workers and family aids	Total	Employees	Employers, own-account workers and family aids	Total
1. Agriculture[b]	3·3	4·4	7·6	17	16	17
2. Industry and construction	3·3	5·9	9·2	16	54	29
3. Mining, transport	0·4		0·4	14	3	13
4. Trade	1·3	4·3	5·6	48	73	65
5. Clerical work	2·5	0·1	2·5	49	75	50
6. Administration	0·1	0·4	0·4	9	21	18
7. Professions	2·3	0·2	2·4	66	49	64
8. Private domestic services ⎫ 9. Other services ⎭	14·2	0·9	15·1	86	82	86
10. Unspecified		6·7	6·7	41	61	61
11. All economically active	27·3	22·7	50·0	39	39	39

[a] The number of adult women (i.e. women of 15 years and over) was 0·5 million or 53 per cent of all adults.
[b] Including animal husbandry, hunting, fishing and forestry.

Table 63

SIZE AND OCCUPATIONAL DISTRIBUTION OF THE FEMALE LABOUR FORCE IN THE DOMINICAN REPUBLIC, 1960

Occupation:	Women occupied in given group as percentage of all adult women in the country[a]			Percentage of women among:		
	Employees	Employers, own-account workers and family aids	Total	Employees	Employers, own-account workers and family aids	Total
1. Agriculture[b]	0·3	0·8	1·1	2	2	2
2. Industry and construction	0·8	0·8	1·6	9	23	13
3. Mining, transport						
4. Trade	0·2	0·9	1·1	14	23	20
5. Clerical work	0·9		0·9	27	34	27
6. Administration				6	20	12
7. Professions	1·5	0·1	1·5	58	19	53
8. Private domestic services }	4·2	0·4	4·6	75	48	72
9. Other services						
10. Unspecified	0·1		0·1	2	8	2
11. All economically active	8·0	3·0	11·0	18	5	11

[a] The number of adult women (i.e. women of 15 years and over) was 0·8 million or 50 per cent of all adults.
[b] Including animal husbandry, hunting, fishing and forestry.

Table 64

SIZE AND OCCUPATIONAL DISTRIBUTION OF THE FEMALE LABOUR FORCE IN PUERTO RICO, 1960

Occupation:	Women occupied in given group as percentage of all adult women in the country[a]			Percentage of women among:		
	Employees	Employers, own-account workers and family aids	Total	Employees	Employers, own-account workers and family aids	Total
1. Agriculture[b]	0·2	0·1	0·3	1	3	2
2. Industry and construction	5·0	1·0	6·0	24	26	25
3. Mining, transport	0·1		0·1	3		2
4. Trade	0·7	0·2	0·9	19	15	18
5. Clerical work }	3·2	0·5	3·8	39	16	32
6. Administration	3·1	0·2	3·2	52	28	50
7. Professions	2·5		2·5	94		94
8. Private domestic services	1·5	0·6	2·2	31	51	35
9. Other services	0·5	0·5	1·0	51	32	40
10. Unspecified						
11. All economically active	16·8	3·2	20·0	26	19	24

a The number of adult women (i.e. women of 15 years and over) was 0·7 million or 51 per cent of all adults.
b Including animal husbandry, hunting, fishing and forestry.

Notes to Tables and Figures

General Notes

Where no other source for the figures are given in the notes below, the figures refer to population censuses or manpower surveys and are taken either directly from the national data or from tables in the Demographic Yearbook of the United Nations, or from the Yearbook or Labour Statistics, of the International Labour Office.

The occupational grouping is that of the international standard classification by occupations, except for columns 3–5 in Table 9, which refer to the international standard classification by industry.

The information refers to the most recent year available, in most cases 1960 or a later year (see Tables 31–64). For lack of more up to date information figures from earlier years were inserted for the following countries: Nigeria (1953), Mozambique (1950), Sudan (1955–6), Algeria (1954), Tunisia (1956), Iraq (1957), Iran (1956), Burma (1953), Malaya, (1957), Singapore (1957), Taiwan (1956), Cuba (1953). For some countries e.g. Korea, the information about status (employee, own-account worker and family aids) refers to another year than the information about total labour force.

The industrialized countries for which information is included in Figures 6, 10, 11 and 13 are: United States (1960), Canada (1961), France (1962), Belgium (1961), Denmark (1960), Norway (1960), Sweden (1960), Japan (1965), New Zealand (1961).

Table 1. Senegal, Boutillier 1962, 107–10, sample of thirty families in Podor and Boghé districts, 1957–8. *Gambia: Sample A and B*, Haswell, 23, 88, samples of 324 and 361 persons in Genieri, 1949 and 1962. *Dahomey:* Guillard 1965, Annex II, 41, sample of twelve families in three months in Ouémé, 1960–1. *Nigeria:* Galetti 399, 663–5, 668–70, sample of 718 persons in Yoruba region, 1950–1. *Cameroon:* Guillard 1958, 423, sample of twenty-nine persons in Toupouri. *Central African Republic: Sample A and B*, Georges, 12, 44, 52, sample of sixty persons in Pouyamba and Madomale, 1959–60. *Sample C*, Guet, 71, 73, sample of twenty-eight persons in Dario, 1960. *Congo:* (Brazzaville), Vennetier, 168, sample of thirty-seven persons in one week in Northern district, 1960–1. *Uganda: Sample A*, Winter, 29–30, sample of ninety-nine persons in Bwamba, 1951–2. *Sample B*, Pudsey, 7, sample of 107 persons in Toro, 1958–9. *Sample C–F*, Katarikawe, 2, 8–13, samples of fifty-nine families in Kiga resettlement schemes, 1965–6. *Sample G*,

Forbes-Watt, 4, sample of fifty-two adults and thirty-three children in Lango district, 1963–4. *Kenya:* Wills, Time Allocation, 17, sample of twenty-five women in Embu district, 1966–7.

Table 2. Western India: Sample A, Dandekar, 82–9, sample of 2,379 households in the old Bombay Deccan, 1949–50. *Sample B and C*, Farm Survey Bombay, 14, 87, 117, 344–50, sample of 158 farms in Ahmednagar and Nazik districts (1956–7). *Central India: Sample A and B*, Farm Survey Madhya Pradesh, 126–7, 143–4, 149, 152, sample of 160 farms in Akola and Amraoti districts, 1956–7. *Southern India:* Farm Survey Madras 16–7, 39–43, sample of 199 farms in Salem and Coimbatore districts, 1956–7. *Delhi territory:* Chaudhuri 647, sample of twenty-seven families in village close to Delhi. *Malaya: Sample A and B*, Wharton, 5–6, sample of fifty families in Province Wellesley in 1962–3. *Philippines:* Survey of Households, 25, a representative sample of 5,123 households, October 1960. *China:* Buck, 290–3, sample of 15,316 farms, 1929–33.

Table 3. See general note.

Table 4. Senegal: Sample A and B, UN. ECA. Polygamy, 9–10, 70,000 persons in Dakar in 1955 and 1960. *Sample C*, Boutillier, 1962, 31, 33; 1,265 persons in the Valley of Senegal, 1957–8. *Sierra Leone:* Little 1948, 9–10n, 842 households in Mende Country, 1937. *Ivory Coast:* Boutillier 1960, 45, sample of 3,764 persons, 1955–6. *Nigeria: Sample A*, Galetti, 71–2; 776 families in the Yoruba region, 1950–1. *Sample B*, Mortimore, 679, sample of 5,103 persons in Kano district, 1964. *Cameroon:* Gouellain, 260, population in New-Bell, Douala, 1956. *Congo: Sample A and B*, Balandier 1955, 136. Brazzaville and Delisie, 1952. *South Africa:* Reynders 260, sample of 1,180 households in Bantu areas, 1950–1. *Uganda: Sample A*, Winter, 23, sample of seventy-one families in Bwamba, 1951. *Sample B*, Katarikawe, 8, sample of fifty-nine families in Kiga resettlement schemes, 1965–6.

Table 5. Galetti 77, sample of 144 women in seventy-three families in Yoruba region, 1951–2.

Table 6. UN. ECA. Polygamy, Annex, I, 7. Original source I.F.A.N. Institute, Dakar, Senegal.

Table 7. Tanner, 14–20, sample of 960 plots of land in three villages in Tanzania coastal area.

Tables 8–10. See general note.

Table 11. India Min. of Food, Madhya Pradesh, 143–4, sample of 160 farms in 1956–7.

Table 12. Thirteen Indian States, India Min. of Labour 1960, 117–19, *Sixteen villages in Uttar Pradesh*, India Min. of Food, Uttar Pradesh, 124.

Table 13–20. See general note.

Table 21. ILO *Review* 1959, Vol. II, 480.

Table 22. See general note.

Table 23. ILO *Review* 1958, Vol. II, 30 and 35.

Table 24. Kenya: Ray, 210–13. *South Africa:* population census 1960.

Table 25. Tables 23 and 24.

Table 26. Reynders, 252–3, survey of 1,180 households in Bantu areas, 1950–1.

Table 27. Dahomey: Guillard 1965, Annex II, 41, twelve families in Fanvi, three months in 1960–1. *Nigeria:* Galetti, 663–4, sample of 187 families in Yoruba region, 1950–1. *Central African Republic: Samples A and B*, Georges, 17, 19, 44, 52, sample of sixty persons in Pouyamba and Madomale, 1959–60. *Sample C*, Guet, 71, 73, sample of twenty-eight persons in Dario, 1960. *Uganda:* Winter, 29–32, sample of ninety-nine persons in Bwamba, 7 weeks in 1951–2. Domestic work estimate. *Kenya:* Wills, Household Sit., 3, sample of thirty-three women in Embu district, 1966–7.

Table 28. Tables 31–64.

Table 29. See general note.

Table 30. Dahomey: Guillard 1965, Annex II, 41, twelve families in Fanvi, three months in 1960–1. *Nigeria:* Galetti, 663–4, sample of 187 families in Yoruba region, 1950–1. *Cameroon:* Guillard 1958, 423, sample of twenty-nine persons, Toupouri. *Central African Republic: Sample A and B*, Georges, 17, 19, 44, 52, sample of sixty persons in Pouyamba and Madomale, 1959–60. *Sample C*, Guet, 71, 73, sample of twenty-eight persons in Dario, 1960. *Uganda:* Winter, 32, sample of ninety-nine persons in Bwamba, 1951–2. Domestic work by estimate. *Kenya:* Wills household sit., 3, sample of thirty-three women in Embu district, 1966–7. *India:* Chaudhuri, 647, sample of twenty-seven families in village close to Delhi. *Philippines:* Diaz, 13–15, 40–2, 69–71, sample of three households in Laguna Province, four to six weeks in 1960.

Tables 31–64. See general note.

Figure 1. Baumann, 303.

Figure 2. Left: Table 3. Right: Sharma, 259–61.

Figure 3. Mitchel, *Soc. Backgr.*, 80.

Figure 4. Table 13 supplemented by estimates.

Figure 5. Tables 31–64.

Figure 6. Table 28 and basic material for Tables 31–64.

Figure 7. Tables 31–64 supplemented by estimates.

Figure 8. Table 16.

Figure 9. Left: Tables 17 and 19. Right: Tables 17 and 18.

Figure 10. Table 18 and basic material for Tables 31–64.

Figure 11. Tables 18 and 19.

Figure 13. Table 28 and basic material to Tables 31–64.

Figure 14. Table 28 supplemented by estimates.

Figure 15. Table 28.

List of Works Cited

Albert, Ethel M., 'La Femme en Urundi', in Paulme, Denise (ed.) *Femmes d'Afrique Noire*, Paris 1960.

Andrus, J. Russel, *Burmese Economic Life*, Stanford 1948.

Appadorai, A., *The Status of Women in South Asia*, Bombay 1954.

Arnaldez, Roger, 'Le Coran et L'emancipation de la Femme', in Mury, Gilbert (ed.) *La Femme à la Recherche d'elle-même*, Paris 1966.

Aziz, U. A. *Survey of Five Villages in Nyalas*, Department of Economics, University of Malaya, Singapore 1957, processed.

Baeck, L., 'An Expenditure Study of the Congolese Evolués of Leopold-ville', Belgian Congo, in Southall, A. W. (ed.), *Social Change in modern Africa*, London 1961.

Baker, Tanya, 'Report on Nigeria', in International Institute of Differing Civilizations, *Women's Role in the Development of Tropical and Sub-Tropical Countries*, Brussels 1959.

Balandier, Georges, *Sociologie des Brazzavilles Noires*, Paris 1955.

Bastide, Roger, Les Amériques Noires, Paris 1967.

Bauer, P. T., *West African Trade*, London 1954.

Baumann, Hermann, 'The Division of Work according to Sex in African Hoe Culture', in *Africa*, Vol. I, 1928.

Beaujeu-Garnier, Jacqueline, 'Les Grandes Villes Surpeuplées dans les Pays Sous-Developpés', paper to *The International Geographical Union's Symposium*, Pennsylvania 1967, processed.

Becker, G. S., *The Economics of Discrimination*, Chicago 1957.

Belshaw, Cyril S., *Traditional Exchange and Modern Markets*, London 1965.

Bhatnagar, K. S., *Dikpatura, Village Survey*, Monographs No. 4, Madhya Pradesh, Part VI, Census of India 1961, Delhi 1964, processed.

Boismenu, Mlle de, *Projet d'Animation Feminine Rurale dans la Préfecture de l'Ouham, République Central Africaine*, Bureau pour le Developpement de la Production Agricole, Paris 1965, processed.

Bose, Ashish, 'Migration Streams in India', in *International Union for the Scientific Study of Population Sydney Conference 1967*, processed.

Bose, Ashish, 'Problems of Urbanization in Countries of the ECAFE Region', paper to the *Expert Working Group on Problems of Internal Migration and Urbanization*. United Nations Economic Commission for Asia and The Far East, Bangkok 1967, processed.

Boserup, Ester, *The Conditions of Agricultural Growth*, London 1965.

Boutillier, J. L., *Bongouanou Côte d'Ivoire*, Paris 1960.

Boutillier, J. L., et al., *La Moyenne Vallée de Sénégal*, Paris 1962.

Buck, John Lossing, *Land Utilization in China*, London 1937.

Carlebach, Julius, 'The Position of Women in Kenya', United Nations Economic Commission for Africa, *Workshop on Urban Problems*, Addis Ababa, 1963, processed.

Carr-Saunders, Sir Alexander, 'Women's Role in the Development of Tropical and Sub-Tropical Countries, Economic Aspect', in International Institute of Differing Civilizations, *Women's Role in the Development of Tropical and Sub-Tropical Countries*, Brussels 1959.

Chaudhury, T. P. S. and Sharma, B. M. 'Female Labour of the Farm Family in Agriculture' in *Agricultural Situation in India*, September 1961.

Clignet, R., 'Les Attitudes de la Société à L'égard des Femmes en Côte-d'Ivoire' in Chombart de Lauwe, Paul-Henri (ed.), *Images de la Femme dans la Société*, Paris 1964.

Collver, Andrew and Langlois, Eleanor, 'The Female Labour Force in Metropolitan Areas, an International Comparison' in *Economic Development and Cultural Change*, January 1962.

Comhaire-Sylvain, Suzanne, *Food and Leisure among the African Youth of Leopoldville*, Cape Town 1950, processed.

Commission for Technical Cooperation in Africa South of the Sahara, (CCTA) *Labour: Inter African Conference 5 Meeting, Lusaka 1957*, Report L 5.

Cormack, Margaret, *The Hindu Woman*, London 1961.

Corredor, Berta, *La Familia en América Latina*, Bogota 1962.

Coughlin, Richard J., 'The Position of Women in Vietnam', in Appadorai, A. (ed.), *The Status of Women in South Asia*, Bombay 1954.

d'Aby, F. J. Amon, 'Report on Côte d'Ivoire', in International Institute of Differing Civilizations, *Women's Role in the Development of Tropical and Sub-Tropical Countries*, Brussels 1959.

Dandekar, V. M. 'Employment and Unemployment of Adult Rural Population' in *Artha Vijnana*, March 1962.

Das, Parimal, 'Women under India's Community Development Programme' in *International Labour Review*, Vol. II, 1959.

Datar, Shri B. N., 'Demographic Aspects of Unemployment and Under-Employment with Particular Reference to India', Meeting A 5 *United Nations World Population Conference 1965*, unprinted paper, processed.

Dean, Edwin, *The Supply Responses of African Farmers*, Amsterdam 1966.

Delalande, Phillippe, *L'aide Étrangère à la Vulgarisation Agricole au Sénégal*, Université de Dakar 1966, typescript.

de la Rivière, M. T., *La Formation des Femmes Rurales Malgaches*, Bureau pour le Developpement de la Production Agricole, Paris 1962, processed.

de Moulety, Henri, *Femmes de Tunisie*, Paris 1958.

Desai, P. B., 'Variation in Population Sex Ratios in India 1901–61' in Bose, Ashish (ed.), *Patterns of Population Change in India 1951–61*, Bombay, 1967.

Deshmukh, M. B., 'A Study of Floating Migration', in UNESCO, Research Centre in South Asia, *Five Studies in Asia*, Calcutta 1956.

Deshpande, S. R., 'The Position of Women in Different Social Stratifications and Occupations in India' in Appadorai, A. (ed.), *The Status of Women in South Asia*, Bombay 1954.

Diaz, Rolph C. and von Oppenfeld, Horst and Judith, *Case Studies of Farm Families, Laguna Province Philippines*, University of the Phillippines 1960, processed.

Dixit, P. K., *Pipalgote, A Village Survey*, Madhya Pradesh, Part VI, No. 7, Census of India, Vol. VIII, 1961.

Dobby, E. H. G. *Southeast Asia*, London 1950.

Doctor, Kailas C. and Gallis, Hans, 'Modern Sector Employment in Asian Countries: Some Empirical Estimates' in *International Labour Review*, Vol. II, 1964.

Dodge, Norton T., *Women in the Soviet Economy*, Baltimore 1966.

Doucy, A., 'The Unsettled Attitude of Negro Workers in the Belgian Congo' in Meynaud, Jean (ed.), *Social Change and Economic Development*, UNESCO 1963.

Dube, S. C., *Indian Village*, London 1956.

Dupire, Marguerite, 'Situation de la Femme dans une Société Pastorale (Peul Wo Da Be-Nomades du Niger)' in Paulme, Denise (ed.) *Femmes d'Afrique Noire*, Paris 1960.

Earthy, E. Dora, *Valence Women, The Social and Economic Life of the Valence Women of Portuguese East Africa*, Oxford 1933.

Eckstein, Alexander, 'Manpower and Industrialization in Communist China' in Milbank Memorial Fund, *Population Trends in Eastern Europe, the USSR and Mainland China*, New York 1960.

Ehrenfels, U. R., 'The Anthropological Background of Matrilineal Societies' in Appadorai, A. (ed.), *The Status of Women in South Asia*, Bombay 1954.

Elizago, Juan C., 'The Demographic Aspect of Unemployment and Underemployment in Latin America', in *United Nations World Population Conference 1965* Vol. IV.

Evans-Pritchard, E. E., *The Position of Women in Primitive Societies and other Essays in Social Anthropology*, London 1965.

Farrag, Abdelmegid M., 'The Occupational Structure of the Labour Force. Patterns and Trends in Selected Countries', in *Population Studies*, July 1964.

Finnegan, R. H., *Survey of the Limba People of Northern. Sierra Leone*, London 1965.

Floyd, Barry N., 'Changing Patterns of African Land Use in Southern Rhodesia', in *Rhodes-Livingstone Journal*, March 1959.

Fonseca, A. J., *Wage Determination and Organized Labour in India*, Oxford 1964.

Forbes-Watt, D., 'Programming and Special Aspects in the Productive Environment of Peasant Farm Decision Makers', *Research Paper Makerere University College* R.D.R. 24, processed.

Forde, Daryll, 'The Rural Economies' in Perham, Margery (ed.), *The Native Economies of Nigeria*, London 1946.

Forget, Nelly, 'Femmes et Professions au Maroc' in Chombart de Lauwe, Paul Henri (ed.), *Images de la Femme dans la Société*, Paris 1964.

Forthomme, Georges, *Mariage et Industrialisation*, Liège 1957.

Fox, Robert, 'Men and Women in the Philippines' in Ward, Barbara (ed.), *Women in the New Asia. The Changing Social Roles of Men and Women in South and South-East Asia*, UNESCO 1963.

Friedan, Betty, *La Femme Mystifiée*, Paris 1964.

Fuller, Anne H., *Buorij, Portrait of a Lebanese Muslim Village*, Cambridge Mass. 1961.

Gadgil, D. R., *Women in the Working Force in India*, Delhi 1965.

Galletti, R., Baldwin, K. D. S. and Dina, I. O., *Nigerian Cocoa Farmers*, London 1956.

Geertz, Clifford, *Peddlers and Princes. Social Change in Economic Modernization in Two Indonesian Towns*, Chicago-London 1963.

Gendell, Murray, 'The Influence of Family-building Activity on Women's Rate of Economic Activity, in *United Nations World Population Conference 1965*, Vol. IV.

Georges, M. M. and Guet, Gabriel, *L'emploi du Temps du Paysan dans une Zone de L'oubangui Central 1959–60*, Bureau pour le Developpement de la Production Agricole, Paris 1961, processed.

Germany, Gino, 'Inquiry into the Social Effects of Urbanization in a Working Class Sector of Greater Buenos Aires', in Hauser, Philip (ed.), *Urbanization in Latin America*, UNESCO 1961.

Giri, V. V. *Labour Problems in Indian Industry*, Delhi 1965.

Gosselin, Gabriel, 'Pour une Anthropologie du Travail Rural en Afrique Noire', in *Cahiers d'Études Africaines*, Vol. III, 1962–3.

Gouellain, R., 'Parenté et affinités ethniques dans l'écologie du "Grand Quartier" de New-Bell, Douala' in Southall, A. (ed.), *Social Change in Modern Africa*, London 1961.

Gourou, Pierre, 'La Population et les Ressources Dites Naturelles', paper to the *International Geographical Union's Symposium*, Pennsylvania 1967, processed.

Gregory, Peter, 'The Labour Market in Puerto Rico' in Moore, Wilbert E. and Feldman, Arnold S., *Labor Commitment and Social Change in Developing Areas*, New York 1960.

Guet, Gabriel, *Dario Village de Haute-Sangha*, Bureau pour le Developpement de la Production Agricole, Paris 1965, processed.

Guilbert, Madeleine, *Les Fonctions des Femmes dans L'industrie*, Paris and The Hague 1966.

Guillard, J., 'Essai de Mesure de L'activité d'un Paysan Africain, le Toupouri' in *L'agronomie Tropicale* No. 4, Paris 1958.

Guillard, M. J., *Techniques Rurales en Afrique, 21 les Temps de Travaux*, Bureau pour le Developpement de la Production Agricole, Paris 1965 processed.

Gutkind, Peter C. W., 'African Urban Family Life', in *Cahiers d'Études Africaines*, Vol. III, 1962–3.

Lord Hailey, *An African Survey*, London 1957.

Hanks, Lucien M. Jr. and Hanks, Jane Richardson, 'Thailand: Equality between the Sexes' in Ward, Barbara E. (ed.), *Women in the New Asia. The Changing Social Roles of Men and Women in South and South-East Asia*, UNESCO 1963.

Hansen, Bent, 'Marginal Productivity Wage Theory and Subsistence Wage Theory in Egyptian Agriculture' in *The Journal of Development Studies*, July 1966.

Hamamsy, El L. S., 'Report on Egypt,' in International Institute of Differing Civilizations, *Women's Role in the Development of Tropical and Sub-Tropical Countries*, Brussels 1959.

Haswell, M. R., *The Changing Pattern of Economic Activity in a Gambia Village*, HMS London 1963, processed.

Hellman, E., 'Rooiyard: A Sociological Survey of an Urban Native Slum Yard', in International African Institute, *Social Implications of Industrialization and Urbanization in Africa South of the Sahara*, UNESCO 1956.

Honigman, John J., *Three Pakistan Villages*, Institute for Research in Social Sciences, University of North Carolina 1958, processed.

Horrell, M., 'Report on the Union of South Africa' in International Institute of Differing Civilizations, *Women's Role in the Development of Tropical and Sub-Tropical Countries*, Brussels 1959.

Hunter, M., 'An Urban Community' in International African Institute, *Social Implications of Industrialization and Urbanization in Africa South of the Sahara*, UNESCO 1956.

Husain, A. F. A., *Human and Social Impact of Technological Change in Pakistan*, Dacca 1956.

Husain, A. F. A., *Employment of Middle Class Muslim Women in Dacca*, Dacca 1958.

India, Ministry of Food and Agriculture, *Studies in Economics of Farm Management in Bombay 1956-7*, Delhi 1962.

India, Ministry of Food and Agriculture, *Studies in Economics of Farm Management in Madhya Pradesh 1956-7*, Delhi 1961.

India, Ministry of Food and Agriculture, *Studies in Economics of Farm Management in Madras 1956-7*, Delhi 1960.

India, Ministry of Food and Agriculture, *Studies in Economics of Farm Management in Uttar Pradesh 1956-7*, Delhi 1960.

India, Ministry of Labour, *Outlook on Employment*, Delhi 1959, processed.

India, Ministry of Labour, *Agricultural Labour in India: Report on the Second Agricultural Labour Enquiry, 1956–57*, Vol. I, Delhi 1960.

India, Ministry of Labour, *Women in Employment, 1901–1956*, Simla 1964.

India, Ministry of Labour, *Women in Employment*, Delhi 1964.

India, Planning Commission, *Report of the Village and Small Scale Industries Committee*, Delhi 1955.

267

India, Planning Commission, *Employment Trends and Task for the Fourth Plan*, Delhi 1964, processed.

India, Planning Commission, *Some Characteristics of Women Job Seekers on the Live Register of Employment Exchanges*, Delhi 1966, processed.

India, Labour Department West Bengal, *Unemployment among Women in West Bengal*, Calcutta 1959.

Institute de Science Economique Appliquée Dakar, *La Femme Africaine et les Marchées Dakarois*, Dakar 1963, processed.

Institute of Economic and Social Research, Djakarta, 'Djakarta, A Study of Urbanization', in UNESCO Research Centre in Southern Asia, *Five Studies in Asia*, Calcutta 1956.

International Labour Office India Branch, *Working Women in Changing India*, Delhi 1963, processed.

International Labour Office, 'Report on India's Policy and Action on Behalf of Tribal Populations', in *International Labour Review*, Vol. I, 1956.

International Labour Office, 'Women's Employment in Latin America', in *International Labour Review*, Vol. I, 1956.

International Labour Office, 'Interracial Wage Structure in Certain Parts of Africa', in *International Labour Review*, Vol. II, 1958.

International Labour Office, 'Wages in Viet-Nam', in *International Labour Review*, Vol. II, 1959.

International Labour Office, 'Unemployment and Underemployment in India, Indonesia, Pakistan and the Philippines', in *International Labour Review*, Vol. II, 1962.

International Labour Office, 'Unemployed Youth', in *International Labour Review*, Vol. I, 1963.

International Labour Office, 'Youth and Work in Latin America', in *International Labour Review*, Vol. II, 1964.

International Labour Office, *Report II Second African Regional Conference Addis Ababa 1964. The Employment and Conditions of Work of African Women*, Geneva 1964, processed.

International Labour Office, *Second African Regional Conference Addis Ababa 1964. Record of Proceedings*, Geneva 1965.

International Labour Office, *International Labour Conference Forty-Eight Session, Record of Proceedings*, Geneva 1965.

Irving, James, *Economic Rent and Household Income among Cape Coloureds in Grahamstown*. Occasional Paper No. 1 Rhodes University Grahamstown South Africa, 1958, processed.

Irving, James, *Economic Rent and Household Income among the African Population of Grahamstown*. Occasional paper No. 2 Rhodes University Grahamstown South Africa, 1958, processed.

Izzeddin, Nejla, *The Arab World*, Chicago 1953.

Izzett, Alison, 'Family Life among the Yoruba, in Lagos, Nigeria', in Southall, A. W. (ed.), *Social Change in Modern Africa*, London 1961.

Jaffe, A. J. and Azumi, K., 'The Birth Rate and Cottage Industries in Under-developed Countries', in *Economic Development and Cultural Change*, October 1960.

Janlekha, K. O., *A Study of a Rice Growing Village in Central Thailand*, Bangkok 1955.

Jean, Suzanne, *La Formation des Femmes Rurales Malgaches*, Bureau pour le Developpement de la Production Agricole, Paris 1961, processed.

Jellicoe, M. R., 'An Experiment in Mass Education among Women', in *Occasional Papers on Community Development* 1, Nairobi 1962.

Jimenez, Lilian, *Conditiones de la Mujer en El Salvador*, Mexico 1962.

Kaberry, Phyllis M., *Women of the Grassfields. A Study of the Economic Position of Women in Bamenda, British Cameroons*. Colonial Office, Research Publication No. 14, London 1952.

Karve, Irawati, 'The Indian Woman in 1975' in *Perspectives, Supplement to the Indian Journal of Public Administration*, January–March 1966.

Katarikawe, E., 'Some Preliminary Results of a Survey of Kiga 'Resettlement Schemes' in Kigezi, Ankoll and Toro Districts, Western Uganda', *Research Paper Makerere University College*, R.D.R. 31, processed.

Kay, Georges, 'Population Pressure on Resources in Zambia', paper to *The International Geographical Union's Symposium*, Pennsylvania 1967, processed.

Kenya, *Report of the Agricultural Education Commission*, Nairobi 1967.

Kenya, *Economic Survey 1967*, Nairobi 1967.

Kertanegara, 'The Batik Industry in Central Java' in *Economi Dan Keuangan Indonesia*, July 1958.

Koyama, Takashi, *The Changing Social Position of Women in Japan*, UNESCO 1961.

Kruse, M., 'The Shortage of Nurses and Conditions of Work in Nursing', in *International Labour Review*, Vol. II 1958.

Lakdawala, et. al., *Work, Wages and Well-being in an Indian Metropolis*, Bombay 1963.

Lam, Mithan J., 'Report on India', in International Institute of Differing Civilizations, *Women's Role in the Development of Tropical and Sub-Tropical Countries*, Brussels 1959.

Langly, Kathleen M., *The Industrialization of Iraq*, Cambridge Mass. 1961.

Leblanc, M., *Personnalité de la Femme Katangaise*, Louvain 1960.

Lefaucheux, Marie-Hélène, 'The Contribution of Women to the Economic and Social Development of African Countries', in *International Labour Review*, Vol. II, 1962.

Leith-Ross, Sylvia, *African Women. A Study of the Ibo of Nigeria*, London 1939.

Leroux, H. and Allier, J. P., *Planification en Afrique 4*, Ministère de la Co-opération, Paris 1963, processed.

Leser, C. E. V., 'Trends in Women's Work Participation', in *Population Studies*, November 1958.

Leurquin, Philippe, *Le Niveau de Vie des Populations Rurales du Ruanda-Urundi*, Louvain 1960.

Lévy, Banyen Phimmasone, 'Yesterday and today in Laos: a Girl's Auto-biographical Notes', in Ward, Barbara E. (ed.), *Women in the New Asia, The Changing Social Roles of Men and Women in South and South-East Asia*, UNESCO 1963.

Lewis, Oscar, *Life in a Mexican Village*, University of Illinois Press 1951.

Lewis, W. Arthur, *The Theory of Economic Growth*, London 1957.

Little, K. L., 'The Changing Position of Women in the Sierra Leone Protectorate', in *Africa*, Vol. XVIII, 1948.

Little, K. L., *The Mende of Sierra Leone. A West African People in Transition*, London 1951.

Loomis, C. P., *Turrialba, Social System and the Introduction of Change*, East Lansing, 1953.

Lopes, J. R. B., 'Aspects of the Adjustment of Rural Migrants to Urban-Industrial Conditions in Sao Paulo, Brazil', in Hauser, Philip (ed.), *Urbanization in Latin America*, UNESCO 1961.

McCall, D., 'Trade and the Role of Wife in a Modern West African Town', in Southall, A. W. (ed.), *Social Change in Modern Africa*, London 1961.

Majumdar, D. N., 'About Women in Patrilocal Societies in South Asia', in Appadorai, A. (ed.), *The Status of Women in South Asia*, Bombay 1954.

Mar, J. Matos, 'Three Indian Communities in Peru', in Meynaud, Jean (ed.), *Social Change and Economic Development*, UNESCO 1963.

Mboya, T. J., 'Women's Role in National Development', Keynote Address at the *Conference organized by the East African Institute of Social and Cultural Affairs and the National Council of Women of Kenya*, Nairobi 1967, processed.

Mead, Margaret, *Male and Female*, London 1950.

Mead, Margaret, *Cultural Patterns and Technical Change*, UNESCO 1958.

Mi Mi Khaing, 'Burma: Balance and Harmony', in Ward, Barbara E. (ed.), *Women in the New Asia. The Changing Social Roles of Men and Women in South and South-East Asia*, UNESCO 1963.

Mitchell, J. Clyde, 'Wage Labour and African Population Movements in Central Africa', in Barbour, K. M. and Prothero, R. M. (ed.), *Essays on African Population*, London 1961.

Mitchell, J. Clyde, *Sociological Background to African Labour*, Salisbury 1961.

Mortimore, M. J., 'Land and Population Pressure in the Kano Close-Settled Zone, Northern Nigeria', in *Advancement of Science*, April 1967.

M'Rabet, Fadéla, *La Femme Algérienne*, Paris 1965.

Naigisiki, Saverio, 'Report on Ruanda', in International Institute of Differing Civilizations, *Women's Role in the Development of Tropical and Sub-Tropical Countries*, Brussels 1959.

Nash, Manning, 'Kinship and Voluntary Association', in Moore, Wilbert E. and Feldman, Arnold S. (ed.), *Labor Commitment and Social Change in Developing Areas*, New York 1960.

Nath, Kamla, 'Women in the New Village', in *The Economic Weekly*. May 1965.

Nath, Kamla, 'Urban Women Workers', in *The Economic Weekly*. Bombay, September 1965.

Nouacer, Khadidja, 'Evolution du Travail Professionel de la Femme au Maroc', in Chombart de Lauwe, Paul-Henri (ed.), *Images de la Femme dans la Société*, Paris 1964.

Nye, F .Ivan and Hoffman, Lois Wladis, *The Employed Mother in America*, Chicago 1963.

Olin, Ulla, 'Population Growth and Problems of Employment in Asia and the Far East', in *United Nations World Population Conference 1965*, Vol. IV.

Oloo, Celina and Cone, Virginia, *Kenya Women Look Ahead*, Nairobi 1965.

Ominde, S. H., *The Luo Girl*, London 1952.

Orleans, Leo A., *Professional Manpower and Education in Communist China*, Washington 1961.

Patnaik, R. C., 'Pattern of Employment of Hired Labour in Agriculture in India', in *The Indian Journal of Agricultural Economics*, Vol. XII, No. 2, April 1957.

Pauw, B. A., 'Some Changes in the Social Structure of the Tlhaping of the Taung Reserve', in *African Studies*, Vol. 19, No. 1, 1960.

Pecson, T. G., 'Report on The Philippines', in International Institute of Differing Civilizations, *Women's Role in the Development of Tropical and Sub-Tropical Countries*, Brussels 1959.

Peddler, F. J., 'A Study of Income and Expenditure in Northern Zaria', in *Africa*, Vol. XVIII, 1948.

Penniment, K. J., 'The Influence of Cultural and Socio-Economic Factors on Labour Force Participation Rates', in *United Nations World Population Conference 1965*, Vol. IV.

Phillips, R. E., 'The Bantu in the City: A Study of Cultural Adjustment on the Witwatersrand', in International African Institute, *Social Implications of Industrialization and Urbanization in Africa South of the Sahara*, UNESCO 1956.

Powesland, P. G., 'History of the Migration in Uganda', in Richards, Audrey I. (ed.), *Economic Development and Tribal Change*, Cambridge 1952.

Prabhu, Pandhdri Nath, 'Bombay, A Study on the Social Effects of Urbanization', in UNESCO Research Centre in Asia, *Five Studies in Asia*, Calcutta 1956.

Pudsey, D., 'Farm Management Research and Extension Advice: Possible Developments in Toro', *Research Paper Makerere University College*, 1967, processed.

Purcell, V., 'Report on Burma, Thailand and Malaya', in International Institute of Differing Civilizations, *Women's Role in the Development of Tropical and Sub-Tropical Countries*, Brussels 1959.

Ramachandran, P., *Attitudes of Women to Part Time Employment*, TATA Institute of Social Research, Bombay 1964.

Ranaday, *Attitudes of Women to Part Time Employment*, Institute of Social Research, Delhi 1968.

Ray, Robert S., 'The Structure of Employment in Kenya', in Sheffield, J. R. (ed.), *Education, Employment and Rural Development*, Nairobi 1967.

Razafy-Andriamihaingo, Suzanne, 'Report on Madagascar', in International Institute of Differing Civilizations, *Women's Role in the Development of Tropical and Sub-Tropical Countries*, Brussels 1959.

Redfield, Robert, *A Village that Chose Progress*, Chicago 1957.

Reeves, Z. P., 'Introducing Community Development among the Wabena', in *Occasional Papers on Community Development*, 1, 1962, Nairobi.

Reynders, H. J. J., 'The Geographical Income of the Bantu Areas in South Africa', in Samuels, L. H. (ed.), *African Studies in Income and Wealth*, London 1963.

Richards, Audrey I., *Land, Labour and Diet in Northern Rhodesia. An Economic Study of the Bemba Tribe*, London 1939.

Richards, Audrey I., *Economic Development and Tribal Change*, Cambridge 1952.

Ritzenthaler, Robert E., 'Anlu: A Women's Uprising in The British Cameroons', in *African Studies*, No. 1, 1960.

Ryan, Bryce and Fernando, Sylvia, *The Female Factory Worker in Colombo*, International Labour Office, Geneva 1952.

Samaj, Bharat Sevah, *Slums of Old Delhi, Report of the Socio-Economic Survey of the Slum Dwellers of Old Delhi City*, Delhi 1958.

Seklani, Mahmoud, 'Population Active et Structures Économiques de l'Egypte', in *Population*, July 1962.

Sengupta, Padmini, *Women Workers of India*, Bombay 1960.

Servais, J. J. et Laurend, J. P., *Histoire et Dossier de la Prostitution*, Paris 1965.

Shah, K. T., *Women's Role in Planned Economy*, Bombay 1947.

Sharma, P. S., 'Agricultural Working Force and Cropping Pattern in the Light of 1961 Census', in *Agricultural Situation in India*, August 1963.

Shrivasta, Rama Shanker, *Agricultural Labour in Eastern Districts of Uttar Pradesh*, Delhi 1966.

Sicot, Marcel, *La Prostitution dans le Monde*, Paris 1964.

Simons, H. J., *African Women. Their Legal Status in South Africa*, Evanston 1968.

Singh, V. B., *An Introduction to the Study of Indian Labour Problems*, Agra 1967.

Sinha, J. N., 'Dynamics of Female Participation in Economic Activity in a Developing Economy', in *United Nations World Population Conference*, Vol. IV, 1965.

Sison, P. S., 'The Role of Women in Business and Industry in The Philippines', in *International Labour Review*, Vol. I, 1963.

Sofer, C., 'Urban African Social Structure and Working Group Behaviour at Jinja, Uganda', in International African Institute, *Social Implications of Industrialization and Urbanization in Africa South of the Sahara*, UNESCO 1956.

Som, Ranjen Kumer, 'Intensity of Employment in India', in Mukerjee, Radhakamal (ed.), *Labour and Planning*, Bombay 1964.

Southall, A. W., 'Alur Migrants', in Richards, Audrey I. (ed.), *Economic Development and Tribal Change*, Cambridge 1952.

Southall, A. W., *Social Change in Modern Africa*, London 1961.

Soyer-Poskin, 'Report on Congo Belge', in International Institute of Differing Civilizations, *Women's Role in the Development of Tropical and Sub-Tropical Countries*, Brussels 1959.

Suwondo, Nani, 'Report on Indonesia', in International Institute of Differing Civilizations, *Women's Role in the Development of Tropical and Sub-Tropical Countries*, Brussels 1959.

Sweet, Louise E., *Tell Toqaan. A Syrian Village*, Ann Arbor 1960.

Swift, Michael, 'Men and Women in Malay Society', in Ward, Barbara E. (ed.), *Women in the New Asia. The Changing Social Roles of Men and Women in South and South-East Asia*, UNESCO 1963.

Ta-Chung Liu and Kung-Chia Yeh, *The Economy of the Chinese Mainland, National Income and Economic Development 1933–1959*, Princeton 1965.

Tanner, R. E. S., 'Land Rights on the Tanganyika Coast', *African Studies*, 1960.

Tardits, Claude, 'Réflexions sur le Problème de la Scolarisation des Filles au Dahomey', in *Cahiers d'Études Africaines*, October 1962.

Tharpar, Romila, 'The History of Female Emancipation in Southern Asia', in Ward, Barbara E. (ed.), *Women in the New Asia. The Changing Social Roles of Men and Women in South and South-East Asia*, UNESCO 1963.

Tothill, J. D., *Agriculture in the Sudan*, London 1954.

Tran Van Minh, 'Report on Viet-Nam', in International Institute of Differing Civilizations, *Women's Role in the Development of Tropical and Sub-Tropical Countries*, Brussels 1959.

United Arab Republic, *The Role of Women in the United Arab Republic*, Cairo, no year.

United Nations Bureau of Social Affairs, 'Demographic Aspects of Urbanization in Latin America', in Hauser, Philip M. (ed.), *Urbanization in Latin America*, UNESCO 1961.

United Nations Commission on the Status of Women, *Resources available to Member States for the Advancement of Women*, New York 1966.

United Nations Commission on the Status of Women, *Seminar on the Participation of Women in Public Life in Ulan Bator, Mongolia 1965*, New York 1966.

United Nations Commission on the Status of Women, *The Participation of Women in Community Development Programmes*, New York 1967, processed.

United Nations Commission on the Status of Women, *The Role of Women in the Economic and Social Development of their Countries. Report of the Secretary-General*, New York 1968, processed.

United Nations Department of Economic and Social Affairs, *Proceedings of the World Population Conference 1965*.

United Nations Economic Commission for Africa, Committee on Social Welfare and Community Development, *Urbanization in Tropical Africa*, Addis Ababa 1962, processed.

United Nations Economic Commission for Africa, *Report of the Working Group on the Treatment of Non-Monetary (Subsistence) Transactions within the Framework of National Accounts*, Addis Ababa 1960, processed.

United Nations Economic Commission for Africa Social Development Section, *The Status and Role of Women in East Africa*, New York 1967.

United Nations Economic Commission for Africa, '*The Role of Women in Urban Development*', *Report of the Workshop on Urban Problems*, Addis Ababa 1964, processed.

United Nations Economic Commission for Africa, 'Polygamie, Famille et Fait Urbain (Essai sur le Sénégal); *Workshop on Urban Problems*, Addis Ababa 1963, processed.

United Nations Economic Commission for Africa, 'The Employment and Socio-Economic Situation of Women in some North African Countries' *Workshop on Urban Problems*, Addis Ababa 1963, processed.

United Nations Economic Commission for Africa, 'Women in the Traditional African Societies', *Workshop on Urban Problems*, Addis Ababa 1963, processed.

United Nations Economic Commission for Latin America, 'Creation of Employment Opportunities in Relation to Labour Supply', in Hauser, Philip M. (ed.), *Urbanization in Latin America*, UNESCO 1961.

Usher, Dan, 'Income as a Measure of Productivity', in *Economica*, November 1966.

Van der Horst, Sheila T., *African Workers in Town*, Cape Town 1964.

Van Glinstra Bleeker, R. J. P., 'Three Secrets of Development Magic', in *International Labour Review*, Vol. II, 1964.

Van Velsen, J., 'Labor Migration as a Positive Factor in the Continuity of Tonga Tribal Society', in *Economic Development and Cultural Change*, April 1960.

Vennetier, P., 'Les Hommes et leur Activité dans le Nord du Congo Brazzaville', in *Sciences Humaines*, No. 1, 1965.

Visaria, Pravin M., 'The Sex Ratio of the Population of India and Pakistan and Regional Variations During 1901–61', in Bose, Ashish (ed.), *Pattern of Population Change in India 1951–61*, Bombay 1967.

Ward Barbara, E., *Women in the New Asia. The Changing Social Rules of Men and Women in South and South-East Asia*, UNESCO 1963.

Watson, William, *Tribal Cohesion in a Money Economy*, Manchester 1958.

Wee, Ann E., 'Some Aspects of the Status of Chinese Women in Malaya', in Appadorai, A. (ed.), *The Status of Women in South Asia*, Bombay 1954.

Wells, F. A. and Warmington, W. A. *Studies in Industrialization: Nigeria and the Cameroons*, London 1962.

Weulersse, Jacques, *Paysans de Syrie et du Proche-Orient*, Paris 1946.

Wharton, Clifton R., 'Malay Rice and Rubber Smallholders: "Economic Man" Revisited', *Association for Asian Studies Meeting 1966.*

Wills, Jane, 'A Study of the Time Allocation by Rural Women and their Place in Decision-Making', *Research Paper Makerere University College*, R.D.R. 44, 1967, processed.

Wills, Jane, 'Small-scale Enterprises in Embu District. Beer Making, Maize Milling and Water Carting', *Research Paper Makerere University College* R.D.R. 24, processed.

Wills, Jane, 'Note on the Household Situation in Embu District Kenya', *Research Paper Makerere University College*, 1968, processed.

Wilson, Gordon, 'Mombasa—A Modern Colonial Municipality', in Southall, A. W. (ed.), *Social Change in Modern Africa*, London 1961.

Winter, E. H., 'Bwamba Economy', *East African Studies*, No. 5, Kampala 1955.

Woodsmall, Ruth Frances, *Moslem Women Enter a New World*, New York 1936.

Woodsmall, Ruth Frances, *Women and the New East*, Washington 1960.

Xydias, Nelly, 'Labour: Conditions, Aptitudes, Training', in International African Institute, *Social Implications of Industrialization and Urbanization in Africa South of the Sahara*, UNESCO 1956.

Zinkin, Maurice, *Development of Free Asia*, London 1956.

Author Index

Subject Index

279